Operating Systems Programming

Operating Systems Programming:

The SR Programming Language

Stephen J. Hartley

Drexel University

New York   Oxford

OXFORD UNIVERSITY PRESS

1995

Oxford University Press

Oxford   New York
Athens   Auckland   Bangkok   Bombay
Calcutta   Cape Town   Dar es Salaam   Delhi
Florence   Hong Kong   Istanbul   Karachi
Kuala Lumpur   Madras   Madrid   Melbourne
Mexico City   Nairobi   Paris   Singapore
Taipei   Tokyo   Toronto

and associated companies in
Berlin   Ibadan

Published by Oxford University Press, Inc.,
198 Madison Avenue, New York, New York 10016-4314

Oxford is a registered trademark of Oxford University Press, Inc.

Library of Congress Cataloging-in-Publication Data
Hartley, Stephen J.
Operating systems programming:
the SR programming language /
Stephen J. Hartley.
p.   cm.

ISBN 0-19-509579-0
1. Operating systems (Computers).
2. Systems programming (Computer science).
I. Title.
QA76.76.063H356   1995   005.4'2—dc20   94-41502

9   8   7   6   5   4   3   2
Printed in the United States of America
on acid-free paper

Preface

SR is a language for concurrent programming. This book describes the SR language, presents some examples of SR programs in the context of an operating systems or concurrent programming course, and provides some programming assignments in the form of open Student Laboratories. The SR language can be used by instructors of concurrent programming or operating systems courses to give students experience in writing concurrent programs that use multiple processes, semaphores, monitors, message passing, remote procedure calls, and the rendezvous. The language can also be used for parallel computing in a shared-memory multiprocessor or a distributed memory cluster environment.

The intended audience is undergraduate and graduate students enrolled in concurrent programming and operating systems classes. Prerequisites for students are knowledge of a high-level programming language like C or Pascal and operating systems concepts. See the Instructor's Manual for more detailed prerequisites. This book is designed to be used during an operating systems course in conjunction with one of the standard texts to provide concurrent programming experience. The book can also be used in a full semester follow-on course to operating systems to provide more extensive programming experience. Since most concepts and terms are defined, the book can be used as the sole text in an introductory concurrent programming course that precedes the operating systems course.

The required computing environment is a UNIX platform such as a Sun 3, Sun 4, Sequent Symmetry, DECstation, SGI Iris, NeXT, HP RISC, or PC compatible running Linux.

The SR examples and programming assignments in this book have been used successfully in undergraduate concurrent programming and operating systems courses at Drexel University, Philadelphia, Pennsylvania, and Trinity University, San Antonio, Texas. The book arose out of a collection of handouts and class notes distributed to students during 1991-94 and is a greatly expanded version of [9, 10, 11].

This book has several important features.

- The material is keyed to four standard operating systems texts: Deitel [8], Silberschatz and Galvin [20], Stallings [21], and Tanenbaum [24]. The relevant sections of these texts for the major concepts, such as semaphores and monitors, is indicated.

- Each of the numerous example programs in this book includes output from one or two sample runs to show how the program works.

- Algorithm animation using the animator interpreter from the XTANGO system is described and used in several of the examples.

- Numerous programming assignments in the form of open Student Laboratories are given.

The example programs in this book will be made available by anonymous **ftp** at site **mcs.drexel.edu**. Contact the author for further details. An Instructor's Manual, containing solution programs to most of the Lab Assignments, is available from the publisher.

Acknowledgements

I want to thank Drexel University for the time and computing resources to prepare this book. Many Drexel students have had the opportunity to use early drafts of this material, including the programming assignments, and have provided useful feedback. I want to thank the EMBA Computing Services of the University of Vermont for the use of their SGI Iris shared-memory multiprocessor to run some of the example programs. Eve Glicksman deserves credit for some technical editing of an early draft.

My sincere appreciation is due to Lori Weaver for her understanding and support during the preparation of this book.

This book was prepared using the LaTeX formatting system. My deepest appreciation is due the authors of TeX, LaTeX, and the many user-contributed macro and style files. I also want to thank John T. Stasko and Doug Hayes for designing and developing the XTANGO algorithm animation software package.

Philadelphia, Pennsylvania   — S. J. H.
September 1994

Contents

Operating Systems Programming

Chapter 1

Operating Systems Programming

Standard operating systems textbooks, such as [8, 20, 21, 24], cover the important concepts involved in concurrent process synchronization and interprocess communication. These textbooks describe how critical sections must be identified in the code of processes that execute concurrently and share data so that race conditions can be avoided. Mutual exclusion can be enforced with semaphores or monitors, which can be built into programming languages, as can other facilities that implement interprocess communication, such as message passing and the rendezvous. The above facilities can be used to solve classical process synchronization problems, such as the bounded buffer producers and consumers, the dining philosophers, the sleeping barber, and the database readers and writers.

What an operating systems textbook cannot provide is experience using these concepts in a programming language and running multiprocess programs on a machine. Students need this experience in order to reinforce their understanding of these concepts. The SR language can give students this opportunity in an operating systems class.

This book gives an overview of the SR language, emphasizing its concurrent programming features. The SR language provides an environment for writing programs that contain multiple processes and gives students practical experience in using the concepts learned in an operating systems course. Solutions in SR to the classical synchronization problems using semaphores, monitors, and message passing will be shown, along with many other examples. Programming assignments using SR, in the form of open student laboratories, that can be given to an operating systems class are included.

1.1   Hardware Basics

The following material is a review of the hardware basics needed to understand the rest of the material in this book. It is covered in assembly language programming, computer architecture, and machine organization courses.

A computing system, such as a mainframe or workstation, consists of a bus to which are attached one or more CPUs, several main (physical) memory modules, and devices like disks, printers, network cards for one or more local area networks, terminals, plotters, etc. The CPU contains a set of registers and a memory management unit (MMU) for address translation. Starting from low addresses, main memory contains interrupt vectors, memory-mapped device registers, and the operating system kernel. The rest of memory contains operating system daemon processes and user processes.

3

A process is a program that is executing. A program executes in the context of a logical address space. Starting at the low addresses is the code or instructions of the program, usually read-only, also called the "text." Next comes the program global data, both initialized and uninitialized, followed by the heap, from which dynamic memory allocation is done (`malloc()` in the C standard library), growing towards high addresses. Starting at the high end of the process memory allocation and growing towards the low end is the process stack, containing the storage for procedure local variables, passed parameters, and return addresses.

The operating system kernel keeps track of the state of all processes with a process table. Each existing process has an entry in this table containing the state of the process (running, ready, blocked, suspended, etc.), the contents of the CPU registers from the last time the process was running on the CPU, the process memory allocation, the process identifier (pid), the owner of the process, open files, accounting information, etc. See [8, 20, 21, 24] for more details.

1.1.1   Hardware and Software Interrupts

Hardware interrupts are generated by devices when they need service or have finished performing a service, for example, a disk controller after a DMA operation has been performed due an to earlier request, or a network card controller when a packet arrives. Hardware interrupts are asynchronous, that is, unrelated to whatever process is currently executing on the CPU.

When a hardware interrupt occurs, it may be ignored or left pending if there is an interrupt priority system in effect, but usually the CPU is switched from user mode to kernel (supervisor or privileged) mode so that protected memory like operating system tables can be accessed. Each device has an interrupt vector associated with it, which consists of a new program counter and status code word. The hardware loads the program counter and status register from the interrupt vector, causing the CPU to start fetching and executing instructions at the address of the interrupt handling code. If handling the interrupt will result in a context switch, described below, the handler saves the register contents in the process table slot of the process that was executing when the interrupt occurred.

Depending on the device that generated the interrupt, the interrupt handler code in the operating system kernel will

- save the character typed by the user in the appropriate buffer,

- copy the incoming network packet from the network card to the appropriate buffer, or

- change the state of a process from blocked to ready because a disk DMA operation is now complete and the user process that requested the disk block can continue running.

The CPU scheduler now decides which process should run next, picking from among those in the ready state. It could be the one that was interrupted, or it could be the process that earlier requested a disk block and just had its state changed from blocked to ready during interrupt handling. The CPU scheduler sets a pointer into the process table to the slot of the process chosen to run next. The interrupt handler loads the registers from process table slot. A return from interrupt is executed, causing a switch back to user mode of the CPU.

Software interrupts, also called system calls, are generated by programs, such as user programs and system utilities, with the TRAP instruction. They are synchronous in nature since they are generated by the program currently executing on the CPU. For example, suppose a user program executes

```
date_time = get_date_and_time()
```

or

```
count = read(file, buffer, nbytes)
```

Here `read()` and `get_date_and_time()` are library routines which execute a TRAP instruction after putting parameters, if any, in registers or on the stack. When a TRAP is executed, things proceed much like a hardware interrupt: TRAP has its own interrupt vector and a jump is made to the TRAP interrupt handler. The interrupt handler examines the parameters on the stack or in the registers. If the TRAP was from `get_date_and_time()`, then the handler will copy data from the clock registers into the return register and return from interrupt. If the TRAP was from `read()`, then the handler will

1. call the appropriate device driver to load the disk controller's command registers for a disk read operation,

2. change the state of the process from running to blocked (the kernel keeps tables of which processes are blocked for what events),

3. call the CPU scheduler to pick a different process to run next, and

4. return from interrupt.

Asynchronously, the disk seeks to the track containing the bytes requested by the `read()` and the controller uses DMA to copy the bytes into memory. The controller generates a hardware interrupt after this has been done and the interrupt handler changes the state of the process that called `read()` from blocked to ready.

The above is a simplified description of system calls and hardware and software interrupts. For a more complete description, including the complete source code for the interrupt handlers, device drivers, and file system manager of an operating system, see [23].

1.1.2 Hardware Protection

In a multiprogrammed computer system, many processes are loaded into physical memory and executed concurrently. It is desirable to protect the main memory allocated to one user process from access by another user process. The operating system kernel code and tables, device controller memory-mapped registers, and interrupt vectors must be protected from access by all user processes. Some instructions must be executed only by the operating system while the CPU is in a privileged mode, for example, setting accounting timers, halting the CPU, masking or disabling interrupts, locking the memory bus, and setting the base and limit registers described below.

These protections can be implemented with (1) a dual mode of CPU operation, and (2) a memory management unit (MMU) with an address translation scheme. The two modes the CPU can execute in are user mode and supervisor (kernel) mode. In kernel mode, the CPU can reference all memory and execute all instructions; in user mode, the CPU cannot execute any privileged instructions and memory protection is enforced, such as the base/limit scheme described below.

Operating systems texts discuss memory protection and management schemes, such as multiple variable-sized partitions, segmentation, and paging. One very simple address translation and protection scheme uses a base register and a limit register in the CPU or MMU. A user process executing on the CPU will generate addresses to process logical address space (code, data, heap, and stack described above) in some range 0 to N, where N represents the size of the process. Each process has been loaded into some unique contiguous area of main memory. Whenever a process runs on the CPU, the starting address of its main memory allocation is loaded into the base register and the size of its main memory allocation is loaded into the limit or length register as part of its context switch information. Before an address generated by the CPU as the process runs is placed on the address lines of the memory bus, the address is compared to the value in the length register. If the address is greater than the length register, then a memory protection violation has occurred and the process is aborted. If this check is passed, the value of the base register is added to the address before it is placed on the bus.

1.1.3   CPU Scheduling

To prevent a user program infinite loop from "hanging" the machine and to give each process on a multiprogrammed machine a fair share of the CPU, a hardware clock generates interrupts periodically, such as 60 times a second. This allows the operating system to schedule all processes in main memory to run on the CPU at regular intervals and to maintain time and date information for accounting.

Each time a clock interrupt occurs, the interrupt handler will check how much CPU time the process currently running has used. If it has used up its time slice or time quantum, then the CPU scheduling code on the operating system kernel is called to pick a different process to run. The CPU scheduler can use one of many algorithms to allocate CPU time, such as round-robin or multilevel feedback queues. See Chapter 10 of [8], Chapter 5 of [20], Chapter 6 of [21], or Chapter 2 of [24].

Each switch of the CPU from one process to another is called a *context switch*. The values of the CPU registers are saved in the process table slot of the process that was running just before the interrupt occurred and the registers are loaded from the process table slot of the process picked by the CPU scheduler. In a multiprogrammed uniprocessor computing system, context switches occur frequently enough that all processes appear to be running concurrently, each on its own slower virtual CPU. In a multiprocessor system, each process may have its own CPU if there are enough of them.

Chapter 2

The SR Programming Language

SR, which stands for Synchronizing Resources, is a high-level language for writing concurrent or parallel programs. Free and in the public domain, SR is available by anonymous `ftp` from the University of Arizona at `cs.arizona.edu`. It runs on many different UNIX[1] platforms, such as Sun 3, Sun 4, Sequent Symmetry, DECstation, SGI Iris, NeXT, HP RISC, and PC compatible running Linux. SR was first described in the two papers [1, 2]. A book on SR [4] has been recently published that describes all the features of the language. It is suitable as a textbook for a concurrent programming, parallel computing, or distributed systems course. Two recent articles [9, 10] described the successful use of SR as an environment for concurrent programming in an undergraduate operating systems course. This book shows how to use SR as the programming environment for an operating systems course.

In a concurrent programming or operating systems course, you will study concurrently executing processes and their synchronization with semaphores and monitors. You will also learn about interprocess communication with message passing and the rendezvous. The SR language provides an environment for writing programs that contain multiple processes and will give you practical experience in using the concepts learned in your concurrent programming or operating systems course.

This book describes the sequential and concurrent features of the SR language and presents some example SR programs in the context of an undergraduate concurrent programming or operating systems course. Many programming assignments in the form of open laboratory exercises are given at the ends of major sections.

2.1 Sequential Features

If you are familiar with Pascal, C, or C++, SR will not be difficult to learn. You are in great shape if you know all three because SR is a lot like Pascal, with some of the "nifty" features of C and C++ thrown in. The sequential features of SR support the standard data types: integers, reals, characters, booleans, pointers, and enumerations. Supported structured types are arrays, strings, and records. The language includes the assignment statement :=, the do-while loop do···od, the for-index loop fa···af, and the if-then-else statement if···[]···fi. Input and output can be performed with read and write statements, or with C's scanf and printf. Procedures and functions are implemented with procedure and returns. SR is a strongly-typed language like Pascal and ANSI C. All identifiers, whether they are for variables, functions, or procedures, must be defined before they can be used.

---

[1] UNIX is a Registered Trademark of X/Open, Inc.

7

SR programs are constructed as one or more *resources*, which correspond roughly to modules or objects of other languages, such as C++. Short or simple sequential programs can be written as a single resource: **resource** *name*() ⋯ **end** *name*. Although it depends on how SR is installed, the standard way to compile and run an SR program on a UNIX platform is the sequence of two commands

> **sr** -o *file file*.**sr**
> *file*

where *file*.**sr** is the file containing the SR source code and *file* contains the compiled and linked object code.

The sequential features of the language are best illustrated with examples. Each example includes one or more sample runs appended to the end of the code as a /* */ comment. Program 2.1, based on page 4 in [2], reads a number from the keyboard and computes factorials for 1 up to the number read. Note that **write**(⋯) generates a linefeed, and that **writes**(⋯) suppresses the linefeed, useful for generating prompts. A function returns a value through assignment to the variable named after **returns**. Comments start with #, conclude with the end of the line, and can tag lines of code. C-style /*⋯*/ comments can also be used. SR's /* */ comments can be nested, unlike C.

Program 2.2, based on pages 32-33 in [2], sorts numbers read from the keyboard. This example shows that arrays can be passed to a procedure by reference with **ref**; other ways are copy-in-copy-out with **var**, by value with **val** as in C, and by result with **res**. The default is by value. Arrays are declared *array-name*[*lower-bound*:*upper-bound*], and the bounds can use variables whose value is not determined until run-time (dynamic storage allocation). A procedure formal parameter that is an array can have its upper bound specified when the procedure is called by using * as the upper bound in its declaration. The built-in function **ub**(*array*) returns the actual upper bound. For-all loops may have more than one *quantifier* separated by commas, where a quantifier gives the index variable its initial value, final value, and step size (optional). For-all loops may also have a *such that* clause **st**. The swap statement :=: swaps values. It can be used with arrays.

Program 2.3 shows how to manipulate strings and arrays of characters. This example illustrates how to declare constants **const** and strings, how to declare and initialize a two dimensional array, and how to read until end-of-file. Strings are not the same as one-dimensional arrays of characters. When entering the input to this program from the keyboard, end-of-file is signaled by typing control-D on a line by itself. The C postincrement operator ++ is available. A string can be converted to a one-dimensional array of characters with **chars** and then assigned to a row of a two-dimensional array of characters. If a program's flow of control reaches the **end** of the resource, the program terminates. A **stop** statement is available to terminate a program explicitly.

The next two programs are from the SR software distribution. Program 2.4 illustrates initializing variables, the remainder operator %, and the **else** clause on an **if** statement. A variable can be initialized by placing := *value* after its declaration. In addition, the program shows how to use the built-in function **getarg** to access arguments on the UNIX command line invoking the compiled program. The **getarg**(*i*, *n*) function call will try to access the ith argument, arg_i, on the command line when the program is run:

> **sr** -o *file file*.**sr**
> *file* arg_1 arg_2 ⋯ arg_i ⋯

If the ith argument is present, **getarg** assigns its value to the variable *n* and returns **1**. If there is no i^{th} argument, **getarg** returns **EOF**; it returns **0** if the argument cannot be read and converted to the type of the variable *n*.

In addition to %, mod can also be used as a remainder operator. They work the same way on positive numbers, for example 7 mod 5 and 7 % 5 are both 2, but differently on negative numbers, for example, -7 mod 5 is 3 but -7 % 5 is -2.

Program 2.5 shows that SR supports recursion. It counts the number of ways that N queens can be placed on an N-by-N chessboard such that no queen is attacking any other queen. The variables N and solutions are global to the procedures place and safe. Index variables in fa··· af loops are local to the loop block and should **not** be declared explicitly with var statements; SR can tell the type of the index variable from its context. One may explicitly return from a procedure.

Program 2.1: Compute Factorials.

```
resource factorial()
    procedure fact(k: int) returns f: int
        if k < 0 -> f := -1
        [] k = 0 or k - 1 -> f := 1
        [] k > 1 -> f := k * fact(k-1)
        fi
    end fact

    var n: int
    writes("How many factorials? "); read(n)
    write()   # generate a linefeed, resulting in a blank line
    fa i := 1 to n ->
        write(i, "factorial is", fact(i))
    af
end factorial

/* .............. Example compile and run(s)

% sr -o factorial factorial.sr
% ./factorial
How many factorials? 5

1 factorial is 1
2 factorial is 2
3 factorial is 6
4 factorial is 24
5 factorial is 120
                                    */
```

Program 2.2: Sort Numbers.

```
resource sorter()
    procedure print_array(ref a[1:*] : int)
        fa i := 1 to ub(a) -> writes(" ", a[i]) af
        writes("\n")   # another way to write a linefeed (terminates above line)
    end print_array

    procedure sort(ref a[1:*] : int)    # into non-decreasing order
        fa i := 1 to ub(a)-1,
```

```
            j := i+1 to ub(a) st a[i] > a[j] ->
               a[i] :=: a[j]   /* swap */
       af
    end sort

    var n : int
    writes("number of integers? "); read(n)
    var nums[1:n] : int
    write("input integers, separated by white space")
    fa i := 1 to n -> read(nums[i]) af
    write("original numbers")
    print_array(nums)
    sort(nums)
    write("sorted numbers")
    print_array(nums)
end sorter

/* .............. Example compile and run(s)

% sr -o sort sort.sr
% ./sort
number of integers? 5
input integers, separated by white space
-10 2 0 100 -77
original numbers
 -10 2 0 100 -77
sorted numbers
 -77 -10 0 2 100
                                          */
```

Program 2.3: Fiddle with Strings.

```
resource fiddle_string()
    const WIDTH := 70, HEIGHT := 20
    var line : string[WIDTH]
    var screen[1:HEIGHT, 1:WIDTH] : char := ([HEIGHT] ([WIDTH] ' '))
    var line_length : int
    var where : int
    where := 0
    do read(line) != EOF ->
       line_length := length(line)
       where++
       screen[where, 1:line_length] := chars(line)
    od
    if where = 0 -> stop fi
    fa i := 1 to where ->
       write(screen[i])
    af
    stop
end fiddle_string

/* .............. Example compile and run(s)
```

```
% sr -o fiddle_string fiddle_string.sr
% ./fiddle_string
12345
abcdefghijklmnopqrstuvwxyzABCDEFGHIJKLMNOPQRSTUVWXYZ12345678901234567890
This is the last line.
^D
12345
abcdefghijklmnopqrstuvwxyzABCDEFGHIJKLMNOPQRSTUVWXYZ123456789012345678
90
This is the last line.
                                                      */
```

Program 2.4: "Wondrous" Numbers.

```
#   A simple sequential program illustrating the "3n+1" problem,
#   called "wondrous numbers" in Hofstadter's "Godel Escher Bach".
#
#   usage:    a.out n      to trace the integer n
#             a.out m n    to trace all integers from m to n
#   default:  a.out 2 25
#
#   Given a positive integer n, halve it if even, or replace by 3n+1
#   if odd.  Stop at 1.  The sequences are interesting, and nobody has
#   proved that all initial values lead to termination.
#
#   Try "a.out 27".
#
#   For full details see Jeffrey Lagarias, The 3x+1 Problem and
#   Generalizations, American Mathematical Monthly, vol.92 no.1
#   (January, 1986), pp. 3-25.

resource wondrous()
    var lwb: int := 2       # lower bound defaults to 2
    var upb: int := 25      # upper bound defaults to 25
    var n: int              # n is the working value
    if getarg(1, lwb) = 1 -> # if one argument set as lower, upper bounds
        upb := lwb
    fi
    getarg(2, upb)          # reset upper bound to 2nd argument if given
    fa i := lwb to upb ->   # for each integer in selected range:
        writes(i, ":")      # print it
        n := i
        do n > 1 ->         # iterate until we hit 1
            if n % 2 = 1 ->
                n := 3*n+1  # 3n+1 if odd
            [] else ->
                n := n/2    # n/2 if even
            fi
            writes(" ", n)  # write new value
        od
        write()             # terminate line at end of sequence
    af
end wondrous
```

```
/* .............. Example compile and run(s)

% sr -o wondrous wondrous.sr
% ./wondrous
2: 1
3: 10 5 16 8 4 2 1
4: 2 1
5: 16 8 4 2 1
6: 3 10 5 16 8 4 2 1
7: 22 11 34 17 52 26 13 40 20 10 5 16 8 4 2 1
8: 4 2 1
9: 28 14 7 22 11 34 17 52 26 13 40 20 10 5 16 8 4 2 1
10: 5 16 8 4 2 1
11: 34 17 52 26 13 40 20 10 5 16 8 4 2 1
12: 6 3 10 5 16 8 4 2 1
13: 40 20 10 5 16 8 4 2 1
14: 7 22 11 34 17 52 26 13 40 20 10 5 16 8 4 2 1
15: 46 23 70 35 106 53 160 80 40 20 10 5 16 8 4 2 1
16: 8 4 2 1
17: 52 26 13 40 20 10 5 16 8 4 2 1
18: 9 28 14 7 22 11 34 17 52 26 13 40 20 10 5 16 8 4 2 1
19: 58 29 88 44 22 11 34 17 52 26 13 40 20 10 5 16 8 4 2 1
20: 10 5 16 8 4 2 1
21: 64 32 16 8 4 2 1
22: 11 34 17 52 26 13 40 20 10 5 16 8 4 2 1
23: 70 35 106 53 160 80 40 20 10 5 16 8 4 2 1
24: 12 6 3 10 5 16 8 4 2 1
25: 76 38 19 58 29 88 44 22 11 34 17 52 26 13 40 20 10 5 16 8 4 2 1
% ./wondrous 27
27: 82 41 124 62 31 94 47 142 71 214 107 322 161 484 242 121 364 182 91 274 137
412 206 103 310 155 466 233 700 350 175 526 263 790 395 1186 593 1780 890 445
1336 668 334 167 502 251 754 377 1132 566 283 850 425 1276 638 319 958 479 1438
719 2158 1079 3238 1619 4858 2429 7288 3644 1822 911 2734 1367 4102 2051 6154
3077 9232 4616 2308 1154 577 1732 866 433 1300 650 325 976 488 244 122 61 184
92 46 23 70 35 106 53 160 80 40 20 10 5 16 8 4 2 1
% ./wondrous 29 30
29: 88 44 22 11 34 17 52 26 13 40 20 10 5 16 8 4 2 1
30: 15 46 23 70 35 106 53 160 80 40 20 10 5 16 8 4 2 1
                                                       */
```

Program 2.5: N Queens Problem.

```
# Generate all possible solutions to the N queens problem.
# The board is represented by board[1:N], which records
# for each column whether there is a queen in that column,
# and if so, which row it occupies.  In particular,
#    board[j] = i if there is a queen in row i of column j
#             = 0 otherwise

resource EightQueens()
   var N : int := 8
   var solution : int := 0
```

```
procedure safe(row, column: int; board[1:*]: int) returns answer: bool
# Check whether it is safe to place a queen at row, column;
#    i.e., is board[column]=row a safe configuration?
   fa j := 1 to column-1 ->
      if board[column-j] = row
            or board[column-j] = row-j
            or board[column-j] = row+j ->
         answer := false
         return
      fi
   af
   answer := true
end safe

procedure place(column: int; board[1:*]: int)
# Place a queen in all safe positions of column c,
# then try placing a queen in the next column.
# If a position in column N is safe, print the board.
   fa row := 1 to N ->
      board[column] := row  # try placing a queen in (row,column)
      if safe(row, column, board) ->
         if column = N -> solution++   # we have a solution
         [] column<N -> place(column+1, board)  # try next column
         fi
      fi
      board[column] := 0   # unrecord that a queen was placed
   af
end place

getarg(1, N)
var board[1:N]: int := ([N] 0)
write("Solutions to the", N, "queens problem:")
place(1, board)
write("There are", solution, "solutions.")
end EightQueens

/* .............. Example compile and run(s)

% sr -o Nqueens Nqueens.sr
% ./Nqueens
Solutions to the 8 queens problem:
There are 92 solutions.
% time ./Nqueens 10
Solutions to the 10 queens problem:
There are 724 solutions.
68.5u 2.8s 1:50 64% 0+448k 7+0io 5pf+0w
                                              */
```

2.2   Additional Sequential Examples and Features

If you are using a UNIX system to run SR and your shell (command interpreter) is csh (the C-shell), then you can use the csh-builtin time command prefix to tell csh to print out some resource usage statistics of the program you are running. This is done, for example, in the sample run for ten queens in Program 2.5:

```
68.5u 2.8s 1:50 64% 0+448k 7+0io 5pf+0w
```

The meaning of each of the statistics is described in the csh manual page under "Predefined Shell Variables." This particular program run used 68.5 seconds of CPU time in user mode, used 2.8s seconds of CPU time in system mode, used 1 minute and 50 seconds of elapsed (also called wallclock) time, got 64% of the CPU during this elapsed time, used 0 bytes of shared-memory data and 448 kilobytes of unshared-memory data, did 7 block input operations and 0 block output operations, and had 5 page faults and 0 swaps to disk.

The built-in function numargs() returns the number of arguments on the command line invoking the program. Program 2.6 shows how to use the return value of getarg for error processing. It shows how a by clause in a fa loop can be used to increment the loop index variable by more than one each time through the loop. For-all loops fa can go down by using downto instead of to. Notice that a writes statement requires an explicit \n for a linefeed, like C's printf.

Program 2.7 shows how to do file IO in SR. When run as

```
sr -o fileIO fileIO.sr
fileIO file1 file2
```

it will copy *file1* to *file2*. Note the use of stderr in the error message write statements. If the output of an executing SR program is being "piped" (UNIX terminology) into another executing program as the latter's input, then writing the error message to stderr will print the message on the terminal screen, rather than the error message "disappearing" down the pipe.

Built-in procedures printf, sprintf, scanf, and sscanf are available. They are similar to the equivalent C functions (where brackets enclose an optional argument):

```
printf([file,] format, arg...)
sprintf(buffer, format, arg...)
scanf([file,] format, arg...)
sscanf(buffer, format, arg...)
```

The conversion specifier %b can be used to convert boolean values. For scanf and sscanf, the arguments are variables (not pointers to variables as in C).

In some situations it is easier to parse input data with scanf than with read. For example, read(name), where name is a string[12] variable containing at most 12 characters, reads the next 12 characters of the input line into name. So it is not possible to read multiple names per line that are separated by blanks; scanf can be used for this. Program 2.8 can be used to read input data like the following from the 1993 Internet Programming Contest.

```
5
dave laura owen vick amy
dave 200 3 laura owen vick
owen 500 1 dave
amy 150 2 vick owen
```

```
laura 0 2 amy vick
vick 0 0
3
liz steve dave
liz 30 1 steve
steve 55 2 liz dave
dave 0 2 steve liz
```

SR has a "raise to the power" operator **. Program 2.9 shows that both integers and reals can be raised to either an integer or real power. Some programming language designers, for example Wirth (Pascal [25]) and Kernighan and Ritchie (C [15]), specifically excluded a power operator from their languages.

Arrays whose dimension bounds are not known until runtime can be passed to a procedure, as shown in Program 2.10. The upper bound in the declaration of the procedure formal parameter for the array is specified as *. In order to avoid runtime errors, though, the lower bound must be one in both the array variable declaration and in the procedure formal parameter declaration.

As Program 2.11 shows, character arrays and strings can be read and written in one `read` ot `write`, but a compiler error message results if that is tried with integer arrays. Also `%s` in a `printf` can be used to print both SR strings and arrays of characters (these are different things).

Program 2.12 shows that integers are converted to real implicitly but that reals are not converted to integer implicitly (the built-in `int` must be used).

There is an escape character that allows strings to be split across lines. It also places a newline in the middle of the string when printed. For example,

```
write("Hello, \
    world!")
```

Useful built-in functions are:

`int(x)` truncate real `x` to an integer

`real(x)` convert or cast integer `x` to a real

`abs(x)` absolute value of `x`, where `x` can be integer or real

`max(a,b,c,...)` maximum value of arguments, which can be integer or real

`min(a,b,c,...)` minimum value of arguments, which can be integer or real

`low(`*type*`)` the smallest value of *type*, where *type* can be integer or real, for example

`high(`*type*`)` the largest value of *type*

`lb(x,i)` the lower bound of the ith dimension of the array `x` (if `i` is `1`, it can be omitted)

`ub(x,i)` the upper bound of the ith dimension of the array `x` (if `i` is `1`, it can be omitted)

`length(x)` the length of the string currently stored in the string variable `x`

`maxlength(x)` the maximum number of characters the string variable `x` can hold

SR has several math functions. All accept real arguments and return real results unless otherwise noted. Some arguments are optional. The functions are:

`sqrt(x)` square root of `x`

`log(x,b)` log of x to the base b (default 2.7183...)

`exp(x,b)` b (default 2.7183...) to the x power

`sin(x)` also `cos(x)` and `tan(x)`

`ceil(x)` smallest integer not less than x

`floor(x)` largest integer not greater than x

`round(x)` nearest integer to x (even integer if in the middle)

`random()` pseudorandom number between 0.0 and 1.0 (including 0.0, excluding 1.0)

`random(ub)` pseudorandom number between 0.0 and ub (including 0.0, excluding ub)

`random(lb,ub)` pseudorandom number between lb and ub (including lb, excluding ub)

The built-in procedure `seed(x)` seeds the random number generator with the real value x. If x is zero or if `seed` is not called, then `random` generates a different sequence of numbers each time the program is executed. If x is non-zero, then the same sequence of numbers will be produced by `random` each time the program is run (useful during program debugging).

Program 2.6: Processing Command Line Arguments.

```
resource arguments()
   var str : string[64]
   var status, n : int
   write("There are", numargs(), "arguments")
   fa i := 0 to numargs()+1 ->
      status :=  getarg(i, n)
      if status = EOF -> writes("no ", i, "-th argument\n")
      [] status = 0    -> getarg(i, str)
                          write("could not process argument", i,
                             "as an integer -- as a string, it is", str)
      [] else          -> write("argument", i, "is", n)
      fi
   af
   writes("The even numbered arguments are")
   fa i := 0 to numargs() by 2 -> getarg(i, str); writes(" ", str) af
   write()
   writes("And the odd numbered arguments in reverse order are")
   fa i := 2*int((numargs()+1)/2.0)-1 downto 1 by -2 ->
      getarg(i, str); writes(" ", str) af
   write()
end arguments


/* .............. Example compile and run(s)

% sr -o args args.sr
% ./args
There are 0 arguments
could not process argument 0 as an integer -- as a string, it is ./args
no 1-th argument
The even numbered arguments are ./args
And the odd numbered arguments in reverse order are
```

```
% ./args 1
There are 1 arguments
could not process argument 0 as an integer -- as a string, it is ./args
argument 1 is 1
no 2-th argument
The even numbered arguments are ./args
And the odd numbered arguments in reverse order are 1
% ./args 1 b
There are 2 arguments
could not process argument 0 as an integer -- as a string, it is ./args
argument 1 is 1
could not process argument 2 as an integer -- as a string, it is b
no 3-th argument
The even numbered arguments are ./args b
And the odd numbered arguments in reverse order are 1
% ./args 1 2 c 3 e
There are 5 arguments
could not process argument 0 as an integer -- as a string, it is ./args
argument 1 is 1
argument 2 is 2
could not process argument 3 as an integer -- as a string, it is c
argument 4 is 3
could not process argument 5 as an integer -- as a string, it is e
no 6-th argument
The even numbered arguments are ./args 2 3
And the odd numbered arguments in reverse order are e c 1
                                                        */
```

Program 2.7: File Input and Output.

```
resource fileIO()
    var infile_name, outfile_name : string[64]
    var infile, outfile : file
    var line : string[256]
    infile_name := "infile"; outfile_name := "outfile"
    getarg(1, infile_name);  getarg(2, outfile_name)
    infile := open(infile_name, READ)
    if infile = null ->
       write(stderr, "cannot open", infile_name, "for reading"); stop
    fi
    outfile := open(outfile_name, WRITE)
    if outfile = null ->
       write(stderr, "cannot open", outfile_name, "for writing"); stop
    fi
    do read(infile, line) != EOF -> write(outfile, line)
    od
end fileIO

/* .............. Example compile and run(s)

% sr -o fileIO fileIO.sr
% cat >infile
This is a test input file.
```

```
^D
% ./fileIO
% ls -l infile outfile
-rw-r--r--  1 shartley        27 Jul  7 13:57 infile
-rw-r--r--  1 shartley        27 Jul  7 13:58 outfile
% ./fileIO fileIO.sr out
% ls -l fileIO.sr out
-rw-r--r--  1 shartley       704 Jul  7 10:55 fileIO.sr
-rw-r--r--  1 shartley       704 Jul  7 13:58 out
% ./fileIO nofile discard
cannot open nofile for reading
% ls -l nofile discard
nofile not found
discard not found

                                                    */
```

Program 2.8: Parsing Lines of Names with **scanf**.

```
resource gift_givers()
    const MAX := 100
    var n, money, num_friends : int
    var names[1:MAX], friends[1:MAX,1:MAX], name : string[12]
    do read(n) != EOF ->
        if n > MAX -> write("n=", n, "is larger than", MAX); stop fi
        write("n=", n)
        writes("names=")
        fa i := 1 to n ->
            scanf("%s", names[i])
            writes(" ", names[i])
        af
        write()
        fa i := 1 to n ->
            scanf("%s%d%d", name, money, num_friends)
            write("name=", name, "money=", money, "num_friends=", num_friends)
            writes("friends=")
            fa j := 1 to num_friends ->
                scanf("%s", friends[i,j])
                writes(" ", friends[i,j])
            af
            write()
        af
    od
end gift_givers

/* ............. Example compile and run(s)

% sr -o gift_givers gift_givers.sr
% ./gift_givers <input
n= 5
names= dave laura owen vick amy
name= dave money= 200 num_friends= 3
friends= laura owen vick
name= owen money= 500 num_friends= 1
```

```
friends= dave
name= amy money= 150 num_friends= 2
friends= vick owen
name= laura money= 0 num_friends= 2
friends= amy vick
name= vick money= 0 num_friends= 0
friends=
n= 3
names= liz steve dave
name= liz money= 30 num_friends= 1
friends= steve
name= steve money= 55 num_friends= 2
friends= liz dave
name= dave money= 0 num_friends= 2
friends= steve liz
                                                    */
```

Program 2.9: Power Operator **.

```
resource raise_to_power()
   var x, y, z, u, v : real
   var i, j, k : int

   do read(x, y, i, j) != EOF ->
      z := x ** y
      k := i ** j
      u := i ** y
      v := x ** j
      write(x, "**", y, "=", z)
      write(i, "**", j, "=", k)
      write(i, "**", y, "=", u)
      write(x, "**", j, "=", v)
   od
end raise_to_power

/* .............. Example compile and run(s)

% sr -o powers powers.sr
% ./powers
2.5 3.7 3 4
2.50000 ** 3.70000 = 29.6741
3 ** 4 = 81
3 ** 3.70000 = 58.2571
2.50000 ** 4 = 39.0625
-2.0 3.0 3 -2
RTS abort: file powers.sr, line 7:
   i**j with j<0
                                                    */
```

Program 2.10: Passing Arrays to Procedures.

```
resource array_bounds()
   var a[1:13], b[-42:17], c[0:11], d[-7:-3], e[4:8]  : int

#  procedure print_bounds(ref x[*:*] : int)
# is illegal; compiler says "fatal: both bounds are '*'"

   procedure print_bounds_and_clear(ref x[1:*] : int)
      writes("bounds[", lb(x), ":", ub(x), "]\n")
      fa i := lb(x) to ub(x) -> x[i] := 0 af
   end print_bounds_and_clear

   print_bounds_and_clear(a)
   print_bounds_and_clear(b)
   print_bounds_and_clear(c)
   print_bounds_and_clear(d)
   print_bounds_and_clear(e)
end array_bounds

/* .............. Example compile and run(s)

% sr -o array_bounds array_bounds.sr
% array_bounds
bounds[1:13]
bounds[-42:17]
RTS abort: file array_bounds.sr, line 9:
   illegal subscript [-42] of array with bounds [-42:17]
                                                      */
```

Program 2.11: Reading and Writing Arrays.

```
resource print_array()
   var a[1:10] : int
#  read(a); write(a)        # does not compile

   var b : string[10]       # works fine (drops extra input)
   var c[1:10] : char       # works fine (drops extra input)
   read(b); printf("%s", b); write(b)
   read(c); printf("%s", c); write(c)
end print_array

/* .............. Example compile and run(s)

% sr -o print_array print_array.sr
% ./print_array
abcd
abcdabcd
efgh
efgh       efgh
% ./print_array
```

```
abcdefghijklmnopqrstuvwxyz
abcdefghijabcdefghij
klmnopqrstklmnopqrst
                                            */
```

Program 2.12: Converting between Real and Integer.

```
resource testing()
    var m, n : int, x : real
    m := 5
    x := m
#   x := real(m)            # previous statement is equivalent to this
    write("m =", m, "x =", x)
#   n := x                  # compile error: fatal: incompatible assignment
    n := int(x)
    write("n =", n)
end testing

/* .............. Example compile and run(s)

% sr -o testing testing.sr
% ./testing
m = 5 x = 5.00000
n = 5
                                            */
```

2.3 Lab: Sequential SR

Objectives

To learn the sequential programming features of SR, such as data types and statement types.

Preparation Before Lab

Read Section 2.1. Study the sequential programs in Programs 2.1–2.5. Learn how to declare variables of different types, including strings and arrays. Learn how to construct if-then-else statements, do-while loops, and for-all-index-variable loops. Note how IO is performed.

2.3.1 Assignment

Write a sequential single-resource SR program that will read a number from the keyboard and then print all prime numbers that are less than or equal to the number read.

For Every Lab

Do not forget to comment your programs. At the top of the program put a comment block identifying yourself, what class the program is for, the date, etc. Blocks, paragraphs, groups of code should be commented as to their function.

The output of your program should show **clearly** that it is working correctly. This is particularly important in the case of starvation prevention (first applicable in Lab 4.5), if that is part of the assignment. Put write statements at strategic places in your program to show that it is working correctly. This kind of output will be immensely helpful to you for debugging, anyway. Then use a yellow magic-marker highlighter or something to write on the output to show where starvation is occurring or where it is being prevented, if that is part of the assignment. Annotate the yellow highlight, that is, write next to the yellow highlight who is now not starving and why not.

Run your program with several different sets of test data. Most of our programs use the random number generator. In the beginning, put in a **seed**(*your favorite number*) for reproducible program runs for debugging (same sequence of random numbers each time the program is run). After debugging, take it out.

Your program grade will be based on: following directions, correct operation, quality documentation (comments in the code and your attached write-up), modularity, code clarity and quality, thoroughness of testing, doing your own work according to the guidelines in the syllabus, and error checking and handling.

In addition, you are to include a write-up describing the following.

1. What you learned doing this assignment and why you think it was given.

2. What problems you encountered while designing, implementing, and debugging your program and how you solved those problems.

3. Which features of the assignment you successfully implemented and which were not implemented.

4. How the input or random numbers you used tested your program thoroughly for its correct operation.

5. How you analyzed the output of your program to convince yourself that the output of your program shows your program is working correctly.

6. How you determined while running your program that it was preventing starvation (first applicable in Lab 4.5), if that is part of the assignment.

You are to turn in a listing of your program source, your write-up, sample input file(s), and a copy of the output(s) produced by its execution (use the `script` command). Make sure that no lines in your program source, write-up, or output scripts exceed 80 characters in length; the `lpr` command does not wrap long lines. If you want, you may use the `enscript -2r` command to produce PostScript files of your program source, write-up, and output scripts; `enscript` does wrap long lines. In addition, e-mail to me copies of your final print-outs (program source, input data, and output runs) and the above write-up.

2.4   Multiple Resources

Most SR programs consist of multiple resources. With the `op` declaration, a resource can make available to other resources the procedures implemented inside it. To do this, the `procedure` declaration must be split into an `op` and `proc` pair, where the `op` is part of the resource's interface specification and the `proc` is part of the body, as follows.

```
resource abc
   op pqr(...)
body abc()
```

```
      proc pqr(...)
        ...
      end pqr
    end abc
```

Each op is thus paired with a proc declaration containing the code implementing the procedure in the body of the resource. The op is similar to a procedure prototype in ANSI C in that it contains type information for parameters.

Another resource that wants to access the procedures "exported" with the op will import the resource implementing the needed procedures. Before the exported procedures declared with op can be accessed, the resource containing the procedures must be "enlivened" with the create statement. In a file (or collection of files) containing a multiple resource SR program, all resources but the last one physically in the file (or last file) need to be explicitly created with the create statement. The last resource in the (last) file is created implicitly when the compiled program is run.

The example in Program 2.13 (still a sequential program) illustrates these features. For the procedure fact to be accessible from outside the resource factorial, the keyword procedure must be replaced with the op and proc pair. The driver resource imports the factorial resource. The resource factorial is like an object that implements a function with the implementation details hidden. The driver resource creates the factorial resource with the create statement. The create returns a value to the driver resource. This value is called a *capability* to the created resource. The value is saved in the *capability variable* fac_cap for later use when the fact procedure, implemented in the factorial resource, is accessed with fac_cap.fact(n). Note the dot notation used. More than one procedure can be implemented and exported by a resource.

If you are using the dot notation to call a procedure in another resource and that procedure does not take any arguments, be careful not to forget the parentheses.

```
      a_cap.some_op()
```

If you forget them and instead code

```
      a_cap.some_op
```

the compiler will not generate an error message or warning, because the line of code is a legal expression evaluating to a capability to the called procedure in the other resource. But no call of the procedure will be done when the line of code is executed and your program will not work as you expect.

The two resources in Program 2.13 could be placed in separate files, say file_1.sr and file_2.sr, and compiled by the command

```
      sr -o fct2 file_1.sr file_2.sr
```

The program also illustrates that read returns a status value: EOF for end-of-file (the user typed control-D), 0 for illegal input such as an illegal character in a number, and a positive value for correctly-processed input.

Program 2.14 shows that an array can (as can any other type) be passed by reference to a proc in another resource. It also shows the use of exit and next in a do loop in conjunction with error checking of input data. The exit and next of SR are like the break and continue of C, respectively: exit terminates the do loop and continues execution with the statement following the od; next terminates the current iteration of the loop and starts another iteration. They can also be used in a fa loop statement. A different algorithm, called *quicksort*, is used to sort the array. It is faster than the exchange algorithm used in Program 2.2.

The examples in Programs 2.13 and 2.14 show how the main driver resource creates one other resource. The following example, Program 2.15, shows how the main resource creates several other resources and passes capabilities to them so they can call procedures in each other. The `driver` resource creates a resource `piglet` containing a procedure `squeak` that the resources `Strangelove` and `Zhivago` will call. The `driver` resource passes the value of the capability-to-piglet variable `pc` to `Strangelove` and `Zhivago` when they are are created. This shows a feature of SR we will see again: values, even those not known until runtime, can be passed to resources when they are created. The `driver` also passes a capability to itself to the `Strangelove` and `Zhivago` resources so they can access the `done` procedure in the `driver` resource. This is done with the built-in function `myresource()`. Note that two resources can import each other and call routines in each other.

Program 2.13: Two Resource Factorial Program.

```
resource factorial
    op fact(k: int) returns f: int
body factorial()
    proc fact(k) returns f
        if k < 0 -> f := -1
        [] k = 0 or k = 1 -> f := 1
        [] k > 1 -> f := k * fact(k-1)
        fi
    end fact
end factorial

resource driver()
    import factorial
    var n, stat : int
    var fac_cap : cap factorial
    fac_cap := create factorial()

    do true ->
        writes("What factorial to compute? ")
        stat := read(n)
        if stat = EOF ->
            write("no more input")
            stop
        [] stat = 0 ->
            write("illegal input -- try again")
        [] else ->
            write(n, "factorial is", fac_cap.fact(n))
        fi
    od
end driver

/* .............. Example compile and run(s)

% sr -o factorial factorial.sr
% ./factorial
What factorial to compute? 5
5 factorial is 120
What factorial to compute? abc
illegal input -- try again
What factorial to compute? 3
```

```
3 factorial is 6
What factorial to compute? ^D
no more input
                                             */
```

Program 2.14: Two Resource Sort Program.

```
resource sorter
    op print_array(ref a[1:*] : int), sort(ref a[1:*] : int)
body sorter()
    proc print_array(a)
        fa i := 1 to ub(a) -> writes(" ", a[i]) af;  writes("\n")
    end print_array

    procedure qs(ref nums[1:*] : int; val left, right : int)  # quicksort
        if right-left <= 0 -> return fi
        var pivot := nums[left]
        var l := left, r := right

        var not_done := true
        do not_done ->
            if nums[l+1] > pivot ->    # needs to be moved to other end of nums
                do (r > l+1) and (nums[r] > pivot) -> r-- od  # find one to swap
                if r > l+1 -> l++; nums[r] :=: nums[l]; not_done := l < r-1
                [] else -> not_done := false   # if can't find one to swap, then
                fi                             # nums now partitioned; we are done
            [] else -> l++; not_done := l < r  # need not be moved to other end
            fi
        od  # when this loop finishes, nums[left] is the pivot,
            # nums[left:l] <= pivot and nums[l+1,right] > pivot
            #
            #                        #   [pivot, <= | > ]
            #                        #     ^         ^ ^ ^
            #                        #     |         | | |
            #                        # left        l r right
            #                        #     |         | | |
            #                        #     v         v v v
        nums[left] :=: nums[l]      #    [<=, pivot | > ]

            # nums[left,l-1] <= pivot, nums[l] = pivot, and nums[l+1,right] > pivot
            # if right-(l+1) = 0, nums[l+1:right] is singleton so sorted
        qs(nums, l+1, right)
            # nums[l] = pivot is singleton so sorted
        qs(nums, left, l-1)
            # if (l-1)-left = 0, nums[left:l-1] is singleton so sorted
    end qs

    proc sort(a)    # into non-decreasing order
        qs(a, 1, ub(a))
    end sort
end sorter

resource user()
```

```
    import sorter
    var sort_cap : cap sorter
    sort_cap := create sorter()
    var stat, n : int
    do true ->
        writes("number of integers to sort? ")
        stat := read(n)
        if stat = EOF -> write("no more input"); exit
        [] stat = 0   -> write("malformed input -- try again"); next
        [] n <= 0     -> write("enter a positive number"); next
        fi
        var nums[1:n] : int  #storage reallocated each time through loop
        write("input integers, separated by white space")
        fa i := 1 to n -> read(nums[i]) af
        write("original numbers");    sort_cap.print_array(nums)
        sort_cap.sort(nums)
        write("sorted numbers");      sort_cap.print_array(nums)
    od
end user

/* .............. Example compile and run(s)

% sr -o quicksort quicksort.sr
% ./quicksort
number of integers to sort? 5
input integers, separated by white space
22 -33 -11 0 1
original numbers
 22 -33 -11 0 1
sorted numbers
 -33 -11 0 1 22
number of integers to sort? abc
malformed input -- try again
number of integers to sort? -1
enter a positive number
number of integers to sort? ^D
no more input
                                                    */
```

Program 2.15: Multiple Resources.

```
resource piglet
    op squeak(message : string[*])
body piglet()
    write("piglet resource is alive")
    proc squeak(message) write("I am", message) end squeak
end piglet

resource Strangelove
    import piglet, driver
    op goodbye()
body Strangelove(pc : cap piglet; dc : cap driver)
    proc goodbye() write("Goodbye!") end goodbye
```

```
      write("Dr. Strangelove is alive")
      pc.squeak("Dr. Strangelove")
      dc.done("Dr. Strangelove")
end Strangelove

resource Zhivago
    import piglet, driver
body Zhivago(pc : cap piglet; dc : cap driver)
    write("Dr. Zhivago is alive")
    pc.squeak("Dr. Zhivago")
    dc.done("Dr. Zhivago")
end Zhivago

resource driver
    import piglet, Strangelove, Zhivago
    op done(message: string[*])
body driver()
    proc done(message) write(message, "is done") end done
    var pc : cap piglet, dc : cap driver, sc : cap Strangelove
    write("main driver resource is alive")
    pc := create piglet()
    dc := myresource()
    sc := create Strangelove(pc, dc)
    create Zhivago(pc, dc)
    sc.goodbye()
end driver

/* .............. Example compile and run(s)

% sr -o multiple multiple.sr
% ./multiple
main driver resource is alive
piglet resource is alive
Dr. Strangelove is alive
I am Dr. Strangelove
Dr. Strangelove is done
Dr. Zhivago is alive
I am Dr. Zhivago
Dr. Zhivago is done
Goodbye!
                                    */
```

2.5   Lab: Resources and Capabilities

Objectives

To learn how one resource can create another and about capability variables.

Preparation Before Lab

Read Section 2.4. Study the sequential examples in Programs 2.13 and 2.15. Note that if an SR program consists of several resources in one file, the physically last resource in the file is started up automatically when the program is compiled and run, but all other resources need to be created explicitly. Observe that the `create` operation returns a *capability* to the resource created and that this capability is needed to access any of the operations (`op` declaration) implemented in the resource.

2.5.1 Assignment

Rewrite your prime generating program from Lab 2.3 so that it consists of two or more resources.

2.6 Additional Features

Program 2.14 shows that an array (`nums`) can be declared inside a loop ("do forever" loop in `user` resource) and that the size of the array so declared can vary. The storage is deallocated before being reallocated each time through the loop.

All created instances of resources are deallocated and destroyed when a program terminates or a `stop` statement is executed. A created instance of a resource can be destroyed explicitly with the `destroy` statement. For example, inside a loop a resource can be created with parameters read from the input data, then later destroyed inside the loop to deallocate its storage.

```
do read(a, b, c) != EOF ->
    fcap := create foo(a, b, c)
    ...
    destroy(fcap)
od
```

A resource can have a `final` block, a block of code that is executed when an instance of the resource is destroyed explicitly with the `destroy` statement. See Program 2.16 for an example of the interactions of the `stop` statement, the `destroy` statement, and the `final` block. If the main resource has a `final` block, it is executed when the main resource terminates or a `stop` statement is executed (either of these implicitly destroys the main resource). The main resource terminates after all instances of resources it has created have terminated. An instance of a created resource terminates when its top-level code terminates (and when all its processes, described in Chapter 3, have terminated). Use of `stop(1)` (or `stop(`*status*`)` for a non-zero *status*) rather than just `stop` will suppress execution of the `final` block in the main resource.

Program 2.17 illustrates a special type of resource called a `global` resource. Variables, constants, types, and `ops` that are global to several resources can be placed here and imported by the resources that need them. It does not have to be created. The dot notation, using the `global` resource name instead of a capability as is done with created (i.e., non-`global`) resources, can be used to reference operations in the `global` resource, but is not needed if there is no ambiguity.

A (non-`global`) resource can be parameterized and can be created multiple times, as shown in Program 2.18. A pointer to each instance of the resource created is stored in a capability variable. In this example, storage for an array is allocated inside each instance of the resource, based on the parameter value passed in the `body` statement (obtained from the value passed in the `create` statement).

Type information can be shared by a collection of (non-`global`) resources without having to set up a `global` resource, as the following example shows.

```
resource calculate
  type person = rec(...
  op calc_friend(...
body calculate()
  ...
end calculate

resource driver
  import calculate
body driver()
  var people[1:test] : person
  ...
end driver
```

When the `driver` resource imports the `calculate` resource, it also gets the `person` type declaration.

It is possible to have arrays in a `global` that are sized dynamically by run-time data. Program 2.19 uses a non-obvious technique to do this. Such a global resource must have an empty () in the body statement, though. It cannot be parameterized when created, like the resource in Program 2.18.

Program 2.16: Resources with `final` Blocks.

```
resource A()
   write("age()=", age(), "resource A is alive")

   final
      write("age()=", age(), "resource A has (been) terminated")
   end final
end A

resource B()
   write("age()=", age(), "resource B is alive")
end B

resource test_final_blocks()
   import A, B
   write("age()=", age(), "main resource is alive")
   var N : int := 1; getarg(1, N)
   var cA : cap A, cB : cap B

   cA := create A(); cB := create B()

   write("age()=", age(), "main resource has created resources A and B")

   if N = 1 -> write("age()=", age(), "normal termination")
   [] N = 2 -> write("age()=", age(), "stop"); stop
   [] N = 3 -> write("age()=", age(), "stop(1)"); stop(1)
   [] N = 4 -> write("age()=", age(), "destroy...")
      destroy(cA); destroy(cB)
      write("age()=", age(), "destroyed")
   fi
```

```
    final
        write("age()=", age(), "main resource has (been) terminated")
    end final
end test_final_blocks

/* .............. Example compile and run(s)

% sr -o test_final_blocks test_final_blocks.sr
% ./test_final_blocks 1
age()= 7 main resource is alive
age()= 17 resource A is alive
age()= 19 resource B is alive
age()= 20 main resource has created resources A and B
age()= 21 normal termination
age()= 32 main resource has (been) terminated
% ./test_final_blocks 2
age()= 6 main resource is alive
age()= 17 resource A is alive
age()= 19 resource B is alive
age()= 20 main resource has created resources A and B
age()= 21 stop
age()= 22 main resource has (been) terminated
% ./test_final_blocks 3
age()= 7 main resource is alive
age()= 19 resource A is alive
age()= 23 resource B is alive
age()= 24 main resource has created resources A and B
age()= 25 stop(1)
% ./test_final_blocks 4
age()= 7 main resource is alive
age()= 17 resource A is alive
age()= 19 resource B is alive
age()= 20 main resource has created resources A and B
age()= 21 destroy...
age()= 22 resource A has (been) terminated
age()= 32 destroyed
age()= 34 main resource has (been) terminated
                                             */
```

Program 2.17: A global Resource.

```
global storage
    var a, b, c : int
    op add()
body storage()
    proc add()
        c := a + b
    end add
end storage

resource read_em()
    import storage
    read(a, b)
```

```
end read_em

resource driver()
    import storage, read_em
    var read_cap : cap read_em
    read_cap := create read_em()
    storage.add()   # storage. is optional if no ambiguity
    printf("a = %d, b = %d, c = %d\n", a, b, c)
end driver

/* .............. Example compile and run(s)

% sr -o global_example global_example.sr
% ./global_example
2 3
a = 2, b = 3, c = 5
                                                    */
```

Program 2.18: A Parameterized Resource Created Multiple Times.

```
resource variable_sized_array
    op increment(), print()
body variable_sized_array(n : int)
    var a[1:n] : int := ([n] n)

    proc increment()
        fa i := 1 to n -> a[i]++ af
    end increment

    proc print()
        fa i := 1 to n -> writes(" ", a[i]) af
        writes("\n")
    end print
end variable_sized_array

resource multiple_creates()
    import variable_sized_array
    var one, two, three : cap variable_sized_array
    one := create variable_sized_array(1)
    two := create variable_sized_array(2)
    three := create variable_sized_array(3)
    one.print(); two.print(); three.print()
    one.increment(); two.increment(); three.increment()
    one.print(); two.print(); three.print()
end multiple_creates

/* .............. Example compile and run(s)

% sr -o multiple_creates multiple_creates.sr
% ./multiple_creates
 1
 2 2
 3 3 3
```

```
2
3 3
4 4 4
```
                                                    */

Program 2.19: Dynamically Sized Arrays in a global Resource.

```
global storage
   const N := 10
   var n : int := N
   var status_not_checked : int := getarg(1,n)    # a non-obvious technique!
   var a[1:n], b[1:n], c[1:n] : int
   op add()
body storage()
   proc add()
      fa i := 1 to n -> c[i] := a[i] + b[i] af
   end add
end storage

resource driver()
   import storage
   writes("Enter a vector of ", n, " integers: ")
   fa i := 1 to n -> read(a[i]) af
   writes("Enter another vector of ", n, " integers: ")
   fa i := 1 to n -> read(b[i]) af
   add()
   writes("The sum of the two vectors is")
   fa i := 1 to n -> writes(" ", c[i]) af
   write()
end driver

/* .............. Example compile and run(s)

% sr -o global_example global_example.sr
% ./global_example
Enter a vector of 10 integers: 1 3 5 7 2 4 10 8 9 11
Enter another vector of 10 integers: 1 1 1 1 1 1 1 1 1 1
The sum of the two vectors is 2 4 6 8 3 5 11 9 10 12
% ./global_example 4
Enter a vector of 4 integers: 2 4 3 5
Enter another vector of 4 integers: 1 2 3 4
The sum of the two vectors is 3 6 6 9
```
                                                    */

2.7   Animating Programs with XTANGO

An undergraduate operating systems course presents the fundamental algorithms and techniques used by the operating system in a computing system to manage concurrently executing processes and the resources they use. Topics studied include mutual exclusion, concurrent process synchronization, CPU scheduling, first fit versus best fit memory allocation, memory compaction, virtual memory and paging, file systems, disk seek scheduling, and deadlock avoidance and detection [8, 20, 21, 24]. Also studied are tools provided by the operating system to support concurrent programming, such as semaphores, monitors, and message passing.

A concurrent programming or parallel computing class looks at parallel versions of symbolic and numerical algorithms used in matrix multiplication, sorting, solving systems of equations, generating prime numbers, and solving the N queens problem.

These operating systems and concurrent programming algorithms are usually presented in the classroom using pseudo-code and drawings on the blackboard or overhead projector screen. Computer programs that implement or simulate these algorithms are usually limited to ASCII terminals or terminal emulators in the ways their generated output is displayed.

Workstations with bit-mapped monitors and graphics packages provide the hardware capability for better ways to display the output of concurrent programs and programs simulating operating systems algorithms. What is needed is a software package that can be used to animate these algorithms.

The presentation in the classroom of just about all operating system classical problems and parallel algorithms would benefit from animation [11]. The package could also be used by students for displaying the output of simulation and parallel programs, greatly facilitating debugging.

John Stasko and Doug Hayes have written a package called XTANGO [22] that can be used on UNIX workstations with bit-mapped color displays running the X11 windowing system. This package provides a platform for constructing algorithm animations. The package includes many sample animation programs, such as matrix multiplication and searching for substrings in a string.

There are two approaches to using the package. Data structures for and library calls to the animation package can be embedded in a C language program that implements a sorting algorithm, such as exchange sort, or that simulates an operating system algorithm, such as first fit memory allocation. The C program is then compiled with the XTANGO library and with the X11 windowing library. Alternatively, a text file of commands to an animation interpreter included in the XTANGO distribution can be constructed. Then the interpreter can be executed with the text file of commands as input. The text file of commands can be constructed with an editor or can be the result of print statements in a program written in any high-level programming language.

In this second alternative, the output of the program can be collected in a file for later input into the animation interpreter or the output of the program can be "piped" (UNIX terminology) directly into the animation interpreter, without the need for an intermediate file. For example, suppose the file **simulation** contains a compiled simulation program of some operating system algorithm, such as first fit memory allocation, in which the programmer has added print statements producing animation commands. Then the command

```
simulation | animator
```

will run the animation, assuming one is logged into a color, bit-mapped display workstation running X-windows (**animator** is the animation interpreter from the **animator** directory in the **xtango** source tree). In the original window on the screen will appear the original simulation output. A new window will be created on the screen in which will appear the animation of the simulation.

Before using **animator**, the command

```
xrdb -merge xtango.res
```

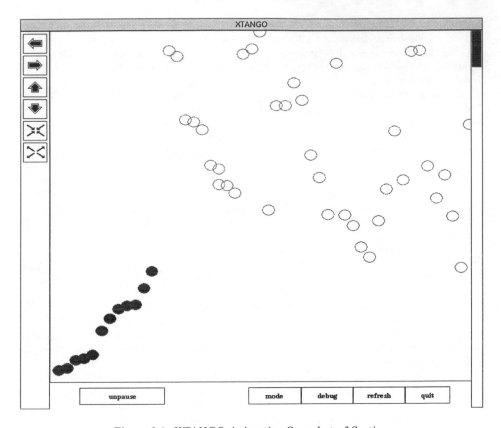

Figure 2.1: XTANGO Animation Snapshot of Sorting.

must be executed, where `xtango.res` is a file from the XTANGO source distribution. This command can be put into the home directory `.login` or `.xinitrc` file.

Program 2.20 draws the string "Hello, world!" in the middle of the XTANGO window. Program 2.21 animates the exchange sort algorithm, first seen in Program 2.2. The comments in the programs describe the animation commands used. The output of these programs is piped into the animation interpreter, as described above. Each `printf` statement consists of a command and its arguments to the animation interpreter. In contrast, normal program output is done with the `write` statement but has to be prefixed with `comment` in order to pass through the animation interpreter and be displayed in the window in which the program is being run. A snapshot of the XTANGO window during the sort animation is shown in Figure 2.1.

A complete list of the animation interpreter commands and their descriptions follows. This material is a copy of the documentation for the `animator` interpreter contained in the XTANGO software distribution. In Section 7.4, it will be shown how to access these commands as procedure calls directly from an SR program.

> This document describes the Animator program which provides an interpreted, interactive animation front-end to XTANGO. The Animator program simply reads an ascii file, one command per line. This is beneficial because you can have the output of any program, be it Pascal, C, Modula-2, etc., drive an

animation. I have used this tool in an undergraduate algorithms class. In addition to implementing an algorithm, students can develop an animation of it just by judiciously placing print statements into their program.

Animations developed with this system will be carried out in a real-valued coordinate system that originally runs from 0.0 to 1.0 from left-to-right and from 0.0 to 1.0 from bottom-to-top. Note, however, that the coordinate system is infinite in all directions. You will create and place graphical objects within the coordinate system, and then move them, change their color, visibility, fill, etc., in order to depict the operations and actions of a computer algorithm.

The format for the individual commands is described below. You can run this program interactively by piping the output of your program to it, e.g.,

    % yourprog | animator

If your program was developed on another system, you can simply import its textual output as a file and read that file as input, e.g.,

    % animator < outfile

What you need to do is augment your implementation of the algorithm under study by a set of output (e.g., `printf`, `writeln`) statements. The statements should be placed in the program at the appropriate positions to provide a trace or depiction of what your program is doing.

Below we summarize the different commands that exist within the system. If there's a command you would like added, just ask. To begin this section, we describe the commands in general.

Each command begins with a unique one word string. Make sure that you spell the strings correctly. Each graphical object that you create should be designated by a unique integer id. You will need to use that id in subsequent commands that move, color, alter, etc., the object. In essence, the id is a handle onto the object. Most of the commands and their parameters should be self-explanatory. Arguments named **steps** and **centered** are of integer type. Arguments named **xpos**, **ypos**, **xsize**, **ysize**, **radius**, **lx**, **by**, **rx**, **ty** are real or floating point numbers. Make sure that they include a decimal point (typing 0 instead of 0.0, for example, will cause an error). The argument **fillval** should be one of the following strings: **outline**, **half** or **solid**. The argument **widthval** should be one of the following strings: **thin**, **medthick**, or **thick**. The parameter **colorval** can be any color string name from the file `/usr/lib/X11/rgb.txt` (one word, no blanks allowed). Note that the **color** command only supports a subset of all these possible colors.

comment A trailing string This command simply prints out any text following the "comment" identifier to the shell in which the animator was invoked.

bg colorval Change the background to the given color. The default starter is white.

coords lx by rx ty Change the displayed coordinates to the given values. You can use repeated applications of this command to pan or zoom the animation view.

delay steps Generate the given number of animation frames with no changes in them.

line id xpos ypos xsize ysize colorval widthval Create a line with one endpoint at the given position and of the given size.

`rectangle id xpos ypos xsize ysize colorval fillval` Create a rectangle with lower left corner at the given position and of the given size (size must be positive).

`circle id xpos ypos radius colorval fillval` Create a circle centered at the given position.

`triangle id v1x v1y v2x v2y v3x v3y colorval fillval` Create a triangle whose three vertices are located at the given three coordinates. Note that triangles are moved (for move, jump, and exchange commands) relative to the center of their bounding box.

`text id xpos ypos centered colorval string` Create text with lower left corner at the given position if `centered` is 0. If `centered` is 1, the position arguments denote the place where the center of the text is put. The text string is allowed to have blank spaces included in it but you should make sure it includes at least one non-blank character.

`bigtext id xpos ypos centered colorval string` This works just like the text command except that this text is in a much larger font.

`move id xpos ypos` Smoothly move, via a sequence of intermediate steps, the object with the given id to the specified position.

`moverelative id xdelta ydelta` Smoothly move, via a sequence of intermediate steps, the object with the given id by the given relative distance.

`moveto id id` Smoothly move, via a sequence of intermediate steps, the object with the first id to the current position of the object with the second id.

`jump id xpos ypos` Move the object with the given id to the designated position in a one frame jump.

`jumprelative id xdelta ydelta` Move the object with the given id by the provided relative distance in one jump.

`jumpto id id` Move the object with the given id to the current position of the object with the second id in a one frame jump.

`color id colorval` Change the color of the object with the given id to the specified color value. Only the colors white, black, red, green, blue, orange, maroon, and yellow are valid for this command.

`delete id` Permanently remove the object with the given id from the display, and remove any association of this id number with the object.

`fill id fillval` Change the object with the given id to the designated fill value. This has no effect on lines and text.

`vis id` Toggle the visibility of the object with the given id.

`lower id` Push the object with the given id backward to the viewing plane farthest from the viewer.

`raise id` Pop the object with the given id forward to the viewing plane closest to the viewer.

`exchangepos id id` Make the two objects specified by the given ids smoothly exchange positions.

`switchpos id id` Make the two objects specified by the given ids exchange positions in one instantaneous jump.

`swapid id id` Exchange the ids used to designate the two given objects.

Program 2.20: Simple XTANGO Example.

```
resource hello_world()
#
# Change coordinates so the window's lower left and upper right corners
# have coordinates (1.0,1.0) and (3.0,3.0), respectively.
#
   printf("coords 1.0 1.0 3.0 3.0\n")
#
# Change the window background color from the default white to azure.
#
   printf("bg azure\n")
#
# Display the string "Hello, world!" in the middle of the window.  The
# text will be red and centered at coordinates (2.0,2.0).  The id of
# the text object is 777.
#
   printf("text 777 2.0 2.0 1 red Hello, world!\n")
#
# Display the same animation frame multiple times.
#
   printf("delay 10000\n")
#
# Delete the text string, identified by id.
#
   printf("delete 777\n")
end hello_world
```

Program 2.21: Animating Sorting with XTANGO.

```
resource sorter()
   procedure print_array(ref a[1:*] : int)
      const MAX_PER_LINE : int := 15
      var count : int := 0
      printf("comment ") # for animator
      fa i := 1 to ub(a) -> writes(" ", a[i]); count++
         if count mod MAX_PER_LINE = 0 -> writes("\n")
            if i < ub(a) -> printf("comment ") /* for animator */ fi
         fi
      af
      if count mod MAX_PER_LINE != 0 -> writes("\n") fi
   end print_array

   var N : int := 10;       getarg(1, N)
   var RANGE : int := 100; getarg(2, RANGE)
   printf("comment ") # for animator
   write("sorting", N, "numbers between 1 and", RANGE)
   var nums[1:N] : int

##### animator #####v
   procedure scale_x(x : int) returns x_scaled : real
```

```
        x_scaled := real(x)/(N+1)
    end scale_x

    procedure scale_y(y : int) returns y_scaled : real
        y_scaled := real(y)/(RANGE+1)
    end scale_y
##### animator #####^

    procedure sort(ref a[1:*] : int)    # into non-decreasing order
        fa i := 1 to ub(a) ->
            fa j := i+1 to ub(a) st a[i] > a[j] ->
                a[i] :=: a[j]
##### animator #####v
                # swap locations and ids of the objects
                printf("move %d %.3f %.3f\n", i, scale_x(j), scale_y(nums[j]))
                printf("move %d %.3f %.3f\n", j, scale_x(i), scale_y(nums[i]))
                printf("swapid %d %d\n", i, j)
##### animator #####^

            af
##### animator #####v
            # fill the object solid to indicate it is in final position
            printf("fill %d solid\n", i)
##### animator #####^
        af
    end sort

    fa i := 1 to N -> nums[i] := int(random(RANGE)+1) af
    printf("comment ") # for animator
    write("original numbers")
    print_array(nums)
##### animator #####v
    # display original numbers
    fa i := 1 to N ->
        printf("circle %d %.3f %.3f %.3f red outline\n",
            i, scale_x(i), scale_y(nums[i]), 0.75*scale_x(1))
    af
##### animator #####^
    sort(nums)
    printf("comment ") # for animator
    write("sorted numbers")
    print_array(nums)
end sorter

/* .............. Example compile and run(s)

% sr -o sort_anim sort_anim.sr
% ./sort_anim 3 10
comment sorting 3 numbers between 1 and 10
comment original numbers
comment  6 10 3
circle 1 0.250 0.545 0.188 red outline
circle 2 0.500 0.909 0.188 red outline
circle 3 0.750 0.273 0.188 red outline
move 1 0.750 0.545
```

```
move 3 0.250 0.273
swapid 1 3
fill 1 solid
move 2 0.750 0.909
move 3 0.500 0.545
swapid 2 3
fill 2 solid
fill 3 solid
comment sorted numbers
comment  3 6 10
% ./sort_anim 50 1000 | animator
Press RUN ANIMATION button to begin

XTANGO Version 1.52

 sorting 50 numbers between 1 and 1000
 original numbers
  443 323 489 928 382 538 748 474 181 945 617 560 40 607 741
  562 146 718 217 62 315 475 934 949 998 220 787 787 853 802
  645 580 77 908 267 353 33 208 456 547 712 573 942 945 613
  522 587 469 67 731
 sorted numbers
  33 40 62 67 77 146 181 208 217 220 267 315 323 353 382
  443 456 469 474 475 489 522 538 547 560 562 573 580 587 607
  613 617 645 712 718 731 741 748 787 787 802 853 908 928 934
  942 945 945 949 998
                                            */
```

2.8   Lab: XTANGO Animation

Objectives

To learn how to use XTANGO's `animator` interpreter to animate a sequential SR program.

Preparation Before Lab

Read Section 2.7 on using XTANGO's `animator` interpreter program. Study Programs 2.20 and 2.21.

2.8.1   Assignment

Three problems usually examined in operating systems classes are memory allocation using first fit, best fit, or next fit; virtual memory paging using LRU, FIFO, MIN, or working set; and disk seek scheduling using FCFS, SSTF, SCAN, or C-SCAN (see Chapters 7-9 and 12 in [8], Chapters 8-9 and 12 in [20], Chapters 5 and 7 in [21], and Chapters 3 and 5 in [24]). Using the `animator` interpreter program described in Section 2.7, add additional print statements to a program simulating one of these algorithms so that an animation of the algorithm can be seen by piping the program output to the animation interpreter.

Chapter 3

Concurrent Programming

In this chapter, we will learn how to write SR programs that contain multiple concurrently executing processes. If the program is running on a uniprocessor computer, the CPU is switched frequently among the processes, as described in Section 1.1.3, so they appear to run concurrently.

If the processes in the program share data, we will see that race conditions on updating the shared data can occur. This is an instance of the critical section and mutual exclusion problem.

We will see several software solutions to the mutual exclusion problem. The next chapter examines a solution, a semaphore, implemented in the operating system.

The mutual exclusion problem is one situation where concurrently executing processes need to be synchronized. Later chapters will examine additional techniques to synchronize processes.

3.1 Multiple Processes in One Resource

Program 3.1 illustrates the **process** declaration in SR. This single-resource program, when executed, will contain two concurrently executing processes or threads of control. When the program is started, the top-level code is executed, starting with the **write** statement. When each of the two **process** declarations is encountered, a new process is created to execute the code in the declaration. Note that if we wanted to add more processes to this program, we would have to type in more code of the form **process** *name* ··· **end** *name*. A quantifier like the ones used in for-all loops can be used to declare a collection of processes executing the same code, as shown in Program 3.2.

Three very useful built-in functions for multiprocess simulation programs of the kind we will be writing are **nap**(*ms*), **random**(*ub*), and **age**(). The first suspends a process for *ms* milliseconds. This will be used in many example programs to simulate a process performing some computation or activity. The random number generator **random** returns a real value in the range zero to the argument passed. It can be used to generate a random time that the simulated activity will take. The third, **age**(), returns the number of milliseconds elapsed since the program was invoked or started. This can be used to tag print statements in processes to get some idea of when during a simulation the print statement was executed.

Program 3.3 shows how to create multiple, identically coded, concurrently executing processes in the context of a single resource, where each process simulates some computation that takes a random amount of time. The quantifier technique of Program 3.2 is used. When Program 3.3 is run, the statements in its top-level block of code are executed. First, a running time and a napping time are set up, with default values overridable from the command line. Then, multiple processes are started up, each doing the same thing: a "do forever" loop that naps for a random amount of time and prints a message. The variable `nap_time` is shared in a read-only fashion by all the processes; each process, though, has its own copy of the variable `napping`. Each process also has its own copy of the variable `i`, initialized to the values 1 through `num_processes`, respectively.

You will see the intermixed output of all the processes on the screen. After the top-level code naps for a while, the whole program (all processes) is terminated with the **stop** statement. Normally an SR program with multiple processes will terminate when all of its processes terminate. Since the processes in Program 3.3 never terminate, an explicit **stop** statement is used.

Notice that the processes in these three programs need not be synchronized in any way because they do not update any shared data and they are not cooperating in the solution of a problem. Thus, there cannot be any race conditions (see Section 3.5).

Program 3.1: Two Processes in One Resource.

```
resource two_processes()
    write("this program creates two processes")

    process process1
        write("this is process 1")
    end process1

    process process2
        write("this is process 2")
    end process2
end two_processes

/* .............. Example compile and run(s)

% sr -o two_processes two_processes.sr
% ./two_processes
this program creates two processes
this is process 1
this is process 2
                                    */
```

Program 3.2: Multiple Processes in One Resource.

```
resource two_processes()
    var N : int := 5
    getarg(1, N)
    write("this program creates", N, "processes")

    process process_i(i := 1 to N)
        write("this is process", i)
    end process_i
end two_processes

/* .............. Example compile and run(s)
```

```
% sr -o N_processes N_processes.sr
% ./N_processes 4
this program creates 4 processes
this is process 1
this is process 2
this is process 3
this is process 4
                                                */
```

Program 3.3: A Multiple-Process Simulation.

```
resource multiple_processes()
    const NUM_PROCESSES := 4, NAP_TIME := 3, RUN_TIME := 60
    var num_processes : int := NUM_PROCESSES
    var nap_time : int := NAP_TIME
    var run_time : int := RUN_TIME
    getarg(1, num_processes); getarg(2, nap_time); getarg(3, run_time)

#   const seeded := 42.0  # Change to 0.0 or leave out these
#   seed(seeded)          # two lines altogether to get
                          # irreproducible random numbers

    write(num_processes, "processes to run for", run_time,
        "seconds with", nap_time, "seconds napping")

    process process_i(i := 1 to num_processes)
        var napping : int
        write("process", i, "is alive")
        do true ->
            napping := int(random(1000*nap_time))
            write("age=", age(), "process", i, "is napping for", napping, "ms")
            nap(napping)
        od
    end process_i

    nap(1000*run_time); write("must stop now"); stop
end multiple_processes

/* .............. Example compile and run(s)

% sr -o multiple_processes multiple_processes.sr
% ./multiple_processes 3 2 10
3 processes to run for 10 seconds with 2 seconds napping
process 1 is alive
age= 35 process 1 is napping for 1325 ms
process 2 is alive
age= 41 process 2 is napping for 1804 ms
process 3 is alive
age= 46 process 3 is napping for 1657 ms
age= 1370 process 1 is napping for 1140 ms
age= 1712 process 3 is napping for 272 ms
age= 1852 process 2 is napping for 1659 ms
```

```
age= 1988 process 3 is napping for 505 ms
age= 2498 process 3 is napping for 1767 ms
age= 2518 process 1 is napping for 1609 ms
age= 3541 process 2 is napping for 916 ms
age= 4139 process 1 is napping for 1858 ms
age= 4278 process 3 is napping for 1325 ms
age= 4470 process 2 is napping for 1357 ms
age= 5609 process 3 is napping for 1385 ms
age= 5835 process 2 is napping for 629 ms
age= 6008 process 1 is napping for 1334 ms
age= 6478 process 2 is napping for 1892 ms
age= 6999 process 3 is napping for 1736 ms
age= 7348 process 1 is napping for 27 ms
age= 7388 process 1 is napping for 160 ms
age= 7556 process 1 is napping for 775 ms
age= 8347 process 1 is napping for 1162 ms
age= 8431 process 2 is napping for 1827 ms
age= 8739 process 3 is napping for 1355 ms
age= 9603 process 1 is napping for 25 ms
age= 9639 process 1 is napping for 568 ms
must stop now
                                            */
```

3.2 Multiple Processes in Multiple Resources

Program 3.4 shows another way to create multiple, identically coded, concurrently executing processes, again without having to type in the code for each one. We write one resource containing the code for the process, then create the resource multiple times. Note how the resource is parameterized. Each time the `helper` resource is created in the `user` resource loop, we pass its identity i and the value of `nap_time`. The latter is no longer a global variable and in fact the instances of the `helper` resource share no variables. The capability values returned by `create` are discarded since they are not needed.

The `reply` statement in Program 3.4 requires more explanation. When a resource is created, any code in its top-level block (any code that is not a `process`, `procedure` or `proc`) is executed until the `end` of the top-level block or a `reply` is encountered. At this point, the `create` returns the capability value to the resource that called `create`. If there is code following the `reply`, that code is executed concurrently with whatever follows the `create` that just returned. Hence, while the `user` resource continues and creates additional `helper` resources, the first `helper` resource concurrently enters its "do forever" loop (`do true ->...od`). The `reply` is necessary for correct operation of this particular program, that is, it cannot be left out of this particular program. If it were left out, the first `create` executed in resource `user` would never return because of the infinite loop in the `helper` resource instance being created.

If the top level code in a resource that is being created eventually terminates, then a `reply` is not strictly necessary for correct operation, but could be inserted to increase concurrent execution. For example, a `reply` statement could be added as the first statement of the `Strangelove` resource in Program 2.15. Then, while the `driver` resource continues and creates the `Zhivago` resource, the `Strangelove` resource concurrently calls the `squeak` procedure in the `piglet` resource. In this program, though, the `reply` is not strictly necessary for correct operation.

Program 3.4: Multiple Processes in Two Resources.

```
resource helper(id, nap_time : int)
   write("helper", id, "is alive, nap_time=", nap_time)
   reply
   var napping : int
   do true ->
      napping := int(random(1000*nap_time))
      writes("age=", age(), ", helper ", id,
        " is napping for ", napping, "ms\n")
      nap(napping)
   od
end helper

resource user()
   import helper
   var num_helpers : int := 5, nap_time : int := 3, run_time : int := 60
   getarg(1, num_helpers); getarg(2, nap_time); getarg(3, run_time)

   write("resource user starting,", num_helpers, "helpers,",
      nap_time, "napping time,", run_time, "running time")

   fa i := 1 to num_helpers -> create helper(i, nap_time)
   af
   nap(1000*run_time); write("must stop now"); stop
end user

/* .............. Example compile and run(s)

% sr -o dynamic dynamic.sr
% ./dynamic 4 2 5
resource user starting, 4 helpers, 2 napping time, 5 running time
helper 1 is alive, nap_time= 2
age=24, helper 1 is napping for 396ms
helper 2 is alive, nap_time= 2
age=37, helper 2 is napping for 438ms
helper 3 is alive, nap_time= 2
age=53, helper 3 is napping for 1674ms
helper 4 is alive, nap_time= 2
age=66, helper 4 is napping for 365ms
age=429, helper 1 is napping for 1042ms
age=441, helper 4 is napping for 1076ms
age=481, helper 2 is napping for 947ms
age=1439, helper 2 is napping for 1837ms
age=1479, helper 1 is napping for 1916ms
age=1529, helper 4 is napping for 1709ms
age=1739, helper 3 is napping for 829ms
age=2571, helper 3 is napping for 1435ms
age=3249, helper 4 is napping for 8ms
age=3269, helper 4 is napping for 1702ms
age=3290, helper 2 is napping for 1089ms
age=3399, helper 1 is napping for 1628ms
age=4019, helper 3 is napping for 817ms
age=4389, helper 2 is napping for 312ms
```

```
age=4710, helper 2 is napping for 822ms
age=4951, helper 3 is napping for 600ms
age=4979, helper 4 is napping for 1737ms
age=5039, helper 1 is napping for 1777ms
must stop now
                                                                    */
```

3.3 Simulated versus Real Concurrency

On a uniprocessor such as a Sun 4, SR implements processes as user-level threads within the
SR runtime library. As far as UNIX is concerned, each SR program (unless it has multiple
virtual machines, described below) is a single UNIX process. When the SR program is
selected to run by UNIX on the CPU, the SR runtime library scheduler will switch the CPU
among the SR processes (threads) in the program. On a shared-memory multiprocessor
machine, such as the Sequent Symmetry and Silicon Graphics Iris, each SR process (thread)
can be assigned its own CPU, up to the number of CPUs available, by setting the UNIX
environment variable SR_PARALLEL to the number of CPUs.

For example, we can execute Program 3.4 on a Sequent Symmetry shared-memory multiprocessor with 8 CPUs as follows.

```
% sr -v -o dynamic dynamic.sr
MultiSR version 2.A, March 1992
dynamic.sr:
dynamic.sr:
+ /bin/cc -w -c -W0,-Nt2000 -Y helper.c
+ /bin/cc -w -c -W0,-Nt2000 -Y user.c
linking:
+ /usr3/SR/install/bin/srl -v -o dynamic helper user
+ /bin/cc -Y -c _dynamic.c
+ /bin/cc -s -Y -o dynamic Interfaces/_dynamic.o Interfaces/user.o
  Interfaces/helper.o /usr3/SR/install/lib/sr/srlib.a -lm /usr/att/lib/libm.a
  -lpps /lib/libc.a /usr/att/lib/libc.a -lseq
% setenv SR_PARALLEL 8
% ./dynamic 8 5 10
resource user starting, 8 helpers, 5 napping time, 10 running time
helper 1 is alive, nap_time= 5
age=370, helper 1 is napping for 1864ms
helper 2 is alive, nap_time= 5
age=380, helper 2 is napping for 4883ms
helper 3 is alive, nap_time= 5
age=430, helper 3 is napping for 799ms
helper 4 is alive, nap_time= 5
age=440, helper 4 is napping for 442ms
helper 5 is alive, nap_time= 5
age=470, helper 5 is napping for 2210ms
helper 6 is alive, nap_time= 5
age=480, helper 6 is napping for 4296ms
helper 7 is alive, nap_time= 5
age=510, helper 7 is napping for 3643ms
helper 8 is alive, nap_time= 5
age=530, helper 8 is napping for 1759ms
age=890, helper 4 is napping for 83ms
```

```
age=990, helper 4 is napping for 4198ms
age=1230, helper 3 is napping for 3488ms
age=2240, helper 1 is napping for 3761ms
age=2290, helper 8 is napping for 2676ms
age=2680, helper 5 is napping for 4532ms
age=4220, helper 7 is napping for 4545ms
age=4720, helper 3 is napping for 154ms
age=4790, helper 6 is napping for 1620ms
age=4880, helper 3 is napping for 675ms
age=4970, helper 8 is napping for 3679ms
age=5190, helper 4 is napping for 4930ms
age=5270, helper 2 is napping for 1899ms
age=5560, helper 3 is napping for 3504ms
age=6010, helper 1 is napping for 4841ms
age=6410, helper 6 is napping for 4847ms
age=7180, helper 2 is napping for 1234ms
age=7220, helper 5 is napping for 3236ms
age=8420, helper 2 is napping for 3213ms
age=8650, helper 8 is napping for 4280ms
age=8780, helper 7 is napping for 1036ms
age=9070, helper 3 is napping for 2106ms
age=9820, helper 7 is napping for 1471ms
age=10120, helper 4 is napping for 3064ms
age=10460, helper 5 is napping for 3617ms
must stop now
```

The same thing can be done with Program 3.3.

The SR language has support for the kind of coarse-grained parallel computing, sometimes called cluster programming, in which the processes of a program run on several workstations connected by a local area network. The processes can synchronize and communicate, if needed, using message passing, covered in Section 6.1. Program 3.5 is a modification of Program 3.4 with code added to start each process running on a machine named on the command line. If violet, rose, and lily are the names of three machines on a local area network, all sharing a common disk partition of user files mounted with NFS, then the command

```
sr -o multiple_machines multiple_machines.sr
multiple_machines 3 2 10 violet rose lily
```

would start three helper processes, one per physical machine.

Only two changes must be made to the original version. The first is adding the block of code bracketed with the comments starts HERE and ends HERE. This block reads in the machine names. In order for a process in an SR program to run on a different physical machine, an environment called a *virtual machine* must be started on the other physical machine with the

```
machine_cap[i] := create vm() on machine_name
```

statement. The create in this case returns a capability to the virtual machine running on the other physical machine. The second change is adding on machine_cap[i] to the statement that creates each helper resource. This addition causes the resource and all its processes (just one here) to run in the virtual machine on the other physical machine.

Program 3.5: Distributed Multiple Processes on a LAN.

```
resource helper(id, nap_time : int)
   write("helper", id, "is alive, nap_time=", nap_time)
   reply
   var napping : int
   do true ->
      napping := int(random(1000*nap_time))
      writes("age=", age(), ", helper ", id,
        " is napping for ", napping, "ms\n")
      nap(napping)
   od
end helper

resource user()
   import helper
   var num_helpers : int := 5, nap_time : int := 3, run_time : int := 60
   getarg(1, num_helpers); getarg(2, nap_time); getarg(3, run_time)

   write("resource user starting,", num_helpers, "helpers,",
      nap_time, "napping time,", run_time, "running time")

   var machine_name : string[64]        # added code starts HERE #####
   var machine_cap[1:num_helpers] : cap vm
   fa i := 1 to num_helpers ->
      getarg(3+i, machine_name)
      machine_cap[i] := create vm() on machine_name
      if machine_cap[i] = null ->
         write("Cannot create vm on", machine_name, "so aborting"); stop
      fi
      write("Virtual machine starting up on machine", machine_name)
   af                                     # added code ends HERE except ...

   fa i := 1 to num_helpers -> create helper(i, nap_time)
        on machine_cap[i]               # ... for this line HERE
   af
   nap(1000*run_time); write("must stop now"); stop
end user

/* .............. Example compile and run(s)

% sr -o multiple_machines multiple_machines.sr
% ./multiple_machines 3 2 10 violet lily rose
resource user starting, 3 helpers, 2 napping time, 10 running time
Virtual machine starting up on machine violet
Virtual machine starting up on machine lily
Virtual machine starting up on machine rose
helper 1 is alive, nap_time= 2
helper 2 is alive, nap_time= 2
helper 3 is alive, nap_time= 2
age=210, helper 3 is napping for 1995ms
age=4010, helper 1 is napping for 1029ms
age=1710, helper 2 is napping for 1938ms
age=5040, helper 1 is napping for 181ms
```

```
age=5260, helper 1 is napping for 1503ms
age=3650, helper 2 is napping for 940ms
age=2210, helper 3 is napping for 1614ms
age=6880, helper 1 is napping for 1776ms
age=4590, helper 2 is napping for 396ms
age=4990, helper 2 is napping for 1523ms
age=3830, helper 3 is napping for 1431ms
age=8750, helper 1 is napping for 78ms
age=8830, helper 1 is napping for 865ms
age=6520, helper 2 is napping for 1514ms
age=5270, helper 3 is napping for 1854ms
age=9710, helper 1 is napping for 1178ms
age=8040, helper 2 is napping for 431ms
age=8480, helper 2 is napping for 1002ms
age=10950, helper 1 is napping for 1581ms
age=7130, helper 3 is napping for 1279ms
age=9490, helper 2 is napping for 358ms
age=9850, helper 2 is napping for 1079ms
age=8410, helper 3 is napping for 1522ms
age=12540, helper 1 is napping for 119ms
age=12660, helper 1 is napping for 1899ms
age=10930, helper 2 is napping for 238ms
age=11170, helper 2 is napping for 483ms
age=9940, helper 3 is napping for 1017ms
age=11660, helper 2 is napping for 1924ms
must stop now
% ./multiple_machines 3 2 10 king queen tweedle
resource user starting, 3 helpers, 2 napping time, 10 running time
Virtual machine starting up on machine king
Virtual machine starting up on machine queen
Cannot create vm on tweedle so aborting
                                       */
```

3.4   Debugging Techniques

The best way to debug an SR program is with the **write** or **printf** statement, as is the case with any high-level programming language. There is no substitute for thinking during design and coding about what you would like to see printed out as the program executes to determine if it is working correctly. In particular, think about what variables you would like to see the values of and where in the program you want to print those values out. Also think about where to insert marker statements, such as

```
write("DEBUG: about to unlink first node in procedure delete")
```

Most of the SR programs you will write will contain multiple processes. The output of all **write** and **printf** statements in all processes will be intermixed on the screen (or in a file if the UNIX **stdout** has been redirected). Therefore, it is useful to tag write statements with a process identifier and with the elapsed time since the program began using the **age()** built-in function. Here is an example.

```
writes("At time ", age(), ", helper ", id, " is napping\n")
```

It is possible to send the output of each process to a different file. Program 3.6 shows how to do this. If you are on a workstation that supports multiple windows on the screen, then you can open up as many shell or command windows as there are output files and execute the UNIX command

```
tail -f helper_i.output
```

in each one (replace i with a number) to see the output of each process in a separate window as the output is generated.

Debugging packages such as dbx and gdb are not going to help much with SR. Even though the SR translator produces C code, which is compiled with the native C compiler, e.g., cc or gcc, the symbol table used by dbx and gdb will contain many unrecognizable names.

The SR runtime system, RTS, will generate error messages before aborting a program. More error conditions are detected than in most C runtime systems. For example, trying to use a subscript value outside the bounds of an array will be detected and a message like the following printed before terminating the program.

```
RTS abort: file testing.sr, line 19:
    illegal subscript [11] of array with bounds [1:10]
```

Some of these runtime checks can be turned off with the -O option:

```
sr -O -o file file.sr
```

This will also activate the C compiler's code optimization phase (the SR compiler produces C code).

The file rts/debug.h in the SR software distribution, shown in Program 3.7, contains information about debugging SR programs that may help. What you can do is set an environment variable, like this,

```
setenv SR_DEBUG 7F
```

to turn on some tracing flags. Then when you run your SR program, various events will be traced on your screen. The debug.h file says to setenv TRACE, but that is wrong; setenv SR_DEBUG instead, as described in the SR manual page. But the hex value flags described in debug.h are the ones to use for setenv SR_DEBUG (7F is a good value to start with; for maximum tracing, use 7FFFFFFF).

Here is sample output, using the value 7F with Program 3.2.

```
% sr -o N_processes N_processes.sr
% setenv SR_DEBUG 7F
% ./N_processes 3
[1] (01FDF8) debug flags set to 7F
[1] (023330) job server 0 alive, pid 12343, ppid 12324
[1] (0232D8) startup code done initializing RTS
this program creates 3 processes
this is process 1
this is process 2
this is process 3
[1] (023388) WE ARE IDLE: activating sr_stop p0232D8
[1] (0232D8) sr_stop(0,1)
[1] (0232D8) finalizing main resource
[1] (0232D8) destroying main VM globals
[1] (0232D8) shutdn(0,1)
[1] (0232D8) exit(0)
```

And more sample output, using the value FFFFF.

```
% sr -o N_processes N_processes.sr
% setenv SR_DEBUG FFFFF
% ./N_processes 3
[1] (01FDF8) debug flags set to FFFFF
[1] (023330) r000000 new_sem  s030BBC ([JSdummy])
[1] (023330) job server 0 alive, pid 12348, ppid 12324
[1] (023330) JS 0 calling sr_scheduler ()
[1] (023330) r000000 switchto p0232D8 prio 0
[1] (0232D8) r000000 new_sem  s030BD8 ([startup])
[1] (0232D8) startup code done initializing RTS
[1] (0232D8) r000000 spawn     p023330
[1] (0232D8) r000000 new_sem  s030BF4 ([startup])
[1] (0232D8) r000000 activate p023330 ([oops])
[1] (0232D8) r000000 P         s030BF4
[1] (0232D8) r000000 *030BF8 block    p0232D8
[1] (0232D8) r000000 switchto p023330 prio 0
this program creates 3 processes
[1] (023330) r0355A4 switchto p023330 prio 0
[1] (023330) two_processe invoke1 00036DF8
[1] (023330) r0355A4 spawn     p0233E0
[1] (023330) r0355A4 activate p0233E0 ([baby proc])
[1] (023330) two_processe invoke1 0003D020
[1] (023330) r0355A4 spawn     p023438
[1] (023330) r0355A4 activate p023438 ([baby proc])
[1] (023330) two_processe invoke1 00043248
[1] (023330) r0355A4 spawn     p023490
[1] (023330) r0355A4 activate p023490 ([baby proc])
[1] (023330) r0355A4 V        s030BF4
[1] (023330) r0355A4 awaken    p0232D8 prio 0 from 030BF8
[1] (023330) r0355A4 switchto p0233E0 prio 0
this is process 1
[1] (0233E0)                  fin_prc 00036DF8
[1] (0233E0) r0355A4 switchto p023438 prio 0
this is process 2
[1] (023438)                  fin_prc 0003D020
[1] (023438) r0355A4 switchto p023490 prio 0
this is process 3
[1] (023490)                  fin_prc 00043248
[1] (023490) r0355A4 switchto p0232D8 prio 0
[1] (0232D8) r000000 kill_sem s030BF4
[1] (0232D8) r000000 switchto p023388 prio -9
[1] (023388) r000000 spawn     p0232D8
[1] (023388) WE ARE IDLE: activating sr_stop p0232D8
[1] (023388) r000000 activate p0232D8 ([shutdown])
[1] (023388) r000000 switchto p0232D8 prio -9
[1] (0232D8) sr_stop(0,1)
[1] (0232D8) finalizing main resource
[1] (0232D8) r000000 spawn     p023490
[1] (0232D8) r000000 new_sem  s030BF4 ([shutdown])
[1] (0232D8) r000000 activate p023490 ([main final])
[1] (0232D8) r000000 P         s030BF4
[1] (0232D8) r000000 *030BF8 block    p0232D8
[1] (0232D8) r000000 switchto p023490 prio -9
[1] (023490) r0355A4 V        s030BF4
```

```
[1] (023490) r0355A4 awaken    p0232D8 prio -9 from 030BF8
[1] (023490) r0355A4 switchto p0232D8 prio -9
[1] (0232D8) destroying main VM globals
[1] (0232D8) shutdn(0,1)
[1] (0232D8) exit(0)
```

As you can see, the best debugging technique is the print statement! Although using XTANGO as described in Section 2.7 to animate programs will itself involve debugging, it can also be used to see if an algorithm is working correctly.

Program 3.6: Sending Each Process Output to a Different File.

```
resource helper(id, nap_time : int; outfile : file)
   write(outfile, "helper", id, "is alive, nap_time=", nap_time)
   reply
   var napping : int
   do true ->
      napping := int(random(1000*nap_time))
      writes(outfile, "age=", age(), ", helper ", id,
        " is napping for ", napping, "ms\n")
      nap(napping)
   od
end helper

resource user()
   import helper
   var number : int := 5, nap_time : int := 3, run_time : int := 60
   getarg(1, number); getarg(3, nap_time); getarg(2, run_time)
   var outfile_name : string[64], outfile : file
   write("resource user starting,", number, "helpers,",
      nap_time, "napping time,", run_time, "running time")
   fa i := 1 to number ->
      sprintf(outfile_name, "helper_%d.output", i)
      outfile := open(outfile_name, WRITE)
      if outfile = null ->
         write("could not open", outfile_name, "for writing"); stop
      fi
      create helper(i, nap_time, outfile)
   af
   nap(1000*run_time); write("must stop now"); stop
end user

/* .............. Example compile and run(s)

% sr -o multiple_outs multiple_outs.sr
% ./multiple_outs
resource user starting, 5 helpers, 3 napping time, 60 running time
must stop now
% ls -l help*
-rw-r--r--  1 shartley      1643 Jul  7 14:41 helper_1.output
-rw-r--r--  1 shartley      1935 Jul  7 14:41 helper_2.output
-rw-r--r--  1 shartley      1647 Jul  7 14:41 helper_3.output
-rw-r--r--  1 shartley      1484 Jul  7 14:41 helper_4.output
-rw-r--r--  1 shartley      1973 Jul  7 14:41 helper_5.output
                                    */
```

Program 3.7: SR file `rts/debug.h`.

```
/*  debug.h -- debugging symbols and macros  */

extern int sr_dbg_flags;              /* currently enabled debugging values */

/*
 *  These flag values are used in the DEBUG macro.
 *  This file may be changed to reflect debugging priorities.
 *
 *  The general philosophy is that each bit should control a particular class
 *  of events, and in each class only the major events are produced (not a
 *  detailed trace).
 *
 *  Debugging is enabled by "setenv TRACE hexvalue".
 */

#define D_ALL_FLAGS       0xFFFFFFFF

/* general */
#define D_GENERAL 0x1              /* startup, shutdown, etc. */
#define D_TEMP          0x2              /* reserved for temporary uses */
#define D_PROG          0x4              /* program calls to SR_DEBUG */

/* resources */
#define D_RESOURCE      0x8              /* resource creation and destruction */

/* virtual machine control */
#define D_SRX_ACT 0x10             /* srx actions */
#define D_SRX_IN  0x20             /* srx inputs */
#define D_SOCKET  0x40             /* misc socket I/O */

/* --- beyond this point the output becomes more voluminous --- */

/* virtual machine messages */
#define D_SENT          0x100            /* packets sent */
#define D_RCVD          0x200            /* packets received */
#define D_TERM          0x400            /* distributed termination */

/* invoke */
#define D_INVOKE  0x800            /* call, send, forward, reply */

/* semaphores */
#define D_V             0x1000           /* V */
#define D_P             0x2000           /* P */
#define D_MKSEM         0x4000           /* create */
#define D_KLSEM         0x8000           /* destroy */

/* processes */
#define D_ACTIVATE      0x10000          /* activate */
#define D_BLOCK         0x20000          /* block */
#define D_SPAWN         0x40000          /* spawn, kill */
#define D_KILL          0x40000          /* spawn, kill */
#define D_RESTART 0x80000          /* restart (context switch) */
```

```
/* I/O and clock */
#define D_CLOCK              0x100000 /* clock events */
#define D_SELECT  0x200000 /* select() calls */

/* MultiSR mutexes */
#define D_QMUTEX  0x400000 /* queue mutex */
#define D_MUTEX              0x800000 /* other mutexes */

/* loops */
#define D_LOOP               0x1000000             /* loop counter expired */

/* memory allocation */
#define D_NEW                0x10000000            /* new/free calls */
#define D_ALLOC              0x20000000            /* low-level allocations */
#define D_ARRAY              0x40000000            /* array & string alloc & init */

/* control flag (this alters behavior rather than selecting tracing) */
#define D_NOFREE  0x80000000             /* inhibit freeing of memory */



/*  Print values v with format f if any debugging flags masked by n are set.  */

#ifndef NDEBUG

#define DBFLAGS(n) (sr_dbg_flags & (n))
#define DEBUG0(n,f) (DBFLAGS(n) ? sr_bugout(f,0,0,0,0,0) : 0)
#define DEBUG(n,f,v1,v2,v3) \
    (DBFLAGS(n) ? sr_bugout(f,(int)(v1),(int)(v2),(int)(v3),0,0) : 0)
#define DEBUG5(n,f,a,b,c,d,e) \
    (DBFLAGS(n) ? sr_bugout(f,(int)(a),(int)(b),(int)(c),(int)(d),(int)(e)) : 0)

#else /*NDEBUG*/

#define DBFLAGS(n) 0
#define DEBUG0(n,f) 0
#define DEBUG(n,f,v1,v2,v3) 0
#define DEBUG5(n,f,v1,v2,v3,v4,v5) 0

#endif /*NDEBUG*/
```

3.5   Race Conditions and Process Synchronization

In a concurrent programming class or in the concurrent process material in an operating systems class, you will learn about the "lost update" problem when two or more processes share data. If two processes share a variable N, if they execute N := N+1 at about the same time on an architecture with CPU registers and load and store register instructions, and if the register loads and stores get interleaved, then one of the updates will be lost and overwritten by the other. This is an example of a *race condition*. Race conditions occur when two or more processes share data, they are reading and writing the shared data concurrently, and the final result depends on which process does what when. Concurrently executing processes that share data need to synchronize their operations and processing in order to avoid race conditions on shared data.

Race conditions can also occur in an operating system. If the ready queue is implemented as a linked list and if the ready queue is being manipulated during the handling of an interrupt, then interrupts will be disabled to prevent another interrupt of the same type being handled before the first one is completed. If interrupts were not disabled then the linked list could become corrupted.

We can create a race condition in an SR program, but not at such a low level as incrementing a variable, since SR may not interleave processes at that fine a granularity. Instead we can interleave the execution of two loops in two processes that share data, as is done in Program 3.8. Each process repeatedly calls the function fn, which updates the shared variable sum with a loop. If two calls to the function by two processes are interleaved, then the variable sum will not be updated the way the programmer desires because the value of sum is passed to the function and the value is stored in the function's local variable f. Updates to sum will be lost during the concurrent execution of sum := fn(sum, i) if the statements of the function fn are interleaved, just as can happen with the concurrent execution of a statement like N := N+1 if its compiled machine language instructions are interleaved.

SR may not interleave the function calls since they are so short. We can force such an interleaving by compiling the program in a certain way. In a lab exercise, you will be asked to store this program in a file named race.sr, and then compile and run it with the following sequence of commands:

```
sr -c race.sr
srl -L 1 -o race_L1 race_2_processes
race_L1
```

The -L 1 argument to srl causes the SR runtime system to do a process context switch after every loop iteration. You will be asked to observe and explain the output.

For future reference, the way to use the srl -L 1 interleaving technique on a multi-resource program in file prog.sr is

```
sr -c prog.sr
srl -L 1 -o prog resource₁ resource₂ ... resourceₘ
prog
```

where $resource_m$ is the name of the last or "main" resource in the file (the one automatically created when the program is run). If there is just one file containing one resource, then the name $resource_1$ on the srl line is the name of the one resource in the file; the file name itself, prog.sr, does not have to match the resource name.

To make the program work under any interleaving scheme, we need to coordinate or synchronize the execution of the processes so they will not try to update a shared variable simultaneously. This is called the *critical section* or *mutual exclusion* problem. In an operating systems or concurrent programming course, you will learn about the various ways to solve this problem, using software, hardware, and system calls to the operating system. Section 3.8 looks at software solutions and the section after that looks at semaphores (usually implemented with system calls to the operating system). But first we need to make explicit our assumptions about the computer architecture and memory system our concurrent programs are running on.

Program 3.8: A Race Condition.

```
resource race_2_processes()
   var sum: int := 0

   procedure fn(j, k: int) returns f: int
      f := j
      fa l := 1 to k ->
         f := f + l
      af
   end fn

   process process1
      write("process1")
      fa i := 1 to 10 ->
         sum := fn(sum, i)
      af
      write("end process1, sum = ", sum)
   end process1

   process process2
      write("process2")
      fa i := 1 to 10 ->
         sum := fn(sum, i)
      af
      write("end process2, sum = ", sum)
   end process2
end race_2_processes

/* .............. Example compile and run(s)

% sr -o race race.sr
% ./race
process1
process2
end process2, sum =   220
end process1, sum =   440
% sr -c race.sr
% srl -L 1 -o race_L1 race_2_processes
% ./race_L1
process1
process2
end process1, sum =   220
end process2, sum =   220
                                          */
```

3.6   Lab: Race Conditions

Objectives

To learn how processes that share data may not execute correctly if their statements are interleaved in certain orders. Race conditions and lost updates can occur.

Preparation Before Lab

Read Sections 3.1–3.2 on multiple processes. Then read Section 3.5 on race conditions. Study Program 3.8.

3.6.1   Assignment

Identify the race condition in Program 3.8. Draw a diagram showing side-by-side the step-by-step interleaved execution of the two processes when the race condition occurs and one of the updates gets lost.

Store Program 3.8 in a file named `race.sr`. Compile and run the program with the usual two commands:

```
sr -o race race.sr
race
```

The program produces the correct output because the normal context switch interval (time between context switches, also called the time quantum) in the SR runtime system is long enough so that the statements of the two processes are not interleaved.

Now compile and run with these commands instead:

```
sr -c race.sr
srl -L 1 -o race_L1 race_2_processes
race_L1
```

The `-L 1` argument to `srl` causes a process context switch after every loop iteration. What is the output of the program this time? Explain exactly how this output can happen and compare this run of the program to the previous one.

3.7   Architecture and Shared Memory Systems

Concurrent programs are those that have several concurrently executing processes. Until we get to Section 6.1 on message passing, we will assume the processes share and update global data and run on a uniprocessor or a shared-memory multiprocessor. Concurrently executing processes that share an entire address space are usually called *threads* or *lightweight processes*. Processes that use message passing to communicate do not need to share their address space, memory, or data.

We will assume that our uniprocessor or shared-memory multiprocessor has a load-store instruction set: instructions use the memory bus to load data from memory into CPU registers or store data from CPU registers into memory. These loads and stores are *atomic*, that is they are done in one uninterruptible memory bus transaction. A context switch cannot occur in the middle of a load or a store; no other instructions from another CPU, if there is one, can be interleaved in the middle of a load or store instruction. If two processes each perform a memory load or store instruction, then their instructions will be serialized by the memory bus, that is, they will be performed in some sequential order.

For a concurrent program to be correct, it has to be written so that it is not dependent in any way on when context switches occur, on how long time slices (times between context switches) are, or on the the relative speeds of the CPUs in a multiprocessor system.

If we have a shared-memory multiprocessor, each CPU may have a cache in order to reduce memory bus traffic and increase the performance of the system. In order to keep the memory system *coherent*, we will assume that the caches are *write-through* and *snoopy* (see Section 9.2 of [24]). If one CPU writes to a memory location, then main memory will be updated and all other caches will either update or invalidate their copy of the item, if they have one. So if several CPUs are caching the same memory location and a process on one of the CPUs writes a value to the memory location and another process on another CPU later reads that location, it will get the updated value. In fact, all the other processes will "see" the updated value at the same time (get the updated value on a read). This is what would happen on a uniprocessor.

We will assume that the shared memory system has the *linearizability* correctness condition described in [12] (also called *atomicity, atomic memory,* and *atomic consistency*). As each process in a collection of concurrent processes runs, it generates a sequence of read and write operations to shared data in memory. Each operation consists of a request (read the value from some address, write a value to some address) and a response (returning the value read, indicating the write was done). The operations of any particular process do not overlap, i.e., the next operation request of process A is not performed until the response to the previous operation of process A has been received by A. In other words, there is no prefetching or pipelining of operations. Each operation (read, write) by each concurrent process on shared memory "takes effect instantaneously at some point between its invocation and its response." In each process, each read or write operation takes effect in the order specified by the code in the process. Furthermore, the "effects" of each process are "seen" or observed in the same order by all processes. Finally, all operations by all processes are interleaved on shared memory in an order that is consistent with the order of each process's operations in its own execution history (sequence of read and write operations). For more details, see [12, 17].

To illustrate this, assume we have a shared-memory multiprocessor. Two processes are executing on two CPUs, a producer process and a consumer process. They share a bounded buffer in which the producer deposits items and from which the consumer fetches items. They need to coordinate their activities so that the producer does not try to deposit an item into a full buffer and the consumer does not try to fetch an item from an empty buffer. This is the *bounded buffer producer consumer* problem we will see again in Section 4.2. Program 3.9 shows a solution that involves *busy waiting*: if the buffer is full the producer spins in a loop until the consumer empties a slot and similarly for the consumer. In SR, `skip` means *noop* or "do nothing" so a `do` *condition* -> `skip` `od` is a busy waiting loop.

This program will not work correctly if the consumer process "sees" the memory updates of the producer's two statements labeled C and D in the program in the reverse order. Likewise, the producer has to see the two memory updates labeled E and F in the same order that they are performed by the consumer. Consequently, this program depends on an atomic memory since it will not work correctly if the `occupied` field is seen by the consumer to be updated by the producer before the `value` field is updated by the producer. A memory system is atomic if the result of executing a collection of processes concurrently is the same as some sequential interleaving of their instructions and if the interleaving preserves the real-time ordering of the operations performed by the processes. In other words, all processes "see" all memory writes to all locations in the same order as they are performed in real time.

Another feature this program needs for correct operation is equal priorities for all processes so that a high priority process, one that is scheduled before lower priority processes, cannot spin in a busy waiting loop waiting for an event to occur and keep a low priority process from being scheduled so it can generate the event. In general, we will always assume all processes have equal priorities, particularly when those processes share a CPU. This will prevent a high-priority busy-waiting processes from starving out a lower priority process that wants to release the resource the high-priority process is waiting for.

As mentioned, the bounded buffer producer and consumer code in Program 3.9 uses busy waiting to synchronize the producer and consumer processes. Besides wasting CPU cycles, this program has two other disadvantages compared to the versions we will see later. Because of race conditions on variables `put_in` and `take_out`, there can only be one producer process and only one consumer process. Also, even with only one producer and consumer process, there would be race conditions on a variable `count` used to maintain a count of full buffer slots. Therefore `count` was commented out.

The program illustrates the use of a record data structure, keyword `rec`, in SR. The statements labeled A and B show how to: declare an array type, declare a record type using the array type, declare an array of the record type, and initialize the array of records as part of its declaration.

Program 3.9: Busy Waiting Bounded Buffer Producer and Consumer.

```
resource user()
    type value_type = [1:2] real                                    # A
    type slot = rec(value : value_type, occupied : bool)            # A
    var num_slots := 10, pnap := 3, cnap := 3, run_time := 60
    getarg(1, num_slots); getarg(2, pnap); getarg(3, cnap); getarg(4, run_time)
    var buffer[0:num_slots-1] : slot := ([num_slots] slot(([2] 0.0), false))  # B
    var take_out := 0, put_in := 0
    ### var count : int := 0

    write("main user resource alive, num_slots=", num_slots,
        "pnap=", pnap, "cnap=", cnap, "run_time=", run_time)

    procedure deposit(item : real)
        do buffer[put_in].occupied -> skip od
        buffer[put_in].value[1] := real(age())/1000.0
        buffer[put_in].value[2] := item                            # C
        buffer[put_in].occupied := true                            # D
        put_in := (put_in + 1) % num_slots
        ### count++                              ### race condition!!!
        write("                          after deposit put_in=", put_in)
    end deposit

    procedure fetch() returns item : real
        do not buffer[take_out].occupied -> skip od
        item := buffer[take_out].value[2]                          # E
        buffer[take_out].occupied := false                         # F
        take_out := (take_out + 1) % num_slots
        ### count--                              ### race condition!!!
        write("                          after fetch take_out=", take_out)
    end fetch

    process producer
```

```
      var item : real, napping : int
      do true ->
         napping := int(random(1000*pnap))
         write("age=", age(), "PRODUCER napping for", napping, "ms")
         nap(napping)
         item := random()
         write("age=", age(), "PRODUCER produced item", item)
         deposit(item)
         writes("PRODUCER deposited item ", item, "; ")
      od
   end producer

   process consumer
      var item : real, napping : int
      do true ->
         napping := int(random(1000*cnap))
         write("age=", age(), "consumer napping for", napping, "ms")
         nap(napping)
         write("age=", age(), "consumer wants to consume ...")
         item := fetch()
         writes("consumer fetched item ", item, "; ")
      od
   end consumer

   nap(1000*run_time); write("must stop now"); stop
end user

/* .............. Example compile and run(s)

% sr -o bounded_buffer bounded_buffer.sr
% ./bounded_buffer 5 3 2 15
main user resource alive, num_slots= 5 pnap= 3 cnap= 2 run_time= 15
age= 59 consumer napping for 123 ms
age= 64 PRODUCER napping for 593 ms
age= 192 consumer wants to consume ...
age= 669 PRODUCER produced item 0.0828345
                              after deposit put_in= 1
PRODUCER deposited item 0.0828345; age= 708 PRODUCER napping for 2368 ms
                              after fetch take_out= 1
consumer fetched item 0.0828345; age= 718 consumer napping for 1914 ms
age= 2642 consumer wants to consume ...
age= 3112 PRODUCER produced item 0.403338
                              after deposit put_in= 2
PRODUCER deposited item 0.403338; age= 3144 PRODUCER napping for 1372 ms
                              after fetch take_out= 2
consumer fetched item 0.403338; age= 3156 consumer napping for 269 ms
age= 3432 consumer wants to consume ...
age= 4522 PRODUCER produced item 0.0881170
                              after deposit put_in= 3
PRODUCER deposited item 0.0881170; age= 4535 PRODUCER napping for 1335 ms
                              after fetch take_out= 3
consumer fetched item 0.0881170; age= 4545 consumer napping for 881 ms
age= 5432 consumer wants to consume ...
age= 5879 PRODUCER produced item 0.805862
                              after deposit put_in= 4
```

```
PRODUCER deposited item 0.805862; age= 5894 PRODUCER napping for 1087 ms
                        after fetch take_out= 4
consumer fetched item 0.805862; age= 5904 consumer napping for 378 ms
age= 6292 consumer wants to consume ...
age= 6994 PRODUCER produced item 0.682286
                        after deposit put_in= 0
PRODUCER deposited item 0.682286; age= 7007 PRODUCER napping for 2772 ms
                        after fetch take_out= 0
consumer fetched item 0.682286; age= 7016 consumer napping for 110 ms
age= 7132 consumer wants to consume ...
age= 9795 PRODUCER produced item 0.367800
                        after deposit put_in= 1
PRODUCER deposited item 0.367800; age= 9807 PRODUCER napping for 2380 ms
                        after fetch take_out= 1
consumer fetched item 0.367800; age= 9817 consumer napping for 1220 ms
age= 11042 consumer wants to consume ...
age= 12194 PRODUCER produced item 0.975605
                        after deposit put_in= 2
PRODUCER deposited item 0.975605; age= 12205 PRODUCER napping for 655 ms
                        after fetch take_out= 2
consumer fetched item 0.975605; age= 12215 consumer napping for 685 ms
age= 12872 PRODUCER produced item 0.276056
                        after deposit put_in= 3
PRODUCER deposited item 0.276056; age= 12883 PRODUCER napping for 1020 ms
age= 12912 consumer wants to consume ...
                        after fetch take_out= 3
consumer fetched item 0.276056; age= 12921 consumer napping for 1805 ms
age= 13912 PRODUCER produced item 0.0169606
                        after deposit put_in= 4
PRODUCER deposited item 0.0169606; age= 13924 PRODUCER napping for 2985 ms
age= 14732 consumer wants to consume ...
                        after fetch take_out= 4
consumer fetched item 0.0169606; age= 14744 consumer napping for 1804 ms
must stop now
                                   */
```

3.8   The Mutual Exclusion Problem

A *critical section* is a section of code in a process that accesses one or more variables in a read-update-write fashion that are shared with other processes. Therefore, there should be *mutual exclusion*: only one process at a time should be allowed to access (read-update-write) a shared variable. The *mutual exclusion problem* is how to keep two or more processes from being in their critical sections at the same time.

When stated as an abstract problem, we make no assumptions about the number of CPUs or their relative speeds. There are some desirable properties that any solution to this problem should have.

- No process outside its critical section should block other processes outside their critical sections from entering.

- There should be no deadlock, also called a "safety" property (absence of unnecessary delay).

process P_i , $i = 1, 2, 3, \ldots$

```
while (true) {
    . . .
    non-critical section code;
    . . .
    mutex_begin(i);    /* pre-protocol */
    . . .
    critical section code;
    . . .
    mutex_end(i);      /* post-protocol */
}
```

Figure 3.1: Pre- and Post-Protocol for Mutual Exclusion.

- No process should have to wait forever to enter its critical section (it should not be blocked forever trying to enter).

- There should be no starvation, also called a "liveness" property (eventual entry).

These last two can be recast as the following three.

- No deadlock: deadlock would occur if two processes tried to enter their critical sections at about the same time, and neither succeeded even though no other processes were in their critical sections.

- No starvation in the absence of contention: this would occur if a process tried to enter its critical section and no other processes were in their critical sections, but it could not enter.

- No starvation in the presence of contention: this would occur if two or more processes were trying to enter their critical sections, but one never gets in while the other(s) gets in over and over again.

In a computer architecture, an *atomic instruction* is a machine language instruction that is executed completely without interruption, that is, with no interleaving of other instructions from another process, no context switching, no hardware interrupts. For example, a register load from memory and register store to memory are both atomic instructions. Some architectures have an instruction that increments a memory location atomically. Some architectures let a processor lock the bus for a sequence of instructions so they are done atomically as a group.

In general, an *atomic action* makes an indivisible state transition: "any intermediate state that might exist in the implementation of the action must not be visible to other processes" (page 60 of [3]). This means nothing from another process can be interleaved in the implementation of the action for it to be atomic. Critical sections need to be done as if they were one atomic action to avoid race conditions.

The mutual exclusion problem then becomes to devise a *pre-protocol* and a *post-protocol*, used as shown in Figure 3.1 and based on either hardware or software, that prevent two processes from being in their critical sections at the same time and that have the desirable no deadlock and no starvation properties described above, given

- a load/store register architecture,

- that multiple concurrently executing processes are sharing data,

- single or multiple CPUs where we cannot make relative speed assumptions,

- that accesses to shared variables can be interleaved if two processes get into their critical sections at the same time,

- that processes may not halt in their pre- or post-protocols,

- that processes may not halt in their critical sections,

- that processes may halt outside their critical sections.

To see more examples of race conditions and to get a better understanding of the mutual exclusion problem, we will look at a sequence of attempts to solve the mutual exclusion problem with software. These examples are based on the ones in [6] (page 28) and have been coded in SR. See also Chapter 4 of [8], Chapter 6 of [20], Chapter 4 of [21], and Chapter 2 of [24].

Except for the first attempt, only the pre-protocol (enter critical section) and post-protocol (exit critical section) code will be shown. The code fragments shown can be inserted into the complete SR code in Program 3.10 for testing.

The first attempt, Program 3.10, is strict alternation using a turn variable. It works but suffers from starvation in the absence of contention. The second attempt, Program 3.11, uses a flag variable to indicate a process's desire to enter its critical section. However it does not work, since two processes can enter their critical sections at the same time.

The third attempt, Program 3.12, tries to fix the second attempt by reversing the order of checking the other process's flag and signaling its own desire to enter its critical section. It fixes the mutual exclusion problem but introduces the possibility of deadlock if both processes try to enter at about the same time.

The fourth attempt, Program 3.13, tries to fix the third attempt by having the processes back off trying to enter their critical sections if they detect they are both trying to enter at about the same time. Unfortunately, this only changes the deadlock problem to a related problem called *livelock*. Clock skew will not get two processes out of deadlock but it will get them out of livelock.

The next attempt, Program 3.14, is the first complete working software solution, due to Dekker. It fixes the fourth attempt by having the processes take turns backing off. Many years later, Peterson discovered a complete working solution shorter than Dekker's (see Section 4.9 of [8], Section 6.2.1.3 of [20], Section 4.2 of [21], or Section 2.2.3 of [24]). It is shown in Program 3.15.

If there are more than two processes, none of the above algorithms will work. Lamport's bakery algorithm (page 39 of [6]) will work in this situation. For two processes, the bakery algorithm is shown in Program 3.16. It is a complete working solution, just like Dekker's and Peterson's. It has the property, though, that no variable is updated by more than one process. For an arbitrary number of processes, the bakery algorithm is shown in Program 3.17.

Program 3.10: First Attempt: Strict Alternation.

```
resource node
    import arbitrator
body node(i : int; scap : cap arbitrator;
    max_outside_cs_time, max_inside_cs_time : int)
    write("node", i, "is alive with max_outside_cs_time of",
        max_outside_cs_time, "and max_inside_cs_time of", max_inside_cs_time)
    reply
```

```
    procedure outside_cs(i : int)
        var napping : int
        napping := int(random(1000*max_outside_cs_time))
        writes("age=", age(), ", node ", i,
            " outside critical section for ", napping, "ms\n")
        nap(napping)
        writes("age=", age(), ", node ", i,
            " wants to enter its critical section\n")
    end outside_cs

    procedure inside_cs(i : int)
        var napping : int
        napping := int(random(1000*max_inside_cs_time))
        writes("age=", age(), ", node ", i,
            " inside critical section for ", napping, "ms\n")
        nap(napping)
    end inside_cs

    do true ->
        outside_cs(i); scap.want_to_enter_cs(i)
        inside_cs(i);  scap.finished_in_cs(i)
    od
end node

resource arbitrator
    op want_to_enter_cs(i : int), finished_in_cs(i : int)
    import node
body arbitrator()
    const TWO_NODES := 2
    var scap : cap arbitrator
    var max_outside_cs_time[1:TWO_NODES] : int := ([TWO_NODES] 8)
    var max_inside_cs_time[1:TWO_NODES] : int := ([TWO_NODES] 2)
    var run_time : int := 60

    procedure other(i: int) returns j : int
        j := (i % TWO_NODES) + 1
    end other

    var turn : int := 1             ### First attempt: strict alternation.

    proc want_to_enter_cs(i)        ### pre-protocol
        do turn != i -> skip od
    end want_to_enter_cs

    proc finished_in_cs(i)          ### post-protocol
        turn := other(i)
    end finished_in_cs              ################################################

    getarg(1, run_time)
    write("arbitrator starting up, run_time =", run_time)
    scap := myresource()
    fa i := 1 to TWO_NODES ->
        getarg(2*i, max_outside_cs_time[i]); getarg(2*i+1, max_inside_cs_time[i])
        create node(i, scap, max_outside_cs_time[i], max_inside_cs_time[i])
```

```
   af

   nap(1000*run_time); write("must stop now"); stop
end arbitrator

/* .............. Example compile and run(s)

% sr -o take_turns take_turns.sr
% ./take_turns 10 1 2
arbitrator starting up, run_time = 10
node 1 is alive with max_outside_cs_time of 1 and max_inside_cs_time of 2
age=36, node 1 outside critical section for 704ms
node 2 is alive with max_outside_cs_time of 8 and max_inside_cs_time of 2
age=62, node 2 outside critical section for 1473ms
age=755, node 1 wants to enter its critical section
age=759, node 1 inside critical section for 460ms
age=1225, node 1 outside critical section for 379ms
age=1545, node 2 wants to enter its critical section
age=1551, node 2 inside critical section for 995ms
age=1615, node 1 wants to enter its critical section
age=2550, node 2 outside critical section for 2044ms
age=2554, node 1 inside critical section for 639ms
age=3205, node 1 outside critical section for 148ms
age=3373, node 1 wants to enter its critical section
age=4604, node 2 wants to enter its critical section
age=4608, node 2 inside critical section for 482ms
age=5113, node 2 outside critical section for 4470ms
age=5117, node 1 inside critical section for 1251ms
age=6375, node 1 outside critical section for 318ms
age=6705, node 1 wants to enter its critical section
age=9703, node 2 wants to enter its critical section
age=9715, node 2 inside critical section for 77ms
age=9799, node 2 outside critical section for 810ms
age=9802, node 1 inside critical section for 1513ms
must stop now
                                                     */
```

Program 3.11: Second Attempt: Check Other's Flag Variable, Then Set Own.

```
   var desires_cs[1:TWO_NODES] : bool := ([TWO_NODES] false)

   proc want_to_enter_cs(i)
      do desires_cs[other(i)] -> skip od
      desires_cs[i] := true
   end want_to_enter_cs

   proc finished_in_cs(i)
      desires_cs[i] := false
   end finished_in_cs
```

Program 3.12: Third Attempt: Set Own Flag Variable, Then Check Other's.

```
var desires_cs[1:TWO_NODES] : bool := ([TWO_NODES] false)

proc want_to_enter_cs(i)
   desires_cs[i] := true
   do desires_cs[other(i)] -> skip od
end want_to_enter_cs

proc finished_in_cs(i)
   desires_cs[i] := false
end finished_in_cs
```

Program 3.13: Fourth Attempt: Back Off.

```
var desires_cs[1:TWO_NODES] : bool := ([TWO_NODES] false)

proc want_to_enter_cs(i)
   desires_cs[i] := true
   do desires_cs[other(i)] ->
      desires_cs[i] := false; desires_cs[i] := true
   od
end want_to_enter_cs

proc finished_in_cs(i)
   desires_cs[i] := false
end finished_in_cs
```

Program 3.14: Dekker's Solution: Take Turns Backing Off.

```
var desires_cs[1:TWO_NODES] : bool := ([TWO_NODES] false)
var turn : int := 1

proc want_to_enter_cs(i)
   desires_cs[i] := true
   do desires_cs[other(i)] ->
      if turn != i ->
         desires_cs[i] := false
         do turn != i -> skip od
         desires_cs[i] := true
      fi
   od
end want_to_enter_cs

proc finished_in_cs(i)
   desires_cs[i] := false
   turn := other(i)
end finished_in_cs
```

Program 3.15: Peterson's Shorter Solution.

```
var desires_cs[1:TWO_NODES] : bool := ([TWO_NODES] false)
var last : int := 1

proc want_to_enter_cs(i)
   desires_cs[i] := true
   last := i
   do desires_cs[other(i)] and last = i -> skip od
end want_to_enter_cs

proc finished_in_cs(i)
   desires_cs[i] := false
end finished_in_cs
```

Program 3.16: Lamport's Bakery Algorithm: Two Processes Only.

```
var number[1:TWO_NODES] : int := ([TWO_NODES] 0)

proc want_to_enter_cs(i)
   number[i] := 1
   number[i] := number[other(i)] + 1
   do not(
                    number[other(i)] = 0 or number[i] < number[other(i)]
                       or # break a tie
                       (number[i] = number[other(i)] and i = 1)
       ) -> skip od
end want_to_enter_cs

proc finished_in_cs(i)
   number[i] := 0
end finished_in_cs
```

Program 3.17: Lamport's Bakery Algorithm: Arbitrary Number of Processes.

```
procedure maxx(number[1:*] : int) returns mx : int
   mx := number[1]
   fa i := 2 to ub(number) -> if number[i] > mx -> mx := number[i] fi af
end maxx

var number[1:num_nodes] : int := ([num_nodes] 0)
var choosing[1:num_nodes] : bool := ([num_nodes] false)

proc want_to_enter_cs(i)
   choosing[i] := true
   number[i] := 1 + maxx(number)
   choosing[i] := false
   fa j := 1 to num_nodes st j != i ->
```

```
        do choosing[j] -> skip od
        do not(
                        number[j] = 0 or number[i] < number[j]
                        or # break a tie
                        (number[i] = number[j] and i < j)
            ) -> skip od
    af
end want_to_enter_cs

proc finished_in_cs(i)
    number[i] := 0
end finished_in_cs
```

Chapter 4

Semaphores

In a concurrent programming or operating systems class, you will learn how *semaphores* can be used to protect and control access to critical sections. A semaphore (see Section 4.12 of [8], Section 6.4 of [20], Section 4.4 of [21], or Section 2.2.5 of [24]) is a non-negative integer variable that can be accessed with only the two operations P and V (called *down* and *up*, respectively, in [23, 24]). If the value of the semaphore S is positive, then a process that does a $P(S)$ decrements S in an atomic action, else the process blocks, waiting for a $V(S)$. If a process does a $V(S)$ and no process is blocked on S, then the value of S is incremented atomically, else a process blocked on S is awakened (usually the first one to have blocked).

Semaphores are abstract synchronization tools that allow processes to block rather than busy-wait for an event to occur. A semaphore can be used to save the number of wakeup signals sent so they are not lost if the process is not sleeping. Another use is for the semaphore value to represent the number of resource units available for allocation. Binary semaphores, those whose value is either zero or one, can be used to solve the critical section mutual exclusion problem described in the previous chapter.

Semaphores can be implemented in an operating system with P and V being system calls.

$P(S)$:   trap to the kernel
         disable interrupts (so semaphore access is atomic)
         if $S > 0$ then $S := S - 1$
         else { queue the process on S, change its state to blocked,
             schedule another process }
         enable interrupts
         return

$V(S)$:   trap to the kernel
         disable interrupts
         if $S = 0$ and queue on S is not empty then
             { pick a process from the queue on S,
               change its state from blocked to ready }
         else $S := S + 1$
         enable interrupts
         return

If we have a shared-memory multiprocessor instead of a uniprocessor, then disabling interrupts to access a semaphore atomically is not sufficient since disabling interrupts on one processor has no effect on another processor. It will be necessary to lock the memory bus or use a busy-waiting loop inside the operating system implemented with a test-and-set or similar instruction.

4.1 SR Semaphores

The SR language provides semaphores and we can eliminate the race condition in Program 3.8 very easily with semaphores, as shown in Program 4.1. The semaphore **mutex** prevents any interleaving of the function calls. In a lab exercise, you will be asked to do the same things (compile and run two different ways) with this example program that you were asked to do with the one in Program 3.8.

Semaphores can be used for *mutual exclusion synchronization* or for *condition synchronization*. Program 4.1 is an example of the former: using semaphores to enforce mutual exclusion and control access to critical sections. In the following section we will define the latter and see more examples of both uses of semaphores.

Semaphores that are used for mutual exclusion are usually initialized to one and take on only two values: one, when the critical section is free and zero, when the critical section is busy. They are called *binary* semaphores for this reason. A true binary semaphore will be restricted to only these two values in the sense that a V operation on a binary semaphore with the value one will have no effect. Counting semaphores can be used as binary semaphores as long as the programmer is careful to avoid a V on a semaphore whose value is one.

Binary semaphores are also called mutual exclusion (mutex) locks. There are two operations on locks: lock (corresponds to P) and unlock (corresponds to V). Unlocking an unlocked lock or binary semaphore has no effect.

SR has no true binary semaphores; all semaphores are general counting ones, although a semaphore can be used as a mutual exclusion lock. But a V on an unlocked SR semaphore will **not** have no effect.

Program 4.1: A Semaphore Prevents the Race Condition.

```
resource no_race_semaphores()
    sem mutex := 1
    var sum: int := 0

    procedure fn(j, k: int) returns f: int
        f := j
        fa l := 1 to k ->
            f := f + 1
        af
    end fn

    process process1
        write("process1")
        fa i := 1 to 10 ->
            P(mutex)                 # pre-protocol: enter CRITICAL SECTION
            sum := fn(sum, i)
            V(mutex)                 # post-protocol: exit CRITICAL SECTION
        af
        write("end process1, sum = ", sum)
    end process1

    process process2
        write("process2")
```

```
    fa i := 1 to 10 ->
        P(mutex)                  # pre-protocol: enter CRITICAL SECTION
        sum := fn(sum, i)
        V(mutex)                  # post-protocol: exit CRITICAL SECTION
    af
    write("end process2, sum = ", sum)
  end process2
end no_race_semaphores

/* .............. Example compile and run(s)

% sr -o no_race no_race.sr
% ./no_race
process1
process2
end process2, sum =  220
end process1, sum =  440
% sr -c no_race.sr
% srl -L 1 -o no_race_L1 no_race_semaphores
% ./no_race_L1
process1
process2
end process1, sum =  385
end process2, sum =  440
                                                           */
```

4.2   Classical Operating Systems Problems

Most operating systems textbooks, for example [8, 20, 21, 23, 24], discuss the following classical synchronization problems: the *bounded buffer producers and consumers*, the *sleeping barber*, the *dining philosophers*, and the database *readers and writers*.

In the bounded buffer problem, a buffer with a finite number of slots holds widgets that are made by the producers. Consumers use widgets by accessing a slot and removing the widget. The synchronization problem is: to suspend the producers when the buffer is full, to suspend the consumers when the buffer is empty, and to make sure that only one process at a time manipulates a buffer slot so there are no race conditions or lost updates.

The sleeping barber problem is to synchronize the barber and customers in a barber shop. The shop has a barber, a barber chair, and a waiting room with several chairs. When the barber finishes cutting a customer's hair, the barber will fetch another customer from the waiting room if there is one or stand by the barber chair and daydream if the waiting room is empty. Customers who need a haircut enter the waiting room. If the waiting room is full, the customer comes back later. If the barber is busy but there is a chair available, the customer takes a seat. If the waiting room is empty and the barber is daydreaming, the customer sits in the barber chair and wakes the barber.

The dining philosophers problem involves five philosophers sitting at a round table with five forks interleaved between them. Philosophers think for a while, then get hungry and try to eat. After eating for a while, a philosopher is ready to think again and the cycle repeats. A philosopher needs both forks to eat, the one on its right and the one on its left. Only one philosopher at a time can use a fork. The synchronization problem is to coordinate the use of the forks so that: only one philosopher at a time uses a fork, there is no deadlock (each philosopher holding a fork and refusing to relinquish it), there is maximal parallelism (a hungry philosopher gets to eat if its forks are not being used by other philosophers to eat), and no philosopher starves (due to its neighbors collaborating).

In the readers and writers problem, readers can read a database simultaneously as long as no writer writes, but only one writer at a time can write (if there are no active readers). The synchronization problem is: to coordinate the processes so that readers can read simultaneously but writers write one at a time, and to prevent starvation (a continual stream of incoming readers preventing writer access).

4.3 Semaphore Solutions

This section presents solutions to the classical operating systems synchronization problems using SR's semaphores.

4.3.1 The Producers and Consumers

Program 4.2 solves the bounded buffer producers and consumers problem with semaphores. The program is a direct translation into SR of the classical semaphore solution presented in operating systems textbooks, such as the one on page 43 of [24]. Notice that there is only one producer process and only one consumer process. Each one naps for a random amount of time, then tries to access the buffer. Programs 2.15 and 3.4 show how to change the program to have multiple producer and consumer processes created from separate producer and consumer resources (see Lab Assignment 4.5.2). If this program did not have the statement pair nap(*runtime*); stop at the end of the main driver resource user or if enough output has been seen before the program stops during a run, control-C can be typed to abort the program.

In this program, the semaphore **mutex** is used to synchronize access to the shared variable **count** in critical section code where **count** is updated. This semaphore is used for mutual exclusion synchronization. The other two semaphores, **elements** and **spaces**, are used to synchronize the producer and consumer processes so the producer does not try to put something into a full buffer and the consumer does not try to take something from an empty buffer. These semaphores are used for condition synchronization, also called event synchronization.

The bounded buffer data structure and the **fetch** and **deposit** routines could have been placed inside a **global** resource instead. However, since a **global** resource cannot be parameterized, the size of the buffer array (number of slots) would have to be declared inside the **global** resource, along with checking the command line for possible default value override. Also, the program would lose the ability to create several different sized bounded buffers with multiple **create** statements.

To illustrate the use of a **global** resource, we will change the program somewhat and implement an unbounded buffer with a linked list, shown in Program 4.3. This program also shows how to use pointers in SR. Storage for a new buffer element is allocated with **new** and deallocated with **free**. The semaphore **elements** is used to block a consumer process if the buffer is empty. This program also has multiple producer and consumer processes. The single binary semaphore **mutex** is used to prevent race conditions on the linked list: two producers trying to add an element at the same time, two consumer trying to remove an element at the same time, or a producer and a consumer trying to manipulate a single element list at the same time.

Program 4.2: Bounded Buffer Producers and Consumers.

```
resource bounded_buffer
    op deposit(item : real)
    op fetch() returns item : real
body bounded_buffer(size : int)
    var buf[0:size-1] : real
    var count : int := 0
    var take_out : int := 0
    var put_in : int := 0
    sem elements := 0
    sem spaces := size
    sem mutex := 1

    write("bounded buffer resource with", size, "slots is alive")

    proc deposit(item)
        P(spaces)
        buf[put_in] := item
        put_in := (put_in + 1) % size
        P(mutex)
        count++
        write("deposit: there are now", count, "items in the buffer")
        V(mutex)
        V(elements)
    end deposit

    proc fetch() returns item
        P(elements)
        item := buf[take_out]
        take_out := (take_out + 1) % size
        P(mutex)
        count--
        write("fetch: there are now", count, "items in the buffer")
        V(mutex)
        V(spaces)
    end fetch
end bounded_buffer

resource user()
    import bounded_buffer
    var bb : cap bounded_buffer
    var slots : int := 20, pnap : int := 3, cnap : int := 3
    var run_time : int := 60

    getarg(1, slots); getarg(2, pnap); getarg(3, cnap); getarg(4, run_time)
    writes("main user resource alive, slots = ", slots, ", pnap = ", pnap,
        ", cnap = ", cnap, ", and run_time = ", run_time, "\n")
    bb := create bounded_buffer(slots)

    process producer
        var it : real
        var napping : int
        do true ->
```

```
            it := random()
            writes("age=", age(), ", PRODUCER produced item ", it, "\n")
            bb.deposit(it)
            napping := int(random(1000*pnap))
            writes("age=", age(), ", PRODUCER deposited item ", it,
               " and napping for ", napping, "ms\n")
            nap(napping)
        od
    end producer

    process consumer
        var it : real
        var napping : int
        do true ->
            writes("age=", age(), ", consumer wants to consume ...\n")
            it := bb.fetch()
            napping := int(random(1000*cnap))
            writes("age=", age(), ", consumer fetched item ", it,
               " and napping for ", napping, "ms\n")
            nap(napping)
        od
    end consumer

    nap(1000*run_time); write("must stop now"); stop
end user

/* .............. Example compile and run(s)

% sr -o bb bb.sr
% ./bb 5 1 3 10
main user resource alive, slots = 5, pnap = 1, cnap = 3, and run_time = 10
bounded buffer resource with 5 slots is alive
age=50, consumer wants to consume ...
age=53, PRODUCER produced item 0.356596
deposit: there are now 1 items in the buffer
age=66, PRODUCER deposited item 0.356596 and napping for 364ms
fetch: there are now 0 items in the buffer
age=73, consumer fetched item 0.356596 and napping for 316ms
age=418, consumer wants to consume ...
age=449, PRODUCER produced item 0.00800780
deposit: there are now 1 items in the buffer
age=456, PRODUCER deposited item 0.00800780 and napping for 654ms
fetch: there are now 0 items in the buffer
age=464, consumer fetched item 0.00800780 and napping for 2152ms
age=1118, PRODUCER produced item 0.755083
deposit: there are now 1 items in the buffer
age=1131, PRODUCER deposited item 0.755083 and napping for 19ms
age=1158, PRODUCER produced item 0.339312
deposit: there are now 2 items in the buffer
age=1165, PRODUCER deposited item 0.339312 and napping for 138ms
age=1308, PRODUCER produced item 0.212412
deposit: there are now 3 items in the buffer
age=1316, PRODUCER deposited item 0.212412 and napping for 567ms
age=1888, PRODUCER produced item 0.00888645
deposit: there are now 4 items in the buffer
```

```
age=1894, PRODUCER deposited item 0.00888645 and napping for 324ms
age=2229, PRODUCER produced item 0.204411
deposit: there are now 5 items in the buffer
age=2253, PRODUCER deposited item 0.204411 and napping for 501ms
age=2629, consumer wants to consume ...
fetch: there are now 4 items in the buffer
age=2636, consumer fetched item 0.755083 and napping for 2215ms
age=2759, PRODUCER produced item 0.727478
deposit: there are now 5 items in the buffer
age=2818, PRODUCER deposited item 0.727478 and napping for 707ms
age=3539, PRODUCER produced item 0.569443
age=4860, consumer wants to consume ...
fetch: there are now 4 items in the buffer
age=4864, consumer fetched item 0.339312 and napping for 1523ms
deposit: there are now 5 items in the buffer
age=4868, PRODUCER deposited item 0.569443 and napping for 732ms
age=5608, PRODUCER produced item 0.989578
age=6398, consumer wants to consume ...
fetch: there are now 4 items in the buffer
age=6407, consumer fetched item 0.212412 and napping for 2838ms
deposit: there are now 5 items in the buffer
age=6411, PRODUCER deposited item 0.989578 and napping for 462ms
age=6879, PRODUCER produced item 0.996745
age=9362, consumer wants to consume ...
fetch: there are now 4 items in the buffer
age=9371, consumer fetched item 0.00888645 and napping for 1097ms
deposit: there are now 5 items in the buffer
age=9375, PRODUCER deposited item 0.996745 and napping for 68ms
age=9448, PRODUCER produced item 0.0306415
must stop now
% ./bb 5 3 1 10
main user resource alive, slots = 5, pnap = 3, cnap = 1, and run_time = 10
bounded buffer resource with 5 slots is alive
age=73, consumer wants to consume ...
age=77, PRODUCER produced item 0.382618
deposit: there are now 1 items in the buffer
age=88, PRODUCER deposited item 0.382618 and napping for 1857ms
fetch: there are now 0 items in the buffer
age=96, consumer fetched item 0.382618 and napping for 867ms
age=980, consumer wants to consume ...
age=1950, PRODUCER produced item 0.0659844
deposit: there are now 1 items in the buffer
age=1956, PRODUCER deposited item 0.0659844 and napping for 133ms
fetch: there are now 0 items in the buffer
age=1960, consumer fetched item 0.0659844 and napping for 669ms
age=2100, PRODUCER produced item 0.714716
deposit: there are now 1 items in the buffer
age=2111, PRODUCER deposited item 0.714716 and napping for 2716ms
age=2640, consumer wants to consume ...
fetch: there are now 0 items in the buffer
age=2647, consumer fetched item 0.714716 and napping for 517ms
age=3180, consumer wants to consume ...
age=4840, PRODUCER produced item 0.653636
deposit: there are now 1 items in the buffer
age=4846, PRODUCER deposited item 0.653636 and napping for 2656ms
```

```
fetch: there are now 0 items in the buffer
age=4849, consumer fetched item 0.653636 and napping for 927ms
age=5780, consumer wants to consume ...
age=7510, PRODUCER produced item 0.992305
deposit: there are now 1 items in the buffer
age=7516, PRODUCER deposited item 0.992305 and napping for 2629ms
fetch: there are now 0 items in the buffer
age=7520, consumer fetched item 0.992305 and napping for 76ms
age=7600, consumer wants to consume ...
must stop now
                                                        */
```

Program 4.3: Unbounded Buffer Producers and Consumers using a **global**.

```
global unbounded_buffer
   op deposit(item : real), fetch() returns item : real
body unbounded_buffer()
   type buffer_entry_type =
      rec(value : real; next_entry : ptr buffer_entry_type)
   var head, tail, new_one, old_one : ptr buffer_entry_type
   var count : int := 0
   sem elements := 0
   sem mutex := 1
   head := tail := new_one := old_one := null
   write("unbounded buffer global is alive")

   proc deposit(item)
      P(mutex)
      new_one := new(buffer_entry_type)    # no need to check return value of
      new_one^.value := item               # new for null; RTS aborts first
      new_one^.next_entry := null
      if tail = null ->    # add to an empty list
         if head != null -> write("head not null when tail null"); stop fi
         head := tail := new_one
      [] else ->           # add to end of list
         tail^.next_entry := new_one
         tail := new_one
      fi
      count++
      write("deposit: there are now", count, "items in the buffer")
      V(mutex)
      V(elements)
   end deposit

   proc fetch() returns item
      P(elements)
      P(mutex)
      if head = null or tail = null ->
         write("head null or tail null and should not be"); stop
      fi
      if head = tail ->  # delete from a singleton list
         old_one := head
         head := tail := null
```

```
      [] else ->          # delete from beginning of list
         old_one := head
         head := old_one^.next_entry
      fi
      item := old_one^.value
      free(old_one)
      count--
      write("fetch: there are now", count, "items in the buffer")
      V(mutex)
   end fetch
end unbounded_buffer

resource user()
   import unbounded_buffer
   var num_producers : int := 5, num_consumers : int := 5
   var pnap : int := 3, cnap : int := 3, run_time : int := 60

   getarg(1, num_producers); getarg(2, num_consumers)
   getarg(3, pnap); getarg(4, cnap); getarg(5, run_time)
   writes("main user resource alive, num_producers = ", num_producers,
      ", num_consumers = ", num_consumers, ",\n pnap = ", pnap,
      ", cnap = ", cnap, ", and run_time = ", run_time, "\n")

   process producer(i := 1 to num_producers)
      var it : real
      var napping : int
      do true ->
         it := random()
         writes("age=", age(), ", PRODUCER ", i, " produced item ", it, "\n")
         unbounded_buffer.deposit(it)
         napping := int(random(1000*pnap))
         writes("age=", age(), ", PRODUCER ", i, " deposited item ", it,
            " and napping for ", napping, "ms\n")
         nap(napping)
      od
   end producer

   process consumer(j := 1 to num_consumers)
      var it : real
      var napping : int
      do true ->
         writes("age=", age(), ", consumer ", j, " wants to consume ...\n")
         it := unbounded_buffer.fetch()
         napping := int(random(1000*cnap))
         writes("age=", age(), ", consumer ", j, " fetched item ", it,
            " and napping for ", napping, "ms\n")
         nap(napping)
      od
   end consumer

   nap(1000*run_time); write("must stop now"); stop
end user

/* .............. Example compile and run(s)
```

```
% sr -o unbb unbb.sr
% ./unbb 3 3 3 3 10
unbounded buffer global is alive
main user resource alive, num_producers = 3, num_consumers = 3,
  pnap = 3, cnap = 3, and run_time = 10
age=58, PRODUCER 1 produced item 0.110759
deposit: there are now 1 items in the buffer
age=69, PRODUCER 1 deposited item 0.110759 and napping for 2730ms
age=74, PRODUCER 2 produced item 0.227981
deposit: there are now 2 items in the buffer
age=80, PRODUCER 2 deposited item 0.227981 and napping for 1598ms
age=84, PRODUCER 3 produced item 0.733602
deposit: there are now 3 items in the buffer
age=94, PRODUCER 3 deposited item 0.733602 and napping for 1185ms
age=98, consumer 1 wants to consume ...
fetch: there are now 2 items in the buffer
age=105, consumer 1 fetched item 0.110759 and napping for 296ms
age=109, consumer 2 wants to consume ...
fetch: there are now 1 items in the buffer
age=115, consumer 2 fetched item 0.227981 and napping for 1461ms
age=119, consumer 3 wants to consume ...
fetch: there are now 0 items in the buffer
age=124, consumer 3 fetched item 0.733602 and napping for 1006ms
age=411, consumer 1 wants to consume ...
age=1141, consumer 3 wants to consume ...
age=1291, PRODUCER 3 produced item 0.695014
deposit: there are now 1 items in the buffer
age=1298, PRODUCER 3 deposited item 0.695014 and napping for 1405ms
fetch: there are now 0 items in the buffer
age=1305, consumer 1 fetched item 0.695014 and napping for 381ms
age=1581, consumer 2 wants to consume ...
age=1691, consumer 1 wants to consume ...
age=1694, PRODUCER 2 produced item 0.125459
deposit: there are now 1 items in the buffer
age=1698, PRODUCER 2 deposited item 0.125459 and napping for 1478ms
fetch: there are now 0 items in the buffer
age=1702, consumer 3 fetched item 0.125459 and napping for 1257ms
age=2711, PRODUCER 3 produced item 0.250267
deposit: there are now 1 items in the buffer
age=2717, PRODUCER 3 deposited item 0.250267 and napping for 1301ms
fetch: there are now 0 items in the buffer
age=2721, consumer 2 fetched item 0.250267 and napping for 2327ms
age=2811, PRODUCER 1 produced item 0.132776
deposit: there are now 1 items in the buffer
age=2816, PRODUCER 1 deposited item 0.132776 and napping for 2542ms
fetch: there are now 0 items in the buffer
age=2820, consumer 1 fetched item 0.132776 and napping for 910ms
age=2961, consumer 3 wants to consume ...
age=3181, PRODUCER 2 produced item 0.670967
deposit: there are now 1 items in the buffer
age=3186, PRODUCER 2 deposited item 0.670967 and napping for 1073ms
fetch: there are now 0 items in the buffer
age=3190, consumer 3 fetched item 0.670967 and napping for 2328ms
age=3741, consumer 1 wants to consume ...
age=4021, PRODUCER 3 produced item 0.0909903
```

```
deposit: there are now 1 items in the buffer
age=4030, PRODUCER 3 deposited item 0.0909903 and napping for 1430ms
fetch: there are now 0 items in the buffer
age=4034, consumer 1 fetched item 0.0909903 and napping for 2494ms
age=4261, PRODUCER 2 produced item 0.955670
deposit: there are now 1 items in the buffer
age=4266, PRODUCER 2 deposited item 0.955670 and napping for 1878ms
age=5051, consumer 2 wants to consume ...
fetch: there are now 0 items in the buffer
age=5056, consumer 2 fetched item 0.955670 and napping for 1451ms
age=5361, PRODUCER 1 produced item 0.122986
deposit: there are now 1 items in the buffer
age=5366, PRODUCER 1 deposited item 0.122986 and napping for 2442ms
age=5471, PRODUCER 3 produced item 0.123644
deposit: there are now 2 items in the buffer
age=5478, PRODUCER 3 deposited item 0.123644 and napping for 2188ms
age=5521, consumer 3 wants to consume ...
fetch: there are now 1 items in the buffer
age=5525, consumer 3 fetched item 0.122986 and napping for 2042ms
age=6151, PRODUCER 2 produced item 0.838933
deposit: there are now 2 items in the buffer
age=6157, PRODUCER 2 deposited item 0.838933 and napping for 721ms
age=6511, consumer 2 wants to consume ...
fetch: there are now 1 items in the buffer
age=6516, consumer 2 fetched item 0.123644 and napping for 1441ms
age=6531, consumer 1 wants to consume ...
fetch: there are now 0 items in the buffer
age=6535, consumer 1 fetched item 0.838933 and napping for 42ms
age=6581, consumer 1 wants to consume ...
age=6881, PRODUCER 2 produced item 0.0194425
deposit: there are now 1 items in the buffer
age=6887, PRODUCER 2 deposited item 0.0194425 and napping for 2447ms
fetch: there are now 0 items in the buffer
age=6890, consumer 1 fetched item 0.0194425 and napping for 1204ms
age=7571, consumer 3 wants to consume ...
age=7675, PRODUCER 3 produced item 0.158038
deposit: there are now 1 items in the buffer
age=7680, PRODUCER 3 deposited item 0.158038 and napping for 2979ms
fetch: there are now 0 items in the buffer
age=7684, consumer 3 fetched item 0.158038 and napping for 1939ms
age=7811, PRODUCER 1 produced item 0.767538
deposit: there are now 1 items in the buffer
age=7816, PRODUCER 1 deposited item 0.767538 and napping for 2207ms
age=7961, consumer 2 wants to consume ...
fetch: there are now 0 items in the buffer
age=7970, consumer 2 fetched item 0.767538 and napping for 2732ms
age=8101, consumer 1 wants to consume ...
age=9341, PRODUCER 2 produced item 0.685172
deposit: there are now 1 items in the buffer
age=9347, PRODUCER 2 deposited item 0.685172 and napping for 2164ms
fetch: there are now 0 items in the buffer
age=9350, consumer 1 fetched item 0.685172 and napping for 335ms
age=9631, consumer 3 wants to consume ...
age=9694, consumer 1 wants to consume ...
age=10031, PRODUCER 1 produced item 0.0719983
```

```
deposit: there are now 1 items in the buffer
age=10040, PRODUCER 1 deposited item 0.0719983 and napping for 1827ms
fetch: there are now 0 items in the buffer
age=10044, consumer 3 fetched item 0.0719983 and napping for 2815ms
must stop now
RTS warning: process blocked on killed sem: unbounded_buffer.fetch
                              */
```

4.3.2 The Sleeping Barber

Program 4.4 solves the sleeping barber problem. It is a direct translation into SR of the C-like solution that appears on page 62 of [24]. The barber waits for the next customer on the semaphore **customers**, then decrements the count of waiting customers using the mutual exclusion semaphore **mutex**. The barber then signals the semaphore **barber**, allowing the next customer into the chair. A customer who needs a haircut accesses the count of waiting customers using the mutual exclusion semaphore **mutex** and increments the count if there is a free waiting room chair. If there was room, the customer signals the semaphore **customers**, which will wake a daydreaming barber, and then waits for the barber on the semaphore **barber**.

This program is written as a single resource and uses the technique shown in Program 3.3,

```
process Customer(j := 1 to num_customers)
```

to create multiple customer processes inside the one resource. The program also shows a good way to give the parameters of a simulation default values and also shows one way for a program to print out what its default values are, a so-called "usage" statement.

Program 4.4: The Sleeping Barber.

```
resource sleeping_barber()
   var num_chairs : int := 5
   var num_customers : int := 10
   var cut_time : int := 2
   var grow_time : int := 4
   var run_time : int := 60

   var temp : string[5] := ""; getarg(1, temp)
   if (temp = "usage") ->
      write("Usage: sleeping_barber",
        "num_chairs num_customers cut_time grow_time run_time")
      printf("defaults: %21d %13d %8d %9d %8d\n",
         num_chairs, num_customers, cut_time, grow_time, run_time)
      stop
   fi

   var arg : int := 1
   getarg(arg++, num_chairs)
   getarg(arg++, num_customers)
   getarg(arg++, cut_time)
   getarg(arg++, grow_time)
   getarg(arg++, run_time)
```

```
write("sleeping barber alive with")
write("   num_chairs=", num_chairs)
write("   num_customers=", num_customers)
write("   cut_time=", cut_time)
write("   grow_time=", grow_time)
write("   run_time=", run_time)

sem customers := 0
sem barber := 0
sem mutex := 1
sem cutting := 0
var waiting : int := 0

procedure cut_hair()
   write("age=", age(), "Barber cutting hair")
   P(cutting)
   write("age=", age(), "Barber finished cutting")
end cut_hair

procedure get_haircut(j : int)
   var napping : int
   napping := int(random(1000*cut_time))
   write("age=", age(), "Customer", j, "haircut for", napping, "ms")
   nap(napping)
   write("age=", age(), "Customer", j, "finished haircut")
   V(cutting)
end get_haircut

process Barber
   write("Barber is alive")
   do true ->
      write("age=", age(), "Barber waiting for a customer")
      P(customers)
      P(mutex)
      waiting--
      V(barber)
      write("age=", age(), "Barber has customer, waiting=", waiting)
      V(mutex)
      cut_hair()
   od
end Barber

process Customer(j := 1 to num_customers)
   var napping : int
   write("Customer", j, "is alive")
   do true ->
      napping := int(random(1000*grow_time))
      write("age=", age(), "Customer", j, "growing", napping, "ms")
      nap(napping)
      write("age=", age(), "Customer", j, "needs a haircut")
      P(mutex)
      if (waiting < num_chairs) ->
         waiting++
         write("age=", age(), "Customer", j, "in room, waiting=", waiting)
         V(customers)
```

```
                V(mutex)
                P(barber)
                get_haircut(j)
          [] else ->
                write("age=", age(), "Customer", j, "room full, waiting=", waiting)
                V(mutex)
            fi
      od
   end Customer

   nap(1000*run_time); write("must stop now"); stop
end sleeping_barber

/* .............. Example compile and run(s)

% sr -o sleeping_barber sleeping_barber.sr
% ./sleeping_barber usage
Usage: sleeping_barber num_chairs num_customers cut_time grow_time run_time
defaults:                 5               10       2         4         60
% ./sleeping_barber 3 6 2 4 10
sleeping barber alive with
   num_chairs= 3
   num_customers= 6
   cut_time= 2
   grow_time= 4
   run_time= 10
Barber is alive
age= 30 Barber waiting for a customer
Customer 1 is alive
age= 75 Customer 1 growing 890 ms
Customer 2 is alive
age= 81 Customer 2 growing 2565 ms
Customer 3 is alive
age= 86 Customer 3 growing 3830 ms
Customer 4 is alive
age= 92 Customer 4 growing 1128 ms
Customer 5 is alive
age= 97 Customer 5 growing 2580 ms
Customer 6 is alive
age= 103 Customer 6 growing 2487 ms
age= 969 Customer 1 needs a haircut
age= 973 Customer 1 in room, waiting= 1
age= 976 Barber has customer, waiting= 0
age= 979 Barber cutting hair
age= 982 Customer 1 haircut for 9 ms
age= 999 Customer 1 finished haircut
age= 1002 Customer 1 growing 1253 ms
age= 1005 Barber finished cutting
age= 1008 Barber waiting for a customer
age= 1229 Customer 4 needs a haircut
age= 1232 Customer 4 in room, waiting= 1
age= 1233 Barber has customer, waiting= 0
age= 1234 Barber cutting hair
age= 1236 Customer 4 haircut for 24 ms
age= 1269 Customer 4 finished haircut
```

```
age= 1272 Customer 4 growing 2288 ms
age= 1273 Barber finished cutting
age= 1274 Barber waiting for a customer
age= 2259 Customer 1 needs a haircut
age= 2263 Customer 1 in room, waiting= 1
age= 2264 Barber has customer, waiting= 0
age= 2265 Barber cutting hair
age= 2266 Customer 1 haircut for 139 ms
age= 2409 Customer 1 finished haircut
age= 2412 Customer 1 growing 1140 ms
age= 2414 Barber finished cutting
age= 2415 Barber waiting for a customer
age= 2599 Customer 6 needs a haircut
age= 2602 Customer 6 in room, waiting= 1
age= 2603 Barber has customer, waiting= 0
age= 2604 Barber cutting hair
age= 2605 Customer 6 haircut for 1163 ms
age= 2649 Customer 2 needs a haircut
age= 2652 Customer 2 in room, waiting= 1
age= 2689 Customer 5 needs a haircut
age= 2692 Customer 5 in room, waiting= 2
age= 3559 Customer 1 needs a haircut
age= 3562 Customer 1 in room, waiting= 3
age= 3564 Customer 4 needs a haircut
age= 3565 Customer 4 room full, waiting= 3
age= 3566 Customer 4 growing 3090 ms
age= 3779 Customer 6 finished haircut
age= 3784 Customer 6 growing 1059 ms
age= 3785 Barber finished cutting
age= 3786 Barber waiting for a customer
age= 3788 Barber has customer, waiting= 2
age= 3789 Barber cutting hair
age= 3790 Customer 2 haircut for 1095 ms
age= 3919 Customer 3 needs a haircut
age= 3922 Customer 3 in room, waiting= 3
age= 4849 Customer 6 needs a haircut
age= 4853 Customer 6 room full, waiting= 3
age= 4854 Customer 6 growing 2587 ms
age= 4889 Customer 2 finished haircut
age= 4892 Customer 2 growing 3278 ms
age= 4893 Barber finished cutting
age= 4894 Barber waiting for a customer
age= 4895 Barber has customer, waiting= 2
age= 4896 Barber cutting hair
age= 4897 Customer 5 haircut for 1473 ms
age= 6379 Customer 5 finished haircut
age= 6383 Customer 5 growing 865 ms
age= 6385 Barber finished cutting
age= 6386 Barber waiting for a customer
age= 6387 Barber has customer, waiting= 1
age= 6388 Barber cutting hair
age= 6389 Customer 1 haircut for 1245 ms
age= 6662 Customer 4 needs a haircut
age= 6665 Customer 4 in room, waiting= 2
age= 7249 Customer 5 needs a haircut
```

```
age= 7253 Customer 5 in room, waiting= 3
age= 7449 Customer 6 needs a haircut
age= 7452 Customer 6 room full, waiting= 3
age= 7453 Customer 6 growing 684 ms
age= 7639 Customer 1 finished haircut
age= 7642 Customer 1 growing 3573 ms
age= 7643 Barber finished cutting
age= 7645 Barber waiting for a customer
age= 7646 Barber has customer, waiting= 2
age= 7647 Barber cutting hair
age= 7648 Customer 3 haircut for 1472 ms
age= 8139 Customer 6 needs a haircut
age= 8142 Customer 6 in room, waiting= 3
age= 8179 Customer 2 needs a haircut
age= 8182 Customer 2 room full, waiting= 3
age= 8183 Customer 2 growing 845 ms
age= 9030 Customer 2 needs a haircut
age= 9034 Customer 2 room full, waiting= 3
age= 9035 Customer 2 growing 1750 ms
age= 9129 Customer 3 finished haircut
age= 9132 Customer 3 growing 2680 ms
age= 9135 Barber finished cutting
age= 9136 Barber waiting for a customer
age= 9137 Barber has customer, waiting= 2
age= 9138 Barber cutting hair
age= 9139 Customer 4 haircut for 1824 ms
must stop now
                                              */
```

4.3.3   The Dining Philosophers

Program 4.5 solves the dining philosophers problem with semaphores. Again, the program is a direct translation into SR of the classical semaphore solution presented in operating systems textbooks, such as page 59 of [24]. We saw in Program 3.4 how to create several processes by putting the code for the process in a separate resource and using **create** to instantiate several instances of the resource, each containing one process.

This program uses an enumerated type,

```
type states = enum(thinking, hungry, eating)
```

a construct similar to C and Pascal.

A philosopher thinks for a random amount of time, gets hungry, then asks a central server **dining_server** for its forks. Once the philosopher obtains its two forks, it eats for a random amount of time, puts down the forks, and then repeats the cycle. The issue of starvation is not addressed. Starvation can be seen if this program is run with the following command line arguments.

```
sr -o dphi dphi.sr
dphi 5 300 1 100 10 1 1 100 100 1 100 1
```

You will be asked to fix the starvation problem in a lab exercise.

Stallings (Problem 4.22 in [21]) criticizes the solution in Program 4.5 because it allows starvation and suggests Program 4.6 as an alternative. Here, each fork is represented by a semaphore and a hungry philosopher will first try to pick up its left fork, blocking if it is in use. After obtaining its left fork it will try to pick up its right fork, again blocking if it is not available while retaining the left fork. Without the room semaphore, this version could deadlock if all philosophers got hungry at the same time and picked up their left forks. The room semaphore allows at most all but one of the philosophers into the room at the same time to eat, preventing deadlock from occurring. This version also does not allow two philosophers to starve the one between them by alternating their eating cycles. The hungry philosopher between them will grab its left fork as soon as it is put down.

As you will do in a lab exercise, it is fairly easy to prevent starvation in Program 4.5. However Stallings' alternative, Program 4.6, has a serious flaw that is not easy to fix: it does not allow *maximal parallelism*. As shown in its second example run, it is possible for the philosophers (assuming they have assigned seats) to enter the room to eat in a "bad" order. The first philosopher eats, but the rest all enter and pick up their left fork and block, waiting for their right fork to become available. Every other one could eat, but only one actually does. Program 4.5 does not have this flaw, that is, it allows maximal parallelism. The starvation fix suggested in Lab Assignment 4.5.5 does not have the flaw either.

Program 4.7 shows that the room semaphore is not the only way to prevent deadlock in Program 4.6. If one philosopher is designated as "odd" and picks up the forks in reverse order from all the others, then deadlock cannot occur. This version also does not allow maximal parallelism, as shown by its second example run.

Program 4.5: The Dining Philosophers.

```
resource philosopher
    import dining_server
body philosopher(i : int; dcap : cap dining_server; thinking, eating: int)
    write("philosopher", i, "alive, max think eat delays", thinking, eating)
    reply

    procedure think()
        var napping : int
        napping := int(random(1000*thinking))
        writes("age=",age(),", philosopher ",i," thinking for ",napping," ms\n")
        nap(napping)
    end think

    procedure eat()
        var napping : int
        napping := int(random(1000*eating))
        writes("age=",age(),", philosopher ",i," eating for ",napping," ms\n")
        nap(napping)
    end eat

    do true ->
        think()
        writes("age=", age(), ", philosopher ", i, " is hungry\n")
        dcap.take_forks(i)
        writes("age=", age(), ", philosopher ", i, " has taken forks\n")
        eat()
        dcap.put_forks(i)
        writes("age=", age(), ", philosopher ", i, " has returned forks\n")
    od
end philosopher
```

```
resource dining_server
    op take_forks(i : int), put_forks(i : int)
body dining_server(num_phil : int)
    write("dining server for", num_phil, "philosophers is alive")
    sem mutex := 1
    type states = enum(thinking, hungry, eating)
    var state[1:num_phil] : states := ([num_phil] thinking)
    sem phil[1:num_phil] := ([num_phil] 0)

    procedure left(i : int) returns lft : int
        if i=1 -> lft := num_phil [] else -> lft := i-1 fi
    end left

    procedure right(i : int) returns rgh : int
        if i=num_phil -> rgh := 1 [] else -> rgh := i+1 fi
    end right

    procedure test(i : int)
        if state[i] = hungry and state[left(i)] ~= eating
            and state[right(i)] ~= eating ->
          state[i] := eating
          V(phil[i])
        fi
    end test

    proc take_forks(i)
        P(mutex)
        state[i] := hungry
        test(i)
        V(mutex)
        P(phil[i])
    end take_forks

    proc put_forks(i)
        P(mutex)
        state[i] := thinking
        test(left(i)); test(right(i))
        V(mutex)
    end put_forks
end dining_server

resource start()
    import philosopher, dining_server
    var num_phil : int := 5, run_time : int := 60
    getarg(1, num_phil); getarg(2, run_time)
    var max_think_delay[1:num_phil] : int := ([num_phil] 5)
    var max_eat_delay[1:num_phil] : int := ([num_phil] 2)
    fa i := 1 to num_phil ->
        getarg(2*i+1, max_think_delay[i]); getarg(2*i+2, max_eat_delay[i])
    af

    var dcap : cap dining_server
    write(num_phil, "dining philosophers running", run_time, "seconds")
    dcap := create dining_server(num_phil)
```

```
    fa i := 1 to num_phil ->
       create philosopher(i, dcap, max_think_delay[i], max_eat_delay[i])
    af
    nap(1000*run_time); write("must stop now"); stop
end start

/* .............. Example compile and run(s)

% sr -o dphi dphi.sr
% ./dphi 5 10
5 dining philosophers running 10 seconds
dining server for 5 philosophers is alive
philosopher 1 alive, max think eat delays 5 2
age=37, philosopher 1 thinking for 491 ms
philosopher 2 alive, max think eat delays 5 2
age=50, philosopher 2 thinking for 2957 ms
philosopher 3 alive, max think eat delays 5 2
age=62, philosopher 3 thinking for 1374 ms
philosopher 4 alive, max think eat delays 5 2
age=74, philosopher 4 thinking for 1414 ms
philosopher 5 alive, max think eat delays 5 2
age=87, philosopher 5 thinking for 1000 ms
age=537, philosopher 1 is hungry
age=541, philosopher 1 has taken forks
age=544, philosopher 1 eating for 1351 ms
age=1097, philosopher 5 is hungry
age=1447, philosopher 3 is hungry
age=1451, philosopher 3 has taken forks
age=1454, philosopher 3 eating for 1226 ms
age=1497, philosopher 4 is hungry
age=1898, philosopher 1 has returned forks
age=1901, philosopher 1 thinking for 2042 ms
age=1902, philosopher 5 has taken forks
age=1903, philosopher 5 eating for 1080 ms
age=2687, philosopher 3 has returned forks
age=2691, philosopher 3 thinking for 2730 ms
age=2988, philosopher 5 has returned forks
age=2991, philosopher 5 thinking for 3300 ms
age=2992, philosopher 4 has taken forks
age=2993, philosopher 4 eating for 1818 ms
age=3017, philosopher 2 is hungry
age=3020, philosopher 2 has taken forks
age=3021, philosopher 2 eating for 1393 ms
age=3947, philosopher 1 is hungry
age=4418, philosopher 2 has returned forks
age=4421, philosopher 2 thinking for 649 ms
age=4423, philosopher 1 has taken forks
age=4424, philosopher 1 eating for 1996 ms
age=4817, philosopher 4 has returned forks
age=4821, philosopher 4 thinking for 742 ms
age=5077, philosopher 2 is hungry
age=5427, philosopher 3 is hungry
age=5431, philosopher 3 has taken forks
age=5432, philosopher 3 eating for 857 ms
age=5569, philosopher 4 is hungry
```

```
age=6298, philosopher 3 has returned forks
age=6301, philosopher 3 thinking for 1309 ms
age=6302, philosopher 5 is hungry
age=6304, philosopher 4 has taken forks
age=6305, philosopher 4 eating for 498 ms
age=6428, philosopher 1 has returned forks
age=6430, philosopher 1 thinking for 1517 ms
age=6432, philosopher 2 has taken forks
age=6433, philosopher 2 eating for 133 ms
age=6567, philosopher 2 has returned forks
age=6570, philosopher 2 thinking for 3243 ms
age=6808, philosopher 4 has returned forks
age=6810, philosopher 4 thinking for 2696 ms
age=6812, philosopher 5 has taken forks
age=6813, philosopher 5 eating for 1838 ms
age=7617, philosopher 3 is hungry
age=7621, philosopher 3 has taken forks
age=7622, philosopher 3 eating for 1251 ms
age=7957, philosopher 1 is hungry
age=8658, philosopher 5 has returned forks
age=8661, philosopher 5 thinking for 4755 ms
age=8662, philosopher 1 has taken forks
age=8664, philosopher 1 eating for 1426 ms
age=8877, philosopher 3 has returned forks
age=8880, philosopher 3 thinking for 2922 ms
age=9507, philosopher 4 is hungry
age=9511, philosopher 4 has taken forks
age=9512, philosopher 4 eating for 391 ms
age=9817, philosopher 2 is hungry
age=9908, philosopher 4 has returned forks
age=9911, philosopher 4 thinking for 3718 ms
age=10098, philosopher 1 has returned forks
age=10100, philosopher 1 thinking for 2541 ms
must stop now
age=10109, philosopher 2 has taken forks
age=10110, philosopher 2 eating for 206 ms
% ./dphi 5 10 1 10 10 1 1 10 10 1 10 1
5 dining philosophers running 10 seconds
dining server for 5 philosophers is alive
philosopher 1 alive, max think eat delays 1 10
age=34, philosopher 1 thinking for 762 ms
philosopher 2 alive, max think eat delays 10 1
age=49, philosopher 2 thinking for 5965 ms
philosopher 3 alive, max think eat delays 1 10
age=61, philosopher 3 thinking for 657 ms
philosopher 4 alive, max think eat delays 10 1
age=74, philosopher 4 thinking for 8930 ms
philosopher 5 alive, max think eat delays 10 1
age=86, philosopher 5 thinking for 5378 ms
age=726, philosopher 3 is hungry
age=731, philosopher 3 has taken forks
age=732, philosopher 3 eating for 3511 ms
age=804, philosopher 1 is hungry
age=808, philosopher 1 has taken forks
age=809, philosopher 1 eating for 3441 ms
```

```
age=4246, philosopher 3 has returned forks
age=4250, philosopher 3 thinking for 488 ms
age=4252, philosopher 1 has returned forks
age=4253, philosopher 1 thinking for 237 ms
age=4495, philosopher 1 is hungry
age=4498, philosopher 1 has taken forks
age=4499, philosopher 1 eating for 8682 ms
age=4745, philosopher 3 is hungry
age=4748, philosopher 3 has taken forks
age=4749, philosopher 3 eating for 2095 ms
age=5475, philosopher 5 is hungry
age=6025, philosopher 2 is hungry
age=6855, philosopher 3 has returned forks
age=6859, philosopher 3 thinking for 551 ms
age=7415, philosopher 3 is hungry
age=7420, philosopher 3 has taken forks
age=7421, philosopher 3 eating for 1765 ms
age=9015, philosopher 4 is hungry
age=9196, philosopher 3 has returned forks
age=9212, philosopher 3 thinking for 237 ms
age=9217, philosopher 4 has taken forks
age=9218, philosopher 4 eating for 775 ms
age=9455, philosopher 3 is hungry
age=9997, philosopher 4 has returned forks
age=10000, philosopher 4 thinking for 2451 ms
age=10002, philosopher 3 has taken forks
age=10004, philosopher 3 eating for 9456 ms
must stop now
                                                      */
```

Program 4.6: The Dining Philosophers Where Each Fork is a Semaphore.

```
#resource philosopher ... end philosopher

resource dining_server
    op take_forks(i : int), put_forks(i : int)
body dining_server(num_phil : int)
    write("dining server for", num_phil, "philosophers is alive")
    type states = enum(thinking, hungry, eating)
    var state[1:num_phil] : states := ([num_phil] thinking)
    sem fork[1:num_phil] := ([num_phil] 1)
    sem room := num_phil - 1

    procedure left(i : int) returns lft : int
        if i=1 -> lft := num_phil [] else -> lft := i-1 fi
    end left

    procedure right(i : int) returns rgh : int
        if i=num_phil -> rgh := 1 [] else -> rgh := i+1 fi
    end right

    proc take_forks(i)
        state[i] := hungry
```

```
        P(room); P(fork[i]); P(fork[right(i)])
        state[i] := eating
    end take_forks

    proc put_forks(i)
        V(fork[i]); V(fork[right(i)]); V(room)
        state[i] := thinking
    end put_forks
end dining_server

#resource start ... end start

/* .............. Example compile and run(s)

% sr -o dphf dphf.sr
% ./dphf 5 10
5 dining philosophers running 10 seconds
dining server for 5 philosophers is alive
philosopher 1 alive, max think eat delays 5 2
age=25, philosopher 1 thinking for 4287 ms
philosopher 2 alive, max think eat delays 5 2
age=34, philosopher 2 thinking for 3536 ms
philosopher 3 alive, max think eat delays 5 2
age=43, philosopher 3 thinking for 2987 ms
philosopher 4 alive, max think eat delays 5 2
age=61, philosopher 4 thinking for 4427 ms
philosopher 5 alive, max think eat delays 5 2
age=74, philosopher 5 thinking for 4045 ms
age=3035, philosopher 3 is hungry
age=3039, philosopher 3 has taken forks
age=3041, philosopher 3 eating for 1979 ms
age=3575, philosopher 2 is hungry
age=4125, philosopher 5 is hungry
age=4129, philosopher 5 has taken forks
age=4130, philosopher 5 eating for 1108 ms
age=4315, philosopher 1 is hungry
age=4495, philosopher 4 is hungry
age=5026, philosopher 3 has returned forks
age=5042, philosopher 3 thinking for 3121 ms
age=5044, philosopher 2 has taken forks
age=5045, philosopher 2 eating for 1169 ms
age=5245, philosopher 5 has returned forks
age=5248, philosopher 5 thinking for 3407 ms
age=5250, philosopher 4 has taken forks
age=5251, philosopher 4 eating for 1801 ms
age=6216, philosopher 2 has returned forks
age=6219, philosopher 2 thinking for 3181 ms
age=6221, philosopher 1 has taken forks
age=6222, philosopher 1 eating for 1064 ms
age=7056, philosopher 4 has returned forks
age=7059, philosopher 4 thinking for 2958 ms
age=7296, philosopher 1 has returned forks
age=7301, philosopher 1 thinking for 4902 ms
age=8166, philosopher 3 is hungry
age=8169, philosopher 3 has taken forks
```

```
age=8171, philosopher 3 eating for 1591 ms
age=8665, philosopher 5 is hungry
age=8669, philosopher 5 has taken forks
age=8670, philosopher 5 eating for 1909 ms
age=9406, philosopher 2 is hungry
age=9766, philosopher 3 has returned forks
age=9770, philosopher 3 thinking for 3449 ms
age=9771, philosopher 2 has taken forks
age=9776, philosopher 2 eating for 1190 ms
age=10026, philosopher 4 is hungry
must stop now
% ./dphf 8 10000 1 10000 263 10 131 10 65 10 31 10 15 10 7 10 3 10
8 dining philosophers running 10000 seconds
dining server for 8 philosophers is alive
philosopher 1 alive, max think eat delays 1 10000
age=35, philosopher 1 thinking for 966 ms
philosopher 2 alive, max think eat delays 263 10
age=76, philosopher 2 thinking for 136701 ms
philosopher 3 alive, max think eat delays 131 10
age=88, philosopher 3 thinking for 70703 ms
philosopher 4 alive, max think eat delays 65 10
age=101, philosopher 4 thinking for 45554 ms
philosopher 5 alive, max think eat delays 31 10
age=114, philosopher 5 thinking for 17368 ms
philosopher 6 alive, max think eat delays 15 10
age=127, philosopher 6 thinking for 11955 ms
philosopher 7 alive, max think eat delays 7 10
age=140, philosopher 7 thinking for 4830 ms
philosopher 8 alive, max think eat delays 3 10
age=152, philosopher 8 thinking for 2805 ms
age=1033, philosopher 1 is hungry
age=1093, philosopher 1 has taken forks
age=1112, philosopher 1 eating for 9779742 ms
age=2963, philosopher 8 is hungry
age=4974, philosopher 7 is hungry
age=12093, philosopher 6 is hungry
age=17495, philosopher 5 is hungry
age=45672, philosopher 4 is hungry
age=70803, philosopher 3 is hungry
^C
                                                       */
```

Program 4.7: The Dining Philosophers Where One is "Odd".

```
#resource philosopher ... end philosopher

#resource dining_server ...

    proc take_forks(i)
        state[i] := hungry
        if i > 1 -> P(fork[i]); P(fork[right(i)])
        [] else  -> P(fork[right(i)]); P(fork[i])
        fi
```

```
        state[i] := eating
    end take_forks

    proc put_forks(i)
        V(fork[i]); V(fork[right(i)])
        state[i] := thinking
    end put_forks

#... end dining_server

#resource start ... end start

/* .............. Example compile and run(s)

% sr -o dpho dpho.sr
% ./dpho 5 10
5 dining philosophers running 10 seconds
dining server for 5 philosophers is alive
philosopher 1 alive, max think eat delays 5 2
age=54, philosopher 1 thinking for 3461 ms
philosopher 2 alive, max think eat delays 5 2
age=67, philosopher 2 thinking for 2990 ms
philosopher 3 alive, max think eat delays 5 2
age=84, philosopher 3 thinking for 3434 ms
philosopher 4 alive, max think eat delays 5 2
age=97, philosopher 4 thinking for 4377 ms
philosopher 5 alive, max think eat delays 5 2
age=116, philosopher 5 thinking for 3939 ms
age=3070, philosopher 2 is hungry
age=3075, philosopher 2 has taken forks
age=3078, philosopher 2 eating for 1721 ms
age=3520, philosopher 1 is hungry
age=3540, philosopher 3 is hungry
age=4062, philosopher 5 is hungry
age=4069, philosopher 5 has taken forks
age=4073, philosopher 5 eating for 1950 ms
age=4489, philosopher 4 is hungry
age=4814, philosopher 2 has returned forks
age=4817, philosopher 2 thinking for 4764 ms
age=6033, philosopher 5 has returned forks
age=6037, philosopher 5 thinking for 4960 ms
age=6041, philosopher 4 has taken forks
age=6042, philosopher 4 eating for 1675 ms
age=6043, philosopher 1 has taken forks
age=6044, philosopher 1 eating for 1976 ms
age=7720, philosopher 4 has returned forks
age=7725, philosopher 4 thinking for 2974 ms
age=7726, philosopher 3 has taken forks
age=7728, philosopher 3 eating for 1165 ms
age=8030, philosopher 1 has returned forks
age=8034, philosopher 1 thinking for 3772 ms
age=8900, philosopher 3 has returned forks
age=8904, philosopher 3 thinking for 2765 ms
age=9591, philosopher 2 is hungry
age=9595, philosopher 2 has taken forks
```

```
age=9596, philosopher 2 eating for 1168 ms
must stop now
% ./dpho 8 10000 1 10000 263 10 131 10 65 10 31 10 15 10 7 10 3 10
8 dining philosophers running 10000 seconds
dining server for 8 philosophers is alive
philosopher 1 alive, max think eat delays 1 10000
age=38, philosopher 1 thinking for 639 ms
philosopher 2 alive, max think eat delays 263 10
age=56, philosopher 2 thinking for 203610 ms
philosopher 3 alive, max think eat delays 131 10
age=70, philosopher 3 thinking for 88146 ms
philosopher 4 alive, max think eat delays 65 10
age=84, philosopher 4 thinking for 43953 ms
philosopher 5 alive, max think eat delays 31 10
age=133, philosopher 5 thinking for 19288 ms
philosopher 6 alive, max think eat delays 15 10
age=175, philosopher 6 thinking for 12721 ms
philosopher 7 alive, max think eat delays 7 10
age=198, philosopher 7 thinking for 3549 ms
philosopher 8 alive, max think eat delays 3 10
age=211, philosopher 8 thinking for 1584 ms
age=682, philosopher 1 is hungry
age=687, philosopher 1 has taken forks
age=690, philosopher 1 eating for 6055740 ms
age=1803, philosopher 8 is hungry
age=3760, philosopher 7 is hungry
age=12910, philosopher 6 is hungry
age=19438, philosopher 5 is hungry
age=44048, philosopher 4 is hungry
age=88289, philosopher 3 is hungry
age=203746, philosopher 2 is hungry
^C
                                              */
```

4.3.4   The Readers and Writers

Program 4.8 solves the readers and writers problem with semaphores, without addressing
starvation. The program is a direct translation into SR of the classical semaphore solution
presented in operating systems textbooks (page 60 of [24]). A number of reader and writer
processes are created, each one napping for a random amount of time and then trying to
read or write by calling Start_Read or Start_Write. After reading or writing for a random
amount of time, each calls End_Read or End_Write. The sample output shows that it is
possible for readers to "starve" a waiting writer if enough readers come along to keep the
database in the concurrent read state. We will see later how to prevent starvation of waiting
writers.

Program 4.8: The Database Readers and Writers.

```
resource server
   op Start_Read(i : int), End_Read(i : int)
   op Start_Write(i : int), End_Write(i : int)
body server()
```

```
      write("readers and writers server is alive")
      var Readers : int := 0
      sem mutex := 1
      sem OK := 1

      proc Start_Read(i)
         P(mutex)
         Readers++
         if Readers = 1 ->
            write("age=", age(), "reader", i, "waiting to read, Readers=",
               Readers)
            P(OK)
         fi
         write("   age=", age(), "reader", i, "has begun reading, Readers=",
            Readers)
         V(mutex)
      end Start Read

      proc End_Read(i)
         P(mutex)
         Readers--
         write("   age=", age(), "reader", i, "finished reading, Readers=",
            Readers)
         if Readers = 0 -> V(OK) fi
         V(mutex)
      end End_Read

      proc Start_Write(i)
         P(OK)
         write("      age=", age(), "WRITER", i, "has begun Writing,")
      end Start_Write

      proc End_Write(i)
         write("   age=", age(), "WRITER", i, "has finished Writing")
         V(OK)
      end End_Write
   end server

resource reader
   import server
body reader(i : int; scap : cap server; nap_time : int)
   write("reader", i, "is alive, nap_time =", nap_time)
   reply
   var napping : int
   do true ->
      napping := int(random(1000*nap_time))
      write("age=", age(), "reader", i, "napping for", napping)
      nap(napping)
      write("age=", age(), "reader", i, "wants to read")
      scap.Start_Read(i)
      napping := int(random(1000*nap_time))
      write("age=", age(), "reader", i, "begins reading for", napping)
      nap(napping)
      scap.End_Read(i)
      write("age=", age(), "reader", i, "finished reading")
```

```
      od
end reader

resource writer
   import server
body writer(i : int; scap : cap server; nap_time : int)
   write("WRITER", i, "is alive, nap_time =", nap_time)
   reply
   var napping : int
   do true ->
      napping := int(random(1000*nap_time))
      write("age=", age(), "WRITER", i, "napping for", napping)
      nap(napping)
      write("age=", age(), "WRITER", i, "wants to write")
      scap.Start_Write(i)
      napping := int(random(1000*nap_time))
      write("age=", age(), "WRITER", i, "is writing for", napping)
      nap(napping)
      write("age=", age(), "WRITER", i, "is finished writing")
      scap.End_Write(i)
   od
end writer

resource start()
   import writer, reader, server
   var readers : int := 10, writers : int := 5, nap_time : int := 3
   var run_time : int := 60
   var scap : cap server
   getarg(1, readers); getarg(2, writers); getarg(3, nap_time)
   getarg(4, run_time)
   write(readers, "readers and", writers,
      "writers starting with nap_time", nap_time, "and run_time", run_time)
   scap := create server()
   fa i := 1 to readers -> create reader(i, scap, nap_time) af
   fa i := 1 to writers -> create writer(i, scap, nap_time) af
   nap(1000*run_time); write("must stop now"); stop
end start

/* .............. Example compile and run(s)

% sr -o rdwr rdwr.sr
% ./rdwr 3 2 1 10
3 readers and 2 writers starting with nap_time 1 and run_time 10
readers and writers server is alive
reader 1 is alive, nap_time = 1
age= 223 reader 1 napping for 506
reader 2 is alive, nap_time = 1
age= 233 reader 2 napping for 694
reader 3 is alive, nap_time = 1
age= 509 reader 3 napping for 27
WRITER 1 is alive, nap_time = 1
age= 641 WRITER 1 napping for 338
age= 658 reader 3 wants to read
age= 670 reader 3 waiting to read, Readers= 1
   age= 727 reader 3 has begun reading, Readers= 1
```

```
age= 732 reader 3 begins reading for 60
WRITER 2 is alive, nap_time = 1
age= 738 WRITER 2 napping for 565
age= 743 reader 1 wants to read
   age= 746 reader 1 has begun reading, Readers= 2
age= 749 reader 1 begins reading for 500
   age= 804 reader 3 finished reading, Readers= 1
age= 815 reader 3 finished reading
age= 822 reader 3 napping for 712
age= 934 reader 2 wants to read
   age= 937 reader 2 has begun reading, Readers= 2
age= 942 reader 2 begins reading for 166
age= 995 WRITER 1 wants to write
   age= 1114 reader 2 finished reading, Readers= 1
age= 1117 reader 2 finished reading
age= 1123 reader 2 napping for 514
   age= 1255 reader 1 finished reading, Readers= 0
age= 1260 reader 1 finished reading
age= 1263 reader 1 napping for 545
      age= 1266 WRITER 1 has begun Writing,
age= 1269 WRITER 1 is writing for 796
age= 1314 WRITER 2 wants to write
age= 1553 reader 3 wants to read
age= 1559 reader 3 waiting to read, Readers= 1
age= 1701 reader 2 wants to read
age= 1825 reader 1 wants to read
age= 2075 WRITER 1 is finished writing
   age= 2146 WRITER 1 has finished Writing
age= 2174 WRITER 1 napping for 555
      age= 2193 WRITER 2 has begun Writing,
age= 2207 WRITER 2 is writing for 964
age= 2754 WRITER 1 wants to write
age= 3212 WRITER 2 is finished writing
   age= 3218 WRITER 2 has finished Writing
age= 3219 WRITER 2 napping for 821
   age= 3221 reader 3 has begun reading, Readers= 1
age= 3222 reader 3 begins reading for 471
   age= 3223 reader 2 has begun reading, Readers= 2
age= 3225 reader 2 begins reading for 286
   age= 3226 reader 1 has begun reading, Readers= 3
age= 3227 reader 1 begins reading for 808
   age= 3515 reader 2 finished reading, Readers= 2
age= 3685 reader 2 finished reading
age= 3733 reader 2 napping for 739
   age= 3784 reader 3 finished reading, Readers= 1
age= 3822 reader 3 finished reading
age= 3883 reader 3 napping for 294
   age= 4044 reader 1 finished reading, Readers= 0
age= 4050 reader 1 finished reading
age= 4053 reader 1 napping for 615
age= 4056 WRITER 2 wants to write
      age= 4059 WRITER 1 has begun Writing,
age= 4062 WRITER 1 is writing for 689
age= 4285 reader 3 wants to read
age= 4289 reader 3 waiting to read, Readers= 1
```

```
age= 4523 reader 2 wants to read
age= 4673 reader 1 wants to read
age= 4763 WRITER 1 is finished writing
   age= 4766 WRITER 1 has finished Writing
age= 4768 WRITER 1 napping for 100
      age= 4769 WRITER 2 has begun Writing,
age= 4770 WRITER 2 is writing for 505
age= 4873 WRITER 1 wants to write
age= 5334 WRITER 2 is finished writing
   age= 5339 WRITER 2 has finished Writing
age= 5340 WRITER 2 napping for 704
   age= 5341 reader 3 has begun reading, Readers= 1
age= 5343 reader 3 begins reading for 575
   age= 5344 reader 2 has begun reading, Readers= 2
age= 5346 reader 2 begins reading for 673
   age= 5347 reader 1 has begun reading, Readers= 3
age= 5348 reader 1 begins reading for 941
   age= 5923 reader 3 finished reading, Readers= 2
age= 5928 reader 3 finished reading
age= 5929 reader 3 napping for 844
   age= 6023 reader 2 finished reading, Readers= 1
age= 6026 reader 2 finished reading
age= 6028 reader 2 napping for 631
age= 6053 WRITER 2 wants to write
   age= 6294 reader 1 finished reading, Readers= 0
age= 6298 reader 1 finished reading
age= 6299 reader 1 napping for 543
       age= 6300 WRITER 1 has begun Writing,
age= 6301 WRITER 1 is writing for 650
age= 6664 reader 2 wants to read
age= 6678 reader 2 waiting to read, Readers= 1
age= 6783 reader 3 wants to read
age= 6935 reader 1 wants to read
age= 6953 WRITER 1 is finished writing
   age= 6956 WRITER 1 has finished Writing
age= 6958 WRITER 1 napping for 837
       age= 6959 WRITER 2 has begun Writing,
age= 6962 WRITER 2 is writing for 12
age= 6986 WRITER 2 is finished writing
   age= 7000 WRITER 2 has finished Writing
age= 7001 WRITER 2 napping for 93
   age= 7002 reader 2 has begun reading, Readers= 1
age= 7004 reader 2 begins reading for 337
   age= 7005 reader 3 has begun reading, Readers= 2
age= 7007 reader 3 begins reading for 448
   age= 7008 reader 1 has begun reading, Readers= 3
age= 7009 reader 1 begins reading for 782
age= 7104 WRITER 2 wants to write
   age= 7344 reader 2 finished reading, Readers= 2
age= 7358 reader 2 finished reading
age= 7360 reader 2 napping for 345
   age= 7466 reader 3 finished reading, Readers= 1
age= 7470 reader 3 finished reading
age= 7471 reader 3 napping for 662
age= 7733 reader 2 wants to read
```

```
   age= 7751 reader 2 has begun reading, Readers= 2
age= 7753 reader 2 begins reading for 391
   age= 7793 reader 1 finished reading, Readers= 1
age= 7797 reader 1 finished reading
age= 7798 reader 1 napping for 660
age= 7799 WRITER 1 wants to write
age= 8143 reader 3 wants to read
   age= 8146 reader 3 has begun reading, Readers= 2
age= 8148 reader 3 begins reading for 478
   age= 8150 reader 2 finished reading, Readers= 1
age= 8151 reader 2 finished reading
age= 8152 reader 2 napping for 790
age= 8467 reader 1 wants to read
   age= 8470 reader 1 has begun reading, Readers= 2
age= 8472 reader 1 begins reading for 687
   age= 8633 reader 3 finished reading, Readers= 1
age= 8636 reader 3 finished reading
age= 8637 reader 3 napping for 812
age= 8943 reader 2 wants to read
   age= 8946 reader 2 has begun reading, Readers= 2
age= 8948 reader 2 begins reading for 458
   age= 9163 reader 1 finished reading, Readers= 1
age= 9166 reader 1 finished reading
age= 9167 reader 1 napping for 399
   age= 9413 reader 2 finished reading, Readers= 0
age= 9416 reader 2 finished reading
age= 9417 reader 2 napping for 884
      age= 9419 WRITER 2 has begun Writing,
age= 9420 WRITER 2 is writing for 737
age= 9453 reader 3 wants to read
age= 9456 reader 3 waiting to read, Readers= 1
age= 9573 reader 1 wants to read
age= 10163 WRITER 2 is finished writing
   age= 10166 WRITER 2 has finished Writing
age= 10168 WRITER 2 napping for 43
      age= 10169 WRITER 1 has begun Writing,
age= 10170 WRITER 1 is writing for 799
age= 10213 WRITER 2 wants to write
age= 10303 reader 2 wants to read
must stop now
                                              */
```

4.4 Binary Semaphores

A common example or exercise in operating systems textbooks is to implement general
counting semaphores using only binary ones (exercise 4.32 in [8], section 6.4.4 of [20], exercise
4.14 in [21], and exercise 6 in chapter 2 of [23]).

To implement a general counting semaphore S and the two operations **down** and **up** on it
using only binary semaphores, we can define two integers, **value** and **waiting**, where **value**
represents the integer value of the semaphore S and **waiting** is the number of processes
blocked on S in a **down** operation. We also need a binary semaphore **mutex** for mutual exclusion and a binary semaphore **blocked** to simulate processes blocking on S. The operations

P and V in the following code are those defined for *binary* semaphores.

```
var value : int := n  /* whatever the initial value of S is to be */
var waiting : int := 0
sem mutex := 1     /* binary */
sem blocked := 0   /* binary */

procedure down(S)
   P(mutex)
   if value = 0 ->
      waiting++
      V(mutex)
      P(blocked)
   [] else ->
      value--
      V(mutex)
   fi
end down

procedure up(S)
   P(mutex)
   if value = 0 and waiting > 0 ->
      waiting--
      V(blocked)
   [] else ->
      value++
   fi
   V(mutex)
end up
```

We can combine `value` and `waiting` into a single integer variable `count` as follows. Here `count` is always equal to the number of up's that have been performed on S minus the number of down's.

```
var count : int := n  /* whatever the initial value of S is to be */
sem mutex := 1     /* binary */
sem blocked := 0   /* binary */

procedure down(S)
   P(mutex)
   count--
   if count < 0 ->
      V(mutex)
      # ...                  # This is "point A" mentioned below.
      P(blocked)
   [] else ->
      V(mutex)
   fi
end down

procedure up(S)
   P(mutex)
   count++
   if count <= 0 ->
      V(blocked)            # This is "point B" mentioned below.
   fi
   V(mutex)
```

```
end up
```

But there is a flaw ([13]; see also problem 4.14 of [21]) in the above implementation of counting semaphores using only binary semaphores. If a context switch occurs at point **A** labeled above in the **down** code, and if before the **down** process resumes, several processes do an **up**, then some signals (V's) at point **B** labeled above will get lost because binary semaphores can have only the values zero and one. This means subsequent **down**'s on S will not work correctly.

We can prevent these "lost signals" from occurring by moving the **else** from the **down** routine to the **up** routine, as follows.

```
var count : int := n   /* whatever the initial value of S is to be */
sem mutex := 1      /* binary */
sem blocked := 0   /* binary */

procedure down(S)
   P(mutex)
   count--
   if count < 0 ->
     V(mutex)
     P(blocked)
   fi
   V(mutex)
end down

procedure up(S)
   P(mutex)
   count++
   if count <= 0 ->
     V(blocked)
   [] else ->
     V(mutex)
   fi
end up
```

The effect is to force a blocked **down** operation to complete for each **up** being done, preventing the V(blocked) signal from getting lost.

This solution still has an undesirable feature. If there are several processes blocked inside of **down** on the binary semaphore **blocked**, then a bunch of **up** operations waking up those processes cannot be executed sequentially but must be strictly interleaved with each process completing its P(blocked) and its **down** operation. As explained in [14], this can have performance penalties because of the extra context switching.

The fix for this is to keep track of the number of V(blocked) operations explicitly as follows.

```
var count : int := n   /* whatever the initial value of S is to be */
sem mutex := 1      /* binary */
sem blocked := 0   /* binary */
var wakeup : int := 0           # new variable

procedure down(S)
   P(mutex)
   count--
   if count < 0 ->
     V(mutex)
     P(blocked)
```

```
        P(mutex)
        wakeup--
        if wakeup > 0 -> V(blocked) fi
     fi
     V(mutex)
  end down

  procedure up(S)
     P(mutex)
     count++
     if count <= 0 ->
        wakeup++
        V(blocked)
     fi
     V(mutex)
  end up
```

Both of these problems can be avoided by adding one more binary semaphore **serial** (page 180-81 of [20]) to the original solution that serializes execution of the **down** code. Therefore at most one process can be at point **A** mentioned above, and there is no restriction on the CPU scheduler.

```
  var count : int := n  /* whatever the initial value of S is to be */
  sem mutex := 1    /* binary */
  sem blocked := 0  /* binary */
  sem serial := 1   /* binary */

  procedure down(S)
     P(serial)
     P(mutex)
     count--
     if count < 0 ->
        V(mutex)
        P(blocked)
     [] else ->
        V(mutex)
     fi
     V(serial)
  end down

  procedure up(S)
     P(mutex)
     count++
     if count <= 0 ->
        V(blocked)                 # This is "point B" mentioned below.
     fi
     V(mutex)
  end up
```

This example shows how difficult it is to write correct programs in the presence of arbitrary context switches, even when binary semaphores or locks are available as a tool.

4.5   Lab: Semaphores

Objectives

To see how semaphores can be used to prevent race conditions and to synchronize the execution of concurrently executing processes that share data.

Preparation Before Lab

Read Sections 4.1-4.3 on semaphores and some of the classical problems in operating systems. Study Programs 4.1, 4.2, 4.5, and 4.8. No busy waiting is allowed in any of these assignments.

4.5.1   Assignment: Fix Race Condition

Compile and run Program 4.1 in the normal way and then again using the `srl -L 1` method. Explain exactly how the semaphore prevents interleaving regardless of the context switch interval length.

4.5.2   Assignment: Multiple Producers and Consumers

Modify Program 4.2 so that there are separate producer and consumer resources. The main driver resource will read two numbers from the command line and create that many producers and consumers, respectively. Refer to Programs 2.15 and 3.4.

In other words, write an SR program that has a single bounded buffer with size of `slots` (default value 20), `num_producers` (default value 3) producer processes, and `num_consumers` (default value 5) consumer processes. The single bounded buffer will be in its own resource. The producers will all be created from one resource, and the consumers will all be created from one resource.

All default values should be overridable with command line arguments:

```
sr -o bbou bbou.sr
bbou slots producer-max-nap consumer-max-nap num-producers num-consumers
```

Watch out for race conditions on the variable `put_in` if multiple producers call `deposit()` at about the same time. Watch out for race conditions on the variable `take_out` if multiple consumers call `fetch()` at about the same time.

Play around with the random number generator arguments, the buffer size, the number of producers, and the number of consumers to get a buffer that drifts between empty and full.

See **For Every Lab** in Lab 2.3 for additional information.

4.5.3   Assignment: Another Classical Problem

Write an SR program that solves, using semaphores, another classical operating systems problem, such as the cigarette smokers (problem 29 on page 73 of [24], problem 6.8 of [20], problem 4.25 of [3]) or the bakery (problem 30 on page 73 of [24]). In the former, each smoker and the agent is to be an SR process. In the latter, each of the m customers and n salespersons is to be an SR process.

4.5.4   Assignment: Multiple Sleeping Barbers

Examine the semaphores and algorithm used for condition synchronization in the sleeping barber program (Program 4.4). Could the algorithm be extended to work with more than one barber (problems 17 and 28 on pages 72 and 73 of [24])? Verify your hypothesis by modifying Program 4.4 and running it with various parameter sets.

4.5.5   Assignment: Dining Philosophers

The SR code for the dining philosophers, Program 4.5, is not completely correct because it allows two philosophers to collaborate and starve a third one (starvation in the presence of contention). Instrument the program so that it detects and prints out when a particular philosopher is starving. A philosopher is starving when the following situation occurs repeatedly without the philosopher being able to eat: the philosopher is hungry and one of its neighbors puts down its forks but the hungry philosopher cannot eat because the neighbor on its other side is eating. If starvation is not prevented, then two philosophers could collaborate and coordinate their eating times so they prevent forever the philosopher between them from eating.

Modify the dining philosophers program so that it is starvation-free. The way to avoid starvation is to add another state, "very hungry" say, and not let a hungry philosopher eat if it has a "very hungry" neighbor. A philosopher enters this new state if its neighbors have put down their forks and the philosopher under consideration has not been able to eat. You can be more elaborate and count the number of times a hungry philosopher has not been able to pick up the forks, and make a philosopher "very hungry" if this number exceeds some specified maximum. You can be even more elaborate and keep separate counts for not being able to pick up the forks because the left fork is in use or the right fork is in use, and change to the starving state when both of these counts exceed the maximum, and the left and right forks not being usable has been alternating.

It is not correct to change the state of a philosopher from hungry to very hungry at any time other than when one of its neighbors puts down one of its forks. If you make the transition when a philosopher gets hungry and is first trying to pick up its forks, then a hungry philosopher goes to be very hungry right away if its forks are not available, and you have gained nothing. It is not correct to have two neighboring philosophers very hungry at the same time because either they will deadlock (if you never allow a philosopher regardless of state to eat if it has a very hungry neighbor) or your solution will still allow starvation (you can construct such a scenario). Finally, the philosophers have very tight grips and forks cannot be taken away from them until they are finished eating.

You may have your philosopher processes eat and think for random amounts of time, but to check for starvation prevention, you will have to exercise more control over the random numbers after compiling your modified version of Program 4.5:

```
sr -o dphi dphi.sr
dphi 5 300 1 100 10 1 1 100 100 1 100 1
```

However, more thorough testing than just the above run is required. Run your program first with starvation prevention disabled, then again with starvation prevention enabled and highlight the difference, as described in **For Every Lab** in Lab 2.3.

4.5.6   Assignment: Fair Readers and Writers

Modify the readers and writers program so that it is fair, i.e., so that a continuous stream of arriving readers cannot starve a writer.

4.5.7 Assignment: Baboons Crossing a Canyon

Write an SR program to coordinate or synchronize baboons crossing a rope over a canyon (problems 15 and 16 on page 264 of [24]) so they do not deadlock. Think of multiple baboons crossing as multiple readers reading a database: many can cross (read) simultaneously. In the readers/writers problem, a reader would read the database for as long or as short a time as it wanted. Allow the same for the baboons: baboons can take as long a time or as short a time to cross as they want, i.e., a baboon can climb over and pass another baboon while crossing if that baboon is going in the same direction. This problem can also be posed as "The Unisex Bathroom" problem (Exercise 4.27 in [3]).

Do this in two steps. First write your program without worrying about a series of eastward-moving baboons holding up the waiting westward-moving baboons indefinitely, or vice versa, that is, do not worry about preventing starvation. However, to see that starvation can actually occur, fiddle with the random number generator parameters to create a situation where starvation occurs. Save the parameters for the next step.

Then modify your program so that there is no starvation. For example, when a baboon that wants to cross to the east arrives at the rope and finds baboons crossing to the west, it waits until the rope is empty, but no more westward-moving baboons are allowed to start until at least one waiting baboon has crossed the other way. Now, run this version of your program with the random number generator parameters that led to starvation in the first version of your program.

4.5.8 Assignment: Fraternity Party

A group of M fraternity brothers and sorority sisters is having a party and drinking from a large communal keg that can hold N servings of soda. When a partier wants to drink, he or she fills a cup from the keg, unless it is empty. If the keg is empty, the partier wakes up the pledge and then waits until the pledge has returned with a new keg. The behavior of the partiers and pledge is specified by the following processes:

Partier:

```
do true ->
    tell_pledge_if_keg_empty(); get_serving_from_keg(); drink()
od
```

Pledge:

```
do true ->
    wait_for_keg_to_empty(); get_new_keg_of_N_servings()
od
```

Develop SR code for the actions of the partiers and pledge. Use semaphores for process synchronization. Your solution should avoid deadlock and awaken the pledge only when the keg is empty. (Adapted from Exercises 4.31 and 6.18 of [3].)

4.5.9 Assignment: Jurassic Park

Jurassic Park consists of a dinosaur museum and a park for safari riding. There are n passengers and m single-passenger cars. Passengers wander around the museum for a while, then line up to take a ride in a safari car. When a car is available, it loads the one passenger it can hold and rides around the park for a random amount of time. If the m cars are all out riding passengers around, then a passenger who wants to ride waits; if a car is ready to load but there are no waiting passengers, then the car waits. Use semaphores to synchronize the n passenger processes and the m car processes. Why is the following code not correct?

```
resource Jurassic_Park()
    var num_passengers : int := 10, num_cars : int := 3
    var wander_time : int := 5, ride_time : int := 4, run_time : int := 60
    sem car_avail := 0, car_taken := 0, car_filled := 0, passenger_released := 0
    getarg(1, num_passengers); getarg(2, num_cars); getarg(3, wander_time)
    getarg(4, ride_time); getarg(5, run_time)

    process passenger(i := 1 to num_passengers)
        do true -> nap(int(random(1000*wander_time)))
            write("age=", age(), "passenger", i, "wants to ride")
            P(car_avail);  V(car_taken);  P(car_filled)
            write("age=", age(), "passenger", i, "taking a ride")
            P(passenger_released)
            write("age=", age(), "passenger", i, "finished riding")
        od
    end passenger

    process car(j := 1 to num_cars)
        do true -> write("age=", age(), "car", j, "ready to load")
            V(car_avail);  P(car_taken);  V(car_filled)
            write("age=", age(), "car", j, "going on safari")
            nap(int(random(1000*ride_time)))
            write("age=", age(), "car", j, "has returned")
            V(passenger_released)
        od
    end car

    nap(1000*run_time); write("must stop now"); stop
end Jurassic_Park
```

Correct the code and write a complete SR program simulating Jurassic Park. Now suppose each car can hold C passengers, $C < n$, instead of just one. Modify your code to reflect this change in the simulation.

4.6   Animating Operating Systems Algorithms

As we saw in Section 4.2, four algorithms or problems usually examined in operating systems classes are the bounded buffer producers and consumers, the database readers and writers, the dining philosophers, and the sleeping barber.

A program that simulates the dining philosophers usually generates its output in the form of lines of philosopher state changes (hungry, eating, thinking) perhaps tagged with a time stamp. The lines from the different philosophers are all intermixed. This makes following the output or debugging the program difficult. An algorithm that lets the philosophers eat in a starvation-free fashion would be much easier to understand if the output could be presented in a graphical or animated form with dining philosopher icons sitting around a circular table, each labeled or colored with its current state.

Using the technique described in Section 2.7, print statements can be added to Program 4.5 to animate the program. The philosophers are represented by small circles equally spaced around a large circle representing the table. The state of each philosopher is repre-

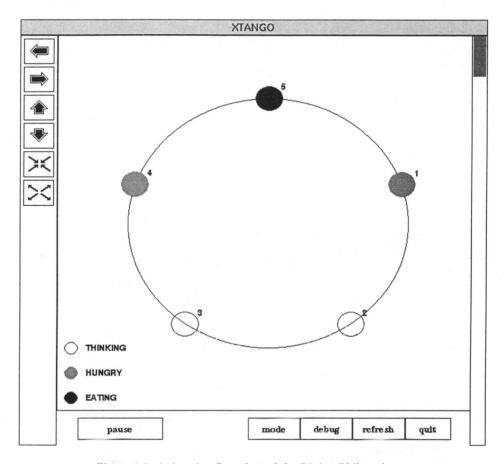

Figure 4.1: Animation Snapshot of the Dining Philosophers.

sented by a different color: green for hungry and blue for eating. Program 4.9 shows the complete code and Figure 4.1 shows a snapshot of the animation.

Program 4.9: Animating the Dining Philosophers with XTANGO.

```
resource philosopher
   import dining_server
body philosopher(i : int; dcap : cap dining_server; thinking, eating: int)
   printf("comment ")                                    # animator
   write("philosopher", i, "alive, max think eat delays", thinking, eating)
   reply

   procedure think()
      var napping : int
      napping := int(random(1000*thinking))
      printf("comment ")                                 # animator
      writes("age=",age(),", philosopher ",i," thinking for ",napping," ms\n")
```

```
          nap(napping)
      end think

   procedure eat()
      var napping : int
      napping := int(random(1000*eating))
      printf("comment ")                                       # animator
      writes("age=",age(),", philosopher ",i," eating for ",napping," ms\n")
      printf("color %d   blue\n", i)                           # animator
      printf("fill   %d solid\n", i)                           # animator
      nap(napping)
   end eat

   do true ->
      think()
      printf("comment ")                                       # animator
      writes("age=", age(), ", philosopher ", i, " is hungry\n")
      printf("color %d green\n", i)                            # animator
      printf("fill   %d solid\n", i)                           # animator
      dcap.take_forks(i)
      printf("comment ")                                       # animator
      writes("age=", age(), ", philosopher ", i, " has taken forks\n")
      eat()
      dcap.put_forks(i)
      printf("comment ")                                       # animator
      writes("age=", age(), ", philosopher ", i, " has returned forks\n")
      printf("fill   %d outline\n", i)                         # animator
      printf("color %d   black\n", i)                          # animator
   od
end philosopher

resource dining_server
   op take_forks(i : int), put_forks(i : int)
body dining_server(num_phil : int)
   printf("comment ")                                          # animator
   write("dining server for", num_phil, "philosophers is alive")
   sem mutex := 1
   type states = enum(thinking, hungry, eating)
   var state[1:num_phil] : states := ([num_phil] thinking)
   sem phil[1:num_phil] := ([num_phil] 0)

   procedure left(i : int) returns lft : int
      if i=1 -> lft := num_phil [] else -> lft := i-1 fi
   end left

   procedure right(i : int) returns rgh : int
      if i=num_phil -> rgh := 1 [] else -> rgh := i+1 fi
   end right

   procedure test(i : int)
      if state[i] = hungry and state[left(i)] ~= eating
            and state[right(i)] ~= eating ->
         state[i] := eating
         V(phil[i])
      fi
```

```
      end test

   proc take_forks(i)
      P(mutex)
      state[i] := hungry
      test(i)
      V(mutex)
      P(phil[i])
   end take_forks

   proc put_forks(i)
      P(mutex)
      state[i] := thinking
      test(left(i)); test(right(i))
      V(mutex)
   end put_forks
end dining_server

resource start()
   import philosopher, dining_server
   var num_phil : int := 5, run_time : int := 60
   getarg(1, num_phil); getarg(2, run_time)
   var max_think_delay[1:num_phil] : int := ([num_phil] 5)
   var max_eat_delay[1:num_phil] : int := ([num_phil] 2)
   fa i := 1 to num_phil ->
      getarg(2*i+1, max_think_delay[i]); getarg(2*i+2, max_eat_delay[i])
   af

   var dcap : cap dining_server
   printf("comment ")                                          # animator
   write(num_phil, "dining philosophers running", run_time, "seconds")
   printf("coords -1.5 -1.5 1.5 1.5\n")                        # animator
   printf("circle 1000  0.0  0.0 1.0  black outline\n")        # animator
   printf("circle 1001 -1.4 -1.0 0.05 black outline\n")        # animator
   printf("text    1002 -1.3 -1.025 0  black THINKING\n")      # animator
   printf("circle 1003 -1.4 -1.2 0.05 green solid\n")          # animator
   printf("text    1004 -1.3 -1.225 0  black HUNGRY\n")        # animator
   printf("circle 1005 -1.4 -1.4 0.05 blue  solid\n")          # animator
   printf("text    1006 -1.3 -1.425 0  black EATING\n")        # animator
   dcap := create dining_server(num_phil)
   const TWO_PI := 2.0*acos(-1.0)                              # animator
   fa i := 1 to num_phil ->
      printf("circle %d %7.2f %7.2f 0.1 black outline\n",      # animator
         i, sin(i*(TWO_PI/num_phil)), cos(i*(TWO_PI/num_phil)))# animator
      printf("text %d %7.2f %7.2f 1 black %d\n",               # animator
         1010+i, sin(i*(TWO_PI/num_phil))+0.1,                 # animator
         cos(i*(TWO_PI/num_phil))+0.1, i)                      # animator
      create philosopher(i, dcap, max_think_delay[i], max_eat_delay[i])
   af
   nap(1000*run_time); printf("comment "); write("must stop now"); stop
end start

/* .............. Example compile and run(s)

% sr -o din_phil din_phil.sr
```

```
% ./din_phil 5 3
comment 5 dining philosophers running 3 seconds
coords -1.5 -1.5 1.5 1.5
circle 1000   0.0   0.0 1.0   black outline
circle 1001 -1.4 -1.0 0.05 black outline
text    1002 -1.3 -1.025 0   black THINKING
circle 1003 -1.4 -1.2 0.05 green solid
text    1004 -1.3 -1.225 0   black HUNGRY
circle 1005 -1.4 -1.4 0.05 blue  solid
text    1006 -1.3 -1.425 0   black EATING
comment dining server for 5 philosophers is alive
circle 1      0.95     0.31 0.1 black outline
text 1011     1.05     0.41 1 black 1
comment philosopher 1 alive, max think eat delays 5 2
comment age=70, philosopher 1 thinking for 4557 ms
circle 2      0.59    -0.81 0.1 black outline
text 1012     0.69    -0.71 1 black 2
comment philosopher 2 alive, max think eat delays 5 2
comment age=94, philosopher 2 thinking for 2019 ms
circle 3    -0.59    -0.81 0.1 black outline
text 1013   -0.49    -0.71 1 black 3
comment philosopher 3 alive, max think eat delays 5 2
comment age=117, philosopher 3 thinking for 758 ms
circle 4    -0.95     0.31 0.1 black outline
text 1014   -0.85     0.41 1 black 4
comment philosopher 4 alive, max think eat delays 5 2
comment age=141, philosopher 4 thinking for 4206 ms
circle 5    -0.00     1.00 0.1 black outline
text 1015    0.10     1.10 1 black 5
comment philosopher 5 alive, max think eat delays 5 2
comment age=165, philosopher 5 thinking for 4084 ms
comment age=887, philosopher 3 is hungry
color 3 green
fill  3 solid
comment age=899, philosopher 3 has taken forks
comment age=903, philosopher 3 eating for 1603 ms
color 3  blue
fill  3 solid
comment age=2127, philosopher 2 is hungry
color 2 green
fill  2 solid
comment age=2518, philosopher 3 has returned forks
fill  3 outline
color 3    black
comment age=2527, philosopher 3 thinking for 2381 ms
comment age=2532, philosopher 2 has taken forks
comment age=2537, philosopher 2 eating for 1954 ms
color 2  blue
fill  2 solid
comment must stop now
% ./din_phil 5 10 | animator
Press RUN ANIMATION button to begin

XTANGO Version 1.52
```

```
5 dining philosophers running 10 seconds
dining server for 5 philosophers is alive
philosopher 1 alive, max think eat delays 5 2
age=54, philosopher 1 thinking for 3381 ms
philosopher 2 alive, max think eat delays 5 2
age=114, philosopher 2 thinking for 393 ms
philosopher 3 alive, max think eat delays 5 2
age=125, philosopher 3 thinking for 1285 ms
philosopher 4 alive, max think eat delays 5 2
age=135, philosopher 4 thinking for 3668 ms
philosopher 5 alive, max think eat delays 5 2
age=150, philosopher 5 thinking for 2779 ms
age=514, philosopher 2 is hungry
age=517, philosopher 2 has taken forks
age=517, philosopher 2 eating for 199 ms
age=732, philosopher 2 has returned forks
age=734, philosopher 2 thinking for 838 ms
age=1416, philosopher 3 is hungry
age=1418, philosopher 3 has taken forks
age=1419, philosopher 3 eating for 1645 ms
age=1597, philosopher 2 is hungry
age=2935, philosopher 5 is hungry
age=2937, philosopher 5 has taken forks
age=2938, philosopher 5 eating for 1428 ms
age=3075, philosopher 3 has returned forks
age=3077, philosopher 3 thinking for 2529 ms
age=3078, philosopher 2 has taken forks
age=3079, philosopher 2 eating for 109 ms
age=3195, philosopher 2 has returned forks
age=3197, philosopher 2 thinking for 1495 ms
age=3437, philosopher 1 is hungry
age=3805, philosopher 4 is hungry
age=4376, philosopher 5 has returned forks
age=4378, philosopher 5 thinking for 4738 ms
age=4379, philosopher 1 has taken forks
age=4380, philosopher 1 eating for 1133 ms
age=4382, philosopher 4 has taken forks
age=4383, philosopher 4 eating for 719 ms
age=4714, philosopher 2 is hungry
age=5105, philosopher 4 has returned forks
age=5106, philosopher 4 thinking for 3695 ms
age=5515, philosopher 1 has returned forks
age=5516, philosopher 1 thinking for 2057 ms
age=5518, philosopher 2 has taken forks
age=5519, philosopher 2 eating for 128 ms
age=5614, philosopher 3 is hungry
age=5655, philosopher 2 has returned forks
age=5657, philosopher 2 thinking for 3637 ms
age=5658, philosopher 3 has taken forks
age=5659, philosopher 3 eating for 1058 ms
age=6725, philosopher 3 has returned forks
age=6727, philosopher 3 thinking for 4475 ms
age=7575, philosopher 1 is hungry
age=7577, philosopher 1 has taken forks
age=7578, philosopher 1 eating for 87 ms
```

```
age=7675, philosopher 1 has returned forks
age=7676, philosopher 1 thinking for 2459 ms
age=8805, philosopher 4 is hungry
age=8814, philosopher 4 has taken forks
age=8815, philosopher 4 eating for 443 ms
age=9125, philosopher 5 is hungry
age=9265, philosopher 4 has returned forks
age=9270, philosopher 4 thinking for 429 ms
age=9271, philosopher 5 has taken forks
age=9272, philosopher 5 eating for 962 ms
age=9295, philosopher 2 is hungry
age=9303, philosopher 2 has taken forks
age=9304, philosopher 2 eating for 270 ms
age=9585, philosopher 2 has returned forks
age=9590, philosopher 2 thinking for 167 ms
age=9705, philosopher 4 is hungry
age=9765, philosopher 2 is hungry
age=9770, philosopher 2 has taken forks
age=9771, philosopher 2 eating for 368 ms
age=10145, philosopher 2 has returned forks
age=10150, philosopher 2 thinking for 146 ms
age=10152, philosopher 1 is hungry
must stop now
                                          */
```

4.7   Lab: Classical Problem Animation

Objectives

To get a better understanding of the classical operating systems problems by animating programs that simulate them.

Preparation Before Lab

Read Section 4.6. Study Program 4.9.

4.7.1   Assignment

Animate one of Program 4.2, 4.4, or 4.8 (bounded buffer producers and consumers, sleeping barber, or database readers and writers, respectively).

Chapter 5

Monitors

Semaphores are like gotos and pointers in that programming with them is prone to mistakes. Semaphores work but they lack structure and "discipline." For example, a disastrous easy-to-make coding mistake is the following.

    V(S)
    critical section
    V(S)

And the following leads to deadlock.

    P(S)
    critical section
    P(S)

Monitors were devised to help avoid these kinds of mistakes and to provide a higher-level programming language construct than semaphores. Monitors are related to objects and object-oriented programming, to abstract data types and data encapsulation.

A *monitor* (see Section 5.3 of [8], Section 6.7 of [20], or Section 2.2.7 of [24]) is a programming language module or package that encapsulates a collection of interface routines and their global and local variables. The only way to access the variables inside the monitor is to call one of the interface procedures. Only one process at a time is allowed to be active inside the monitor, that is executing one of the interface routines. This will prevent race conditions involving the variables inside the monitor if several processes call interface procedures at about the same time.

Mutual exclusion synchronization is therefore implicit in monitors. To provide a mechanism for event or condition synchronization, a monitor can contain *condition variables*. There are two operations on a condition variable: *signal* and *wait*. These are a little like the "up" and "down" operations on binary semaphores. A process that does a wait on a condition variable will temporarily leave the monitor and block until such time as some other process does a signal on that condition variable. Then the process can reenter the monitor and continue execution of the interface routine it had called. A monitor condition variable has no value and is really the name of a queue of processes that are blocked on the condition variable. If a signal is done on a conditional variable that has no blocked processes, then the signal is not remembered and has no effect. This is in contrast to semaphores.

Monitors and condition variables can be implemented with one of several signaling disciplines: *signal and exit*, *signal and wait*, and *signal and continue*. In signal and exit, a process executing inside the monitor that does a signal on a condition variable is required to leave the monitor (return from the interface procedure) immediately after the signal.

The first process in the wait queue of that condition variable will be awakened and will continue executing inside the monitor. It gets priority to execute inside the monitor over all processes queued to enter the monitor via one of its interface procedures. In signal and wait, the signaled process executes inside the monitor while the signaler waits for it to leave the monitor; then the signaler continues. In signal and continue, the signaled process waits for the signaler to leave the monitor before it resumes execution inside the monitor. See Chapter 6 of [3] for a much more thorough treatment of monitors and their various signaling disciplines.

We will use the first one, signal and exit, since it is simpler to understand, particularly for those working with monitors for the first time. Therefore, we will make the following two assumptions about condition variables.

1. The signaler must exit the monitor immediately after signaling a condition variable by executing a return statement so that no variables can change before the signaled process wakes up and continues executing inside the monitor. In this way the signaled process finds the condition still true when it resumes execution inside the monitor.

2. The signaled process is given priority to proceed inside the monitor over those processes waiting to enter the monitor through an interface routine call. Thus, the signaled process finds the condition still true when it resumes execution inside the monitor.

5.1   Monitors and SR

SR provides a way to use monitors. Included with the SR software distribution is a pre-processor program m2sr, which will translate a monitor into equivalent SR code [18]. The translated monitor and an SR program making calls to the monitor can then be compiled together. To use the preprocessor, place the monitor code in a file, say monitor.m, and the rest of the SR program that uses the monitor in another file, say driver.sr. Then execute the following commands.

```
m2sr -sx monitor.m
sr -o prog monitor.sr driver.sr
prog
```

The -sx argument on the m2sr command means use the signal and exit condition variable signaling discipline, described above.

The SR monitor translator m2sr supports arrays of condition variables, used in the dining philosophers, Program 5.4. Below are relevant excerpts from its UNIX manual page (man m2sr command).

Arrays of one or two dimensions of condition variables can be declared, although the syntax is baroque; e.g., condvar1(scan,0:1) declares scan to be a one dimensional array with indices 0 and 1, and condvar2(foo,3,5:9) declares foo to be a two dimensional array with indices 1 through 3 in the first dimension and 5 through 9 in the second dimension.

A number of syntactic limitations exist to ease the implementation. Do not use names of SR predefined functions or reserved words (e.g., free, exit, or skip) as variable names within monitors. Do not use identifiers beginning with m_ within monitor code. Do not use any other SR synchronization or return/reply within a monitor program. Do not use the # form of comment; use only the /* */ form, but do not nest comments. Do not use /% or %/. Spaces in source text, even within string literals, between the following pairs of characters will be deleted: / and %, % and /, / and /, [and], * and *, ˜ and =, and : and =; in addition spaces preceding : and = will also be deleted. Within string literals, use an escape character (\) to retain the desired spacing.

DIAGNOSTICS

Some erroneous monitor code will cause errors from cpp. The line numbers that cpp complains about generally correspond to the ones in the .m file. Other than that, m2sr does nearly no error checking. To flag some errors, m2sr intentionally generates invalid SR code containing the word 'ERROR' followed by an explanation. The SR compiler will detect that as an error later.

Other errors in monitor code are detected by the SR compiler. The line numbers for these errors will not correspond to those in the original source file, but they can be mapped back by looking in the generated code file. That file will be rather ugly, but the cause of the error can be found there. To give some help in tracing back errors to the original source file, the generated code file contains comments of the form /*--X--*/, where X is a line number in the original source file. These comments are generated for any construct that the preprocessor replaces by other text. If, for example, the SR compiler reports an error on line 38, then look at line 38 of the generated SR file. If on that line you find the comment /*--12--*/, examine line 12 of the original source file to see the error's cause. If you see no /*--X--*/ comment on the line itself, you should look for the first /*--X--*/ comment that appears above the line and use that number to point you back to the correct line in the original source file.

The following program has been helpful in working with SR monitors. When m2sr -sx is run on file.m, the file.sr produced has very long lines in it, so the UNIX editor vi cannot be started up on it to see what lines are in error. Program 5.1 will at least give you the line.

Program 5.1: A Utility Program to Print Long Lines.

```
resource print_line_number()
    var which_line : int := 1
    var line : string[8192]
    var status : int
    getarg(1, which_line)
    fa i := 1 to which_line ->
        status := read(line)
        if status = EOF -> write("not that many lines"); stop fi
    af
    write(line)
end print_line_number

/* .............. Example compile and run(s)

% m2sr -sx bb.m
% sr -o bb bb.sr driver.sr
bb.sr:
"bb.sr", line 268: fatal: parse error at keyword 'end'
driver.sr:
% vi bb.sr
"bb.sr" Line too long
:q!
% sr -o print_long_line print_long_line.sr
```

```
% ./print_long_line 268 <bb.sr
  /*--21--*/ send m_mutex(); end
                                                */
```

5.1.1   The Producers and Consumers

The monitor in Program 5.2 is for the bounded buffer producer and consumer problem and is adapted from an example on the SR software distribution. The `_print(cv)` statement prints out the number of processes waiting on the condition variable `cv`. The function `_empty(cv)` returns true if there are no processes waiting on the condition variable `cv`. SR monitors cannot be passed parameters when they are created as can resources; so the size of the buffer is read from the command line with `getarg`.

To use the monitor in Program 5.2 with the program in Program 4.2, place the bounded buffer program in a file, say `driver.sr` and remove the `bounded_buffer` resource from it. Change the two occurrences of `bb` to `bounded_buffer` and delete the `create` statement. Since the size of the buffer is specified inside the monitor, remove all references to `slots`. Program 5.3 shows the modifications. Place the monitor in a file, say `bb.m`. Then execute the following commands.

```
m2sr -sx bb.m
sr -o bb bb.sr driver.sr
bb
```

It is important to note that an SR resource that exports a collection of operations (list of `ops`) and implements them with `procs` in its body, such as the `bounded_buffer` resource in Program 4.2, is not the same thing as a monitor because concurrent calls of the `procs` can be made. We had to use semaphores inside Program 4.2 to prevent race conditions.

Program 5.2: Bounded Buffer Monitor.

```
/* use only this form of commenting, but don't nest */
_monitor(bounded_buffer)
   op deposit(data: real), fetch() returns data: real
_body(bounded_buffer)
   var size : int := 20;   getarg(1, size)
   write("bounded buffer alive with", size, "slots")
   var buf[0:size-1]: real
   var front := 0, rear := 0, count := 0
   _condvar(not_full); _condvar(not_empty)

   _proc( deposit(data) )
      if count = size -> _print(not_full); _print(not_empty); _wait(not_full) fi
      _print(not_full); _print(not_empty)
      buf[rear] := data
      rear := (rear+1) % size
      count := count+1
      write("there are now", count, "items in the buffer")
      if _empty(not_empty) -> write("no consumers are waiting")
      [] else               -> write("consumers are waiting")
      fi
      _signal(not_empty)
```

```
    _proc_end

    _proc( fetch() returns result )
        if count = 0 -> _print(not_full); _print(not_empty); _wait(not_empty) fi
        _print(not_full); _print(not_empty)
        result := buf[front]
        front := (front+1) % size
        count := count-1
        write("there are now", count, "items in the buffer")
        if _empty(not_full) -> write("no producers are waiting")
        [] else                -> write("producers are waiting")
        fi
        _signal(not_full)
    _proc_end
_monitor_end
```

Program 5.3: Bounded Buffer Monitor Driver.

```
resource user()
    import bounded_buffer
    var pnap : int := 3, cnap : int := 3
    var run_time : int := 60
    getarg(2, pnap)              # buffer size is argument 1 and
    getarg(3, cnap)              # is getarg-ed in the monitor!
    getarg(4, run_time)
    writes("main user resource alive, pnap = ", pnap, ", cnap = ", cnap,
        ", and run_time = ", run_time, "\n")

    process producer
        var it : real
        var napping : int
        do true ->
            it := random()
            writes("age=", age(), ", PRODUCER produced item ", it, "\n")
            bounded_buffer.deposit(it)
            napping := int(random(1000*pnap))
            writes("age=", age(), ", PRODUCER deposited item ", it,
                " and napping for ", napping, "ms\n")
            nap(napping)
        od
    end producer

    process consumer
        var it : real
        var napping : int
        do true ->
            writes("age=", age(), ", consumer wants to consume ...\n")
            it := bounded_buffer.fetch()
            napping := int(random(1000*cnap))
            writes("age=", age(), ", consumer fetched item ", it,
                " and napping for ", napping, "ms\n")
            nap(napping)
        od
```

```
    end consumer

    nap(1000*run_time); write("must stop now"); stop
end user

/* .............. Example compile and run(s)

% m2sr -sx bb.m
% sr -o bb bb.sr driver.sr
bb.sr:
driver.sr:
bb.sr:
driver.sr:
linking:
% ./bb 5 1 3 10
bounded buffer alive with 5 slots
main user resource alive, pnap = 1, cnap = 3, and run_time = 10
age=46, PRODUCER produced item 0.606729
age=55, consumer wants to consume ...
        **** Printing for not_full **** 0 waiting process(es)
        **** Printing for not_empty **** 0 waiting process(es)
there are now 1 items in the buffer
no consumers are waiting
age=79, PRODUCER deposited item 0.606729 and napping for 876ms
        **** Printing for not_full **** 0 waiting process(es)
        **** Printing for not_empty **** 0 waiting process(es)
there are now 0 items in the buffer
no producers are waiting
age=114, consumer fetched item 0.606729 and napping for 2825ms
age=974, PRODUCER produced item 0.270639
        **** Printing for not_full **** 0 waiting process(es)
        **** Printing for not_empty **** 0 waiting process(es)
there are now 1 items in the buffer
no consumers are waiting
age=1093, PRODUCER deposited item 0.270639 and napping for 412ms
age=1514, PRODUCER produced item 0.490240
        **** Printing for not_full **** 0 waiting process(es)
        **** Printing for not_empty **** 0 waiting process(es)
there are now 2 items in the buffer
no consumers are waiting
age=1539, PRODUCER deposited item 0.490240 and napping for 92ms
age=1644, PRODUCER produced item 0.679252
        **** Printing for not_full **** 0 waiting process(es)
        **** Printing for not_empty **** 0 waiting process(es)
there are now 3 items in the buffer
no consumers are waiting
age=1669, PRODUCER deposited item 0.679252 and napping for 179ms
age=1854, PRODUCER produced item 0.163522
        **** Printing for not_full **** 0 waiting process(es)
        **** Printing for not_empty **** 0 waiting process(es)
there are now 4 items in the buffer
no consumers are waiting
age=1879, PRODUCER deposited item 0.163522 and napping for 837ms
age=2724, PRODUCER produced item 0.407361
        **** Printing for not_full **** 0 waiting process(es)
```

```
              **** Printing for not_empty **** 0 waiting process(es)
there are now 5 items in the buffer
no consumers are waiting
age=2749, PRODUCER deposited item 0.407361 and napping for 837ms
age=2944, consumer wants to consume ...
              **** Printing for not_full **** 0 waiting process(es)
              **** Printing for not_empty **** 0 waiting process(es)
there are now 4 items in the buffer
no producers are waiting
age=2956, consumer fetched item 0.270639 and napping for 1154ms
age=3594, PRODUCER produced item 0.123102
              **** Printing for not_full **** 0 waiting process(es)
              **** Printing for not_empty **** 0 waiting process(es)
there are now 5 items in the buffer
no consumers are waiting
age=3625, PRODUCER deposited item 0.123102 and napping for 417ms
age=4054, PRODUCER produced item 0.734775
              **** Printing for not_full **** 0 waiting process(es)
              **** Printing for not_empty **** 0 waiting process(es)
age=4114, consumer wants to consume ...
              **** Printing for not_full **** 1 waiting process(es), all with rank 0
              **** Printing for not_empty **** 0 waiting process(es)
there are now 4 items in the buffer
producers are waiting
age=4126, consumer fetched item 0.490240 and napping for 1063ms
              **** Printing for not_full **** 0 waiting process(es)
              **** Printing for not_empty **** 0 waiting process(es)
there are now 5 items in the buffer
no consumers are waiting
age=4136, PRODUCER deposited item 0.734775 and napping for 360ms
age=4504, PRODUCER produced item 0.806480
              **** Printing for not_full **** 0 waiting process(es)
              **** Printing for not_empty **** 0 waiting process(es)
age=5194, consumer wants to consume ...
              **** Printing for not_full **** 1 waiting process(es), all with rank 0
              **** Printing for not_empty **** 0 waiting process(es)
there are now 4 items in the buffer
producers are waiting
age=5207, consumer fetched item 0.679252 and napping for 1546ms
              **** Printing for not_full **** 0 waiting process(es)
              **** Printing for not_empty **** 0 waiting process(es)
there are now 5 items in the buffer
no consumers are waiting
age=5217, PRODUCER deposited item 0.806480 and napping for 987ms
age=6214, PRODUCER produced item 0.679876
              **** Printing for not_full **** 0 waiting process(es)
              **** Printing for not_empty **** 0 waiting process(es)
age=6764, consumer wants to consume ...
              **** Printing for not_full **** 1 waiting process(es), all with rank 0
              **** Printing for not_empty **** 0 waiting process(es)
there are now 4 items in the buffer
producers are waiting
age=6787, consumer fetched item 0.163522 and napping for 570ms
              **** Printing for not_full **** 0 waiting process(es)
              **** Printing for not_empty **** 0 waiting process(es)
```

```
there are now 5 items in the buffer
no consumers are waiting
age=6799, PRODUCER deposited item 0.679876 and napping for 657ms
age=7364, consumer wants to consume ...
          **** Printing for not_full **** 0 waiting process(es)
          **** Printing for not_empty **** 0 waiting process(es)
there are now 4 items in the buffer
no producers are waiting
age=7386, consumer fetched item 0.407361 and napping for 406ms
age=7464, PRODUCER produced item 0.661360
          **** Printing for not_full **** 0 waiting process(es)
          **** Printing for not_empty **** 0 waiting process(es)
there are now 5 items in the buffer
no consumers are waiting
age=7476, PRODUCER deposited item 0.661360 and napping for 924ms
age=7794, consumer wants to consume ...
          **** Printing for not_full **** 0 waiting process(es)
          **** Printing for not_empty **** 0 waiting process(es)
there are now 4 items in the buffer
no producers are waiting
age=7814, consumer fetched item 0.123102 and napping for 357ms
age=8194, consumer wants to consume ...
          **** Printing for not_full **** 0 waiting process(es)
          **** Printing for not_empty **** 0 waiting process(es)
there are now 3 items in the buffer
no producers are waiting
age=8206, consumer fetched item 0.734775 and napping for 1021ms
age=8404, PRODUCER produced item 0.0976776
          **** Printing for not_full **** 0 waiting process(es)
          **** Printing for not_empty **** 0 waiting process(es)
there are now 4 items in the buffer
no consumers are waiting
age=8418, PRODUCER deposited item 0.0976776 and napping for 285ms
age=8705, PRODUCER produced item 0.326485
          **** Printing for not_full **** 0 waiting process(es)
          **** Printing for not_empty **** 0 waiting process(es)
there are now 5 items in the buffer
no consumers are waiting
age=8720, PRODUCER deposited item 0.326485 and napping for 461ms
age=9184, PRODUCER produced item 0.784775
          **** Printing for not_full **** 0 waiting process(es)
          **** Printing for not_empty **** 0 waiting process(es)
age=9234, consumer wants to consume ...
          **** Printing for not_full **** 1 waiting process(es), all with rank 0
          **** Printing for not_empty **** 0 waiting process(es)
there are now 4 items in the buffer
producers are waiting
age=9248, consumer fetched item 0.806480 and napping for 336ms
          **** Printing for not_full **** 0 waiting process(es)
          **** Printing for not_empty **** 0 waiting process(es)
there are now 5 items in the buffer
no consumers are waiting
age=9258, PRODUCER deposited item 0.784775 and napping for 71ms
age=9344, PRODUCER produced item 0.713071
          **** Printing for not_full **** 0 waiting process(es)
```

```
                **** Printing for not_empty **** 0 waiting process(es)
age=9594, consumer wants to consume ...
                **** Printing for not_full **** 1 waiting process(es), all with rank 0
                **** Printing for not_empty **** 0 waiting process(es)
there are now 4 items in the buffer
producers are waiting
age=9607, consumer fetched item 0.679876 and napping for 2830ms
                **** Printing for not_full **** 0 waiting process(es)
                **** Printing for not_empty **** 0 waiting process(es)
there are now 5 items in the buffer
no consumers are waiting
age=9622, PRODUCER deposited item 0.713071 and napping for 39ms
age=9664, PRODUCER produced item 0.524740
                **** Printing for not_full **** 0 waiting process(es)
                **** Printing for not_empty **** 0 waiting process(es)
must stop now
% ./bb 5 3 1 10
bounded buffer alive with 5 slots
main user resource alive, pnap = 3, cnap = 1, and run_time = 10
age=50, PRODUCER produced item 0.964400
age=59, consumer wants to consume ...
                **** Printing for not_full **** 0 waiting process(es)
                **** Printing for not_empty **** 0 waiting process(es)
there are now 1 items in the buffer
no consumers are waiting
age=143, PRODUCER deposited item 0.964400 and napping for 2893ms
                **** Printing for not_full **** 0 waiting process(es)
                **** Printing for not_empty **** 0 waiting process(es)
there are now 0 items in the buffer
no producers are waiting
age=236, consumer fetched item 0.964400 and napping for 764ms
age=1027, consumer wants to consume ...
                **** Printing for not_full **** 0 waiting process(es)
                **** Printing for not_empty **** 0 waiting process(es)
age=3057, PRODUCER produced item 0.472359
                **** Printing for not_full **** 0 waiting process(es)
                **** Printing for not_empty **** 1 waiting process(es), all with rank 0
there are now 1 items in the buffer
consumers are waiting
age=3089, PRODUCER deposited item 0.472359 and napping for 2311ms
                **** Printing for not_full **** 0 waiting process(es)
                **** Printing for not_empty **** 0 waiting process(es)
there are now 0 items in the buffer
no producers are waiting
age=3099, consumer fetched item 0.472359 and napping for 902ms
age=4007, consumer wants to consume ...
                **** Printing for not_full **** 0 waiting process(es)
                **** Printing for not_empty **** 0 waiting process(es)
age=5407, PRODUCER produced item 0.270513
                **** Printing for not_full **** 0 waiting process(es)
                **** Printing for not_empty **** 1 waiting process(es), all with rank 0
there are now 1 items in the buffer
consumers are waiting
age=5434, PRODUCER deposited item 0.270513 and napping for 1533ms
                **** Printing for not_full **** 0 waiting process(es)
```

```
            **** Printing for not_empty **** 0 waiting process(es)
there are now 0 items in the buffer
no producers are waiting
age=5489, consumer fetched item 0.270513 and napping for 754ms
age=6257, consumer wants to consume ...
            **** Printing for not_full **** 0 waiting process(es)
            **** Printing for not_empty **** 0 waiting process(es)
age=6979, PRODUCER produced item 0.00863305
            **** Printing for not_full **** 0 waiting process(es)
            **** Printing for not_empty **** 1 waiting process(es), all with rank 0
there are now 1 items in the buffer
consumers are waiting
age=7011, PRODUCER deposited item 0.00863305 and napping for 1463ms
            **** Printing for not_full **** 0 waiting process(es)
            **** Printing for not_empty **** 0 waiting process(es)
there are now 0 items in the buffer
no producers are waiting
age=7036, consumer fetched item 0.00863305 and napping for 869ms
age=7982, consumer wants to consume ...
            **** Printing for not_full **** 0 waiting process(es)
            **** Printing for not_empty **** 0 waiting process(es)
age=8497, PRODUCER produced item 0.221957
            **** Printing for not_full **** 0 waiting process(es)
            **** Printing for not_empty **** 1 waiting process(es), all with rank 0
there are now 1 items in the buffer
consumers are waiting
age=8520, PRODUCER deposited item 0.221957 and napping for 1745ms
            **** Printing for not_full **** 0 waiting process(es)
            **** Printing for not_empty **** 0 waiting process(es)
there are now 0 items in the buffer
no producers are waiting
age=8530, consumer fetched item 0.221957 and napping for 472ms
age=9018, consumer wants to consume ...
            **** Printing for not_full **** 0 waiting process(es)
            **** Printing for not_empty **** 0 waiting process(es)
must stop now
                                                    */
```

5.1.2   The Dining Philosophers

The monitor in Program 5.4 is for coordinating the dining philosophers. The monitor has an array of condition variables, one array entry for each philosopher to block on if its forks are not both available. A naive form of starvation detection and prevention is included. A philosopher is put into a "very hungry" state if it cannot pick up both forks to eat whenever one of its neighbors puts down its forks. A hungry philosopher is not allowed to eat if it has a very hungry neighbor. The driver program for this monitor is Program 5.5. Since our decision has been to require that a process exit the monitor immediately after signaling on a condition variable, a process cannot perform two signal operations on two condition variables during one call to a monitor interface routine. To handle this situation, we build a routine, put_forks, in an intermediate resource, dining_interface, that is called once by the philosopher code when the philosopher puts down its forks; put_forks does the calls to the interface routines in the monitor.

Program 5.4: Starvation-Free Dining Philosophers Monitor.

```
_monitor(dining_server)
    op hungry_and_get_forks(i : int), finished_eating(i : int)
    op  check_left_fork_down(i : int; check_very_hungry : bool)
    op check_right_fork_down(i : int; check_very_hungry : bool)
_body(dining_server)
    type states = enum(thinking, hungry, very_hungry, eating)
    var num_phils : int := 5; getarg(2, num_phils)
    var state[1:num_phils] : states := ([num_phils] thinking)
    _condvar1(self, 1:num_phils)

    procedure left(i : int) returns lft : int
        if i=1 -> lft := num_phils [] else -> lft := i-1 fi
    end left

    procedure right(i : int) returns rgh : int
        if i=num_phils -> rgh := 1 [] else -> rgh := i+1 fi
    end right

    procedure see_if_very_hunger(k : int)
        if state[k] = hungry and state[left(k)] != very_hungry and
              state[right(k)] != very_hungry ->
            state[k] := very_hungry
            write("*** at age", age(), "philosopher", k, "is VERY HUNGRY")
        fi
    end see_if_very_hunger

    procedure test(k : int; check_very_hungry: bool)
        if state[left(k)] != eating and state[left(k)] != very_hungry and
              (state[k] = hungry or state[k] = very_hungry) and
              state[right(k)] != very_hungry and state[right(k)] != eating ->
            state[k] := eating
            write("*** at age", age(), "philosopher", k, "may eat")
        [] check_very_hungry ->
            see_if_very_hunger(k) /* simplistic naive check for starvation */
        fi
    end test

    _proc(hungry_and_get_forks(i))
        state[i] := hungry
        test(i, false)
        if state[i] != eating -> _wait(self[i]) fi
    _proc_end

    _proc(finished_eating(i))
        state[i] := thinking
    _proc_end

/*
 * Cannot _signal() in a procedure (undefined m_bozo); must be a _proc()
 *
 * procedure check_fork_down(i : int; check_very_hungry : bool)
 *    test(i, check_very_hungry)
```

```
*       if state[i] = eating -> _signal(self[i]) fi
* end check_fork_down
*/

   _proc(check_left_fork_down(i, check_very_hungry))
      /* check_fork_down(left(i)) */
      test(left(i), check_very_hungry)
      if state[left(i)] = eating -> _signal(self[left(i)]) fi
   _proc_end

   _proc(check_right_fork_down(i, check_very_hungry))
      /* check_fork_down(right(i)) */
      test(right(i), check_very_hungry)
      if state[right(i)] = eating -> _signal(self[right(i)]) fi
   _proc_end
_monitor_end
```

Program 5.5: Dining Philosophers Monitor Driver.

```
resource philosopher
   import dining_interface
body philosopher(i : int; dcap : cap dining_interface; thinking, eating: int)
   write("philosopher", i, "alive, max think eat delays", thinking, eating)
   reply

   procedure think()
      var napping : int
      napping := int(random(1000*thinking))
      writes("age=",age(),", philosopher ",i," thinking for ",napping," ms\n")
      nap(napping)
   end think

   procedure eat()
      var napping : int
      napping := int(random(1000*eating))
      writes("age=",age(),", philosopher ",i," eating for ",napping," ms\n")
      nap(napping)
   end eat

   do true ->
      think()
      writes("age=", age(), ", philosopher ", i, " is hungry\n")
      dcap.take_forks(i)
      writes("age=", age(), ", philosopher ", i, " has taken forks\n")
      eat()
      dcap.put_forks(i)
      writes("age=", age(), ", philosopher ", i, " has returned forks\n")
   od
end philosopher

resource dining_interface
   import dining_server
   op take_forks(i : int), put_forks(i : int)
```

```
body dining_interface(check_very_hungry : bool)
   write("dining_interface alive, check_very_hungry is", check_very_hungry)

   proc take_forks(i)
      dining_server.hungry_and_get_forks(i)
   end take_forks

   proc put_forks(i)
      dining_server.finished_eating(i)
      dining_server.check_left_fork_down(i, check_very_hungry)
      dining_server.check_right_fork_down(i, check_very_hungry)
   end put_forks
end dining_interface

resource driver()
   import philosopher, dining_interface
   var check_very_hungry : bool := true
   var num_phils : int := 5, run_time : int := 60
   getarg(1, check_very_hungry); getarg(2, num_phils); getarg(3, run_time)
   var max_think_delay[1:num_phils] : int := ([num_phils] 5)
   var max_eat_delay[1:num_phils] : int := ([num_phils] 2)
   fa i := 1 to num_phils ->
      getarg(2*i+2, max_think_delay[i]); getarg(2*i+3, max_eat_delay[i])
   af

   var dcap : cap dining_interface
   write(num_phils, "dining philosophers running", run_time, "seconds")
   dcap := create dining_interface(check_very_hungry)
   fa i := 1 to num_phils ->
      create philosopher(i, dcap, max_think_delay[i], max_eat_delay[i])
   af
   nap(1000*run_time); write("must stop now"); stop
end driver

/* .............. Example compile and run(s)

% m2sr -sx dp.m
% sr -o dp dp.sr dp_driver.sr
dp.sr:
dp_driver.sr:
dp.sr:
dp_driver.sr:
linking:
% ./dp false 5 45 300 1 1 20 2 2 1 20 300 1
5 dining philosophers running 30 seconds
dining_interface alive, check_very_hungry is false
philosopher 1 alive, max think eat delays 300 1
age=75, philosopher 1 thinking for 284352 ms
philosopher 2 alive, max think eat delays 1 20
age=91, philosopher 2 thinking for 601 ms
philosopher 3 alive, max think eat delays 2 2
age=108, philosopher 3 thinking for 1415 ms
philosopher 4 alive, max think eat delays 1 20
age=125, philosopher 4 thinking for 483 ms
philosopher 5 alive, max think eat delays 300 1
```

```
age=141, philosopher 5 thinking for 29612 ms
age=619, philosopher 4 is hungry
*** at age 625 philosopher 4 may eat
age=629, philosopher 4 has taken forks
age=631, philosopher 4 eating for 18399 ms
age=700, philosopher 2 is hungry
*** at age 710 philosopher 2 may eat
age=714, philosopher 2 has taken forks
age=717, philosopher 2 eating for 16128 ms
age=1529, philosopher 3 is hungry
age=16852, philosopher 2 has returned forks
age=16856, philosopher 2 thinking for 537 ms
age=17399, philosopher 2 is hungry
*** at age 17403 philosopher 2 may eat
age=17404, philosopher 2 has taken forks
age=17405, philosopher 2 eating for 12056 ms
age=19042, philosopher 4 has returned forks
age=19046, philosopher 4 thinking for 635 ms
age=19689, philosopher 4 is hungry
*** at age 19693 philosopher 4 may eat
age=19694, philosopher 4 has taken forks
age=19695, philosopher 4 eating for 7916 ms
age=27621, philosopher 4 has returned forks
age=27625, philosopher 4 thinking for 25 ms
age=27659, philosopher 4 is hungry
*** at age 27663 philosopher 4 may eat
age=27664, philosopher 4 has taken forks
age=27666, philosopher 4 eating for 11719 ms
age=29471, philosopher 2 has returned forks
age=29475, philosopher 2 thinking for 295 ms
age=29759, philosopher 5 is hungry
age=29780, philosopher 2 is hungry
*** at age 29788 philosopher 2 may eat
age=29789, philosopher 2 has taken forks
age=29798, philosopher 2 eating for 19603 ms
must stop now
% ./dp true   5 45 300 1 1 20 2 2 1 20 300 1
5 dining philosophers running 30 seconds
dining_interface alive, check_very_hungry is true
philosopher 1 alive, max think eat delays 300 1
age=110, philosopher 1 thinking for 178842 ms
philosopher 2 alive, max think eat delays 1 20
age=123, philosopher 2 thinking for 859 ms
philosopher 3 alive, max think eat delays 2 2
age=136, philosopher 3 thinking for 483 ms
philosopher 4 alive, max think eat delays 1 20
age=150, philosopher 4 thinking for 292 ms
philosopher 5 alive, max think eat delays 300 1
age=163, philosopher 5 thinking for 263276 ms
age=445, philosopher 4 is hungry
*** at age 519 philosopher 4 may eat
age=523, philosopher 4 has taken forks
age=526, philosopher 4 eating for 9251 ms
age=626, philosopher 3 is hungry
age=986, philosopher 2 is hungry
```

```
*** at age 1259 philosopher 2 may eat
age=1417, philosopher 2 has taken forks
age=1606, philosopher 2 eating for 4476 ms
*** at age 6100 philosopher 3 is VERY HUNGRY
age=6105, philosopher 2 has returned forks
age=6106, philosopher 2 thinking for 591 ms
age=6706, philosopher 2 is hungry
*** at age 9786 philosopher 3 may eat
age=9792, philosopher 4 has returned forks
age=9793, philosopher 4 thinking for 714 ms
age=9795, philosopher 3 has taken forks
age=9796, philosopher 3 eating for 234 ms
*** at age 10036 philosopher 2 may eat
age=10041, philosopher 3 has returned forks
age=10042, philosopher 3 thinking for 1188 ms
age=10044, philosopher 2 has taken forks
age=10046, philosopher 2 eating for 3601 ms
age=10515, philosopher 4 is hungry
*** at age 10519 philosopher 4 may eat
age=10521, philosopher 4 has taken forks
age=10522, philosopher 4 eating for 6002 ms
age=11235, philosopher 3 is hungry
*** at age 13657 philosopher 3 is VERY HUNGRY
age=13661, philosopher 2 has returned forks
age=13662, philosopher 2 thinking for 250 ms
age=13915, philosopher 2 is hungry
*** at age 16527 philosopher 3 may eat
age=16532, philosopher 4 has returned forks
age=16534, philosopher 4 thinking for 473 ms
age=16535, philosopher 3 has taken forks
age=16536, philosopher 3 eating for 60 ms
*** at age 16606 philosopher 2 may eat
age=16618, philosopher 3 has returned forks
age=16623, philosopher 3 thinking for 93 ms
age=16625, philosopher 2 has taken forks
age=16626, philosopher 2 eating for 11215 ms
age=16725, philosopher 3 is hungry
age=17015, philosopher 4 is hungry
*** at age 17019 philosopher 4 may eat
age=17020, philosopher 4 has taken forks
age=17021, philosopher 4 eating for 15353 ms
*** at age 27847 philosopher 3 is VERY HUNGRY
age=27851, philosopher 2 has returned forks
age=27852, philosopher 2 thinking for 251 ms
age=28105, philosopher 2 is hungry
must stop now
                                              */
```

5.1.3   The Readers and Writers

The monitor in Program 5.6 is for the readers and writers problem and is based on Figure 5.5 of [6]. It implements a fair, starvation-free solution, that is a continual stream of arriving readers cannot delay for an arbitrary amount of time a writer from writing. The monitor can be used with Program 4.8 by removing the **server** resource, replacing **server** and **scap** with **Reader_Writer**, and deleting the **create server** statement. Program 5.7 shows the modifications. From the sample output, it can be seen that if a reader wants to read the database and there is a waiting writer, then that reader has to wait. Therefore, writers do not starve.

Program 5.6: Starvation-Free Readers and Writers Monitor.

```
_monitor(Reader_Writer)
    op Start_Read(i : int), End_Read(i : int)
    op Start_Write(i : int), End_Write(i : int)
_body(Reader_Writer)
    var Readers: int := 0
    var Writing: bool := false
    _condvar(OK_to_Read); _condvar(OK_to_Write)

    _proc(Start_Read(i))
        if Writing -> _wait(OK_to_Read)
        [] not _empty(OK_to_Write) ->
            write("   age=", age(), "reader", i, "has to WAIT")
            _wait(OK_to_Read) # new incoming readers cannot starve writers
        fi
        Readers := Readers + 1
        write("   age=", age(), "reader", i, "has begun reading, Readers=",
            Readers)
        _signal(OK_to_Read)   # when a writer finishes, all waiting readers start
    _proc_end

    _proc(End_Read(i))
        Readers := Readers - 1
        write("   age=", age(), "reader", i, "finished reading, Readers=",
            Readers)
        if Readers = 0 -> _signal(OK_to_Write) fi
    _proc_end

    _proc(Start_Write(i))
        if Readers != 0 or Writing -> _wait(OK_to_Write) fi
        Writing := true
        write("      age=", age(), "WRITER", i, "has begun Writing,")
    _proc_end

    _proc(End_Write(i))
        Writing := false
        write("   age=", age(), "WRITER", i, "has finished Writing")
        if not _empty(OK_to_Read) -> _signal(OK_to_Read)
        [] else -> _signal(OK_to_Write)    # nor do writers starve readers
        fi
    _proc_end
```

```
_monitor_end
```

Program 5.7: Starvation-Free Readers and Writers Driver.

```
resource reader
    import Reader_Writer
body reader(i : int; nap_time : int)
    write("reader", i, "is alive, nap_time =", nap_time)
    reply
    var napping : int
    do true ->
        napping := int(random(1000*nap_time))
        write("age=", age(), "reader", i, "napping for", napping)
        nap(napping)
        write("age=", age(), "reader", i, "wants to read")
        Reader_Writer.Start_Read(i)
        napping := int(random(1000*nap_time))
        write("age=", age(), "reader", i, "begins reading for", napping)
        nap(napping)
        Reader_Writer.End_Read(i)
        write("age=", age(), "reader", i, "finished reading")
    od
end reader

resource writer
    import Reader_Writer
body writer(i : int; nap_time : int)
    write("WRITER", i, "is alive, nap_time =", nap_time)
    reply
    var napping : int
    do true ->
        napping := int(random(1000*nap_time))
        write("age=", age(), "WRITER", i, "napping for", napping)
        nap(napping)
        write("age=", age(), "WRITER", i, "wants to write")
        Reader_Writer.Start_Write(i)
        napping := int(random(1000*nap_time))
        write("age=", age(), "WRITER", i, "is writing for", napping)
        nap(napping)
        write("age=", age(), "WRITER", i, "is finished writing")
        Reader_Writer.End_Write(i)
    od
end writer

resource start()
    import writer, reader, Reader_Writer
    var readers : int := 10, writers : int := 5, nap_time : int := 3
    var run_time : int := 60
    getarg(1, readers); getarg(2, writers); getarg(3, nap_time)
    getarg(4, run_time)
    write(readers, "readers and", writers,
        "writers starting with nap_time", nap_time, "and run_time", run_time)
    fa i := 1 to readers -> create reader(i, nap_time) af
```

```
    fa i := 1 to writers -> create writer(i, nap_time) af
    nap(1000*run_time); write("must stop now"); stop
end start

/* .............. Example compile and run(s)

% m2sr -sx rw.m
% sr -o rw rw.sr driver.sr
rw.sr:
driver.sr:
rw.sr:
driver.sr:
linking:
% rw 5 2 1 10
5 readers and 2 writers starting with nap_time 1 and run_time 10
reader 1 is alive, nap_time = 1
age= 64 reader 1 napping for 585
reader 2 is alive, nap_time = 1
age= 80 reader 2 napping for 44
reader 3 is alive, nap_time = 1
age= 106 reader 3 napping for 682
reader 4 is alive, nap_time = 1
age= 137 reader 4 napping for 406
age= 166 reader 2 wants to read
reader 5 is alive, nap_time = 1
age= 174 reader 5 napping for 970
   age= 184 reader 2 has begun reading, Readers= 1
WRITER 1 is alive, nap_time = 1
age= 193 WRITER 1 napping for 809
age= 235 reader 2 begins reading for 124
WRITER 2 is alive, nap_time = 1
age= 248 WRITER 2 napping for 320
   age= 370 reader 2 finished reading, Readers= 0
age= 374 reader 2 finished reading
age= 382 reader 2 napping for 844
age= 552 reader 4 wants to read
   age= 557 reader 4 has begun reading, Readers= 1
age= 566 reader 4 begins reading for 12
age= 579 WRITER 2 wants to write
   age= 586 reader 4 finished reading, Readers= 0
age= 604 reader 4 finished reading
age= 608 reader 4 napping for 861
      age= 611 WRITER 2 has begun Writing,
age= 614 WRITER 2 is writing for 409
age= 659 reader 1 wants to read
age= 800 reader 3 wants to read
age= 1019 WRITER 1 wants to write
age= 1031 WRITER 2 is finished writing
   age= 1035 WRITER 2 has finished Writing
age= 1046 WRITER 2 napping for 498
   age= 1049 reader 1 has begun reading, Readers= 1
age= 1056 reader 1 begins reading for 191
   age= 1068 reader 3 has begun reading, Readers= 2
age= 1078 reader 3 begins reading for 514
age= 1151 reader 5 wants to read
```

```
      age= 1171 reader 5 has to WAIT
age= 1240 reader 2 wants to read
      age= 1245 reader 2 has to WAIT
      age= 1261 reader 1 finished reading, Readers= 1
age= 1279 reader 1 finished reading
age= 1285 reader 1 napping for 520
age= 1479 reader 4 wants to read
      age= 1489 reader 4 has to WAIT
age= 1549 WRITER 2 wants to write
      age= 1607 reader 3 finished reading, Readers= 0
age= 1612 reader 3 finished reading
age= 1615 reader 3 napping for 766
        age= 1620 WRITER 1 has begun Writing,
age= 1628 WRITER 1 is writing for 774
age= 1809 reader 1 wants to read
age= 2389 reader 3 wants to read
age= 2425 WRITER 1 is finished writing
      age= 2430 WRITER 1 has finished Writing
age= 2435 WRITER 1 napping for 582
      age= 2438 reader 5 has begun reading, Readers= 1
age= 2443 reader 5 begins reading for 629
      age= 2459 reader 2 has begun reading, Readers= 2
age= 2464 reader 2 begins reading for 717
      age= 2468 reader 4 has begun reading, Readers= 3
age= 2474 reader 4 begins reading for 565
      age= 2477 reader 1 has begun reading, Readers= 4
age= 2492 reader 1 begins reading for 499
      age= 2497 reader 3 has begun reading, Readers= 5
age= 2506 reader 3 begins reading for 933
      age= 3004 reader 1 finished reading, Readers= 4
 ...
must stop now
                                      */
```

5.2 Implementing Monitors with Semaphores

Monitors can be implemented with semaphores. The description on pages 52-53 of [24] is not correct. The method shown here is based on Section 5.4 of [6].

Each monitor is implemented with a binary semaphore to allow only one interface routine to be called (active) at a time.

> semaphore mutex := 1
> > . . .
> interface procedure i:
> > P(mutex)
> > > . . .
> > V(mutex)
> end
> > . . .

Each condition variable $cond_i$ is implemented with a semaphore SEM_i and an integer counter $COUNT_i$, both initially zero.

wait($cond_i$):
        $COUNT_i++$
        V(mutex)
        P(SEM_i)
        P(mutex)
        $COUNT_i--$
    . . .
signal($cond_i$):
        if $COUNT_i > 0$ then V(SEM_i) fi
        V(mutex)
        exit the monitor, i.e., return

There is a problem with this: a process waiting to enter an interface routine (enter the monitor for the first time) may "sneak" in (due to a context switch or faster CPU) and do a P(mutex) and get in the monitor before the signaled process can do its P(mutex). The process the snuck in may change the condition so when the signaled process does succeed in its P(mutex), the condition may no longer be true.

So, to implement the signal and exit discipline, we change the above to

wait($cond_i$):
        $COUNT_i++$
        V(mutex)
        P(SEM_i)
        $COUNT_i--$
    . . .
signal($cond_i$):
        if $COUNT_i > 0$ then V(SEM_i)
        else V(mutex) fi
        exit the monitor, i.e., return

5.3   Lab: Monitors

Objectives

To learn about monitors in SR.

Preparation Before Lab

Read Section 5.1 on monitors. Look at Programs 5.2 and 5.6. No semaphores are allowed in any of these assignments.

5.3.1   Assignment: Fair Baboons

Write a monitor for the fair baboons program done in Lab 4.5.

5.3.2   Assignment: Sleeping Barber

Write a monitor for the sleeping barber program done in Lab 4.5.

5.3.3 Assignment: Fair Dining Philosophers

Enhance the starvation detection in the monitor in Program 5.4 for the fair dining philosophers so that the two neighbors have to alternate their eating three times before the one in the middle becomes very hungry.

5.3.4 Assignment: Fraternity Party

Write a monitor for the fraternity party program done in Lab 4.5.

5.3.5 Assignment: Bakery

Write a monitor for the bakery program done in Lab 4.5.

Chapter 6

Message Passing and the Rendezvous

Semaphores and monitors can be used in a shared memory environment since they represent variables and data shared by a collection of concurrently executing processes. But they cannot be used in a distributed system, a collection of machines or workstations connected together on a local area network (LAN). For distributed systems, we must use message passing.

6.1   Message Passing

Primitive operations are:

>   send(to, message)

and

>   receive(from, message)

where "from" and "to" specify source and destination addressing.

Message passing can be *blocking* versus *nonblocking*, also called *synchronous* versus *asynchronous*. If receives are blocking and there are no messages are available, the receiver blocks until one arrives. If sends are blocking, the sender blocks if there is no receiver ready to receive the the message being sent. If sends are nonblocking, a send returns control immediately after the message is queued. If receives are nonblocking, a receive returns a failure indicator if no message is available to receive.

If both send and receive are blocking, then a *simple rendezvous* occurs when the message is transferred or copied from the sender to the receiver. Both the sending process and the receiving process are at known points in their code and a unidirectional flow of information is taking place.

We also have *buffered* versus *nonbuffered*. An unbuffered send blocks until a receiver executes a receive. A buffered send usually implies non-blocking. But there is usually an upper limit on buffer size above which the sender will block. There is not much difference between blocking buffered and blocking un-buffered sends.

So we really have three varieties: For send,

1. blocking: wait for receiver or receiver is already waiting;

```
client                          server
. . .                           . . .
send (request)                  receive (service request)
... [wait]                      ... [do requested service]
receive (results)               send (back results)
. . .                           . . .
```

Figure 6.1: Client-to-Server Remote Procedure Call.

2. buffered, non-blocking: message will be buffered but the receiver has not necessarily gotten it yet;

3. non-buffered, non-blocking: return an error if no receiver is ready or waiting, return okay if message was sent and received.

For receive,

1. blocking: wait for message or sender to send;

2. buffered, non-blocking: return an error if no message was waiting;

3. non-buffered, non-blocking: return an error if no sender is ready or waiting, return okay if message was sent and received.

An *extended rendezvous* occurs when

- the sender does a blocking send followed by a blocking receive,

- and the receiver does a blocking receive followed by a blocking send.

Both processes are at known points in their code and a bidirectional flow of information is taking place.

An extended rendezvous is also called a *remote procedure call* (RPC), particularly if the sender and receiver are on two different machines connected by a local area network. In this case, tools may be provided to the programmer to make the code for the rendezvous look like a simple procedure code. See Figure 6.1. For more information, see Section 16.3.1 of [20], Section 9.4 of [21], or Section 10.3 of [24].

6.2 Message Passing in SR

SR supports both synchronous and asynchronous message passing. Both forms use a blocking **receive** operation to receive messages. To send a message and block until it is received, the **call** invocation is used; to send a message without blocking, the **send** invocation is used. If neither **call** nor **send** is used, then the invocation is implicitly a **call**. As noted above, synchronous message passing is also called a simple rendezvous. SR messages are like parameter lists in procedure calls: a list of variables and expressions whose values are sent in the message. The values are placed in corresponding order into the variable list of the **receive**. Program 6.1 is a simple example of sending and receiving messages.

Program 6.2 is another example of sending and receiving messages in SR. Note that if the **reply** in the **chicken** resource were left out, the program would deadlock. The **chicken** resource would be blocked at the **receive peep** while the **fox** resource would be blocked in the **create chicken** statement. This **create** cannot complete until **chicken** does a **reply** or finishes all its top-level code.

Program 6.1: Simple Message Passing.

```
resource messages()
   op sum(p, q : int), answer(r : int)

   process process_a
      var z : int
      send sum(1, 2)
      receive answer(z)
      write("the sum of 1 and 2 is", z)
   end process_a

   process process_b
      var x, y : int
      receive sum(x, y)
      call answer(x+y)
   end process_b

end messages

/* .............. Example compile and run(s)

% sr -o messages messages.sr
% ./messages
the sum of 1 and 2 is 3
                                          */
```

Program 6.2: More Message Passing.

```
resource chicken
   import fox
   op peep(a : int; b : real; c : char)
   op cluck(d : string[*])
body chicken(foxy : cap fox)
   var x : int
   var y : real
   var z : char
   var s : string[64]
   write("chicken is alive")
   reply                          # this reply is necessary
   receive peep(x, y, z)
   write("chicken receive peep, x=", x, "y=", y, "z=", z)
   receive cluck(s)
   write("chicken receive cluck, s=", s)
   send foxy.quick(true)
end chicken

resource fox
   import chicken
   op quick(e : bool)
body fox()
```

```
    var chick : cap chicken
    var y : bool
    write("fox is alive")
    chick := create chicken(myresource())
# call peep blocks until chicken reaches receive peep
    call chick.peep(1, 2.0, 'c')   # "call" can be omitted
    send chick.cluck("non-blocking")
    receive quick(y)
    write("fox receive quick, y=", y)
end fox

/* .............. Example compile and run(s)

% sr -o send_receive send_receive.sr
% ./send_receive
fox is alive
chicken is alive
chicken receive peep, x= 1 y= 2.00000 z= c
chicken receive cluck, s= non-blocking
fox receive quick, y= true
                                              */
```

6.2.1   Concurrent Programs and Message Passing

A parallel version of the Sieve of Eratosthenes is shown in Program 6.3. This program computes the first N prime numbers by creating N filter processes that run in parallel. The first filter is sent, using message passing, all odd numbers. Each filter prints out the first number it receives, which is prime, and then sends to the next filter all numbers it receives that are not multiples of the prime number that it printed out. Finally, filter N gets the Nth prime number, which it prints out, and then executes a **stop** statement. The sample output shows that the first few filters do most of the computation, so there will be limited speed-up if this program is executed on a shared-memory multiprocessor unless the processes are distributed in a load-balanced manner across the CPUs.

A new feature of SR in this program is the **optype** statement. This declares a template for an **op** and a name for the template, much like **type** in Pascal and **typedef** in C. The operation **sieve** is declared as an array,

```
    op sieve[1:n] : pipe
```

The ith filter receives numbers from filter $i - 1$ by doing

```
    receive sieve[i](number)
```

and sends numbers to filter $i + 1$ by doing

```
    send sieve[i+1](number)
```

Program 6.4 contains a more complicated example of message passing, a program that sorts numbers using a pipeline (based on pages 34-35 in [2]). The **sort** procedure first calls the **worker** function, which sends back as its function return value the capability for the **mypipe** operation that **worker** implements. The **reply** in **worker** causes it to return its function value to the caller and continue executing as a concurrent process. Then **sort** sends the numbers to be sorted, one at a time, to **worker** (**sort** uses the capability that **worker** returned to it, and worker receives the numbers in its op of type mypipe). Meanwhile, the worker called by sort, calls worker recursively. So the first worker, the one created by sort, itself creates a second worker process. The second worker passes a capability to its mypipe operation back to the first worker.

The first worker receives all the numbers from sort and then sends all but the smallest to the second worker. Meanwhile, the second worker creates a third and sends all but the smallest it sees to the third. Enough workers are created until the last one receives a single number. Now all the worker processes send their smallest retained numbers back to sort, which puts them into the proper spot of the array.

Program 6.3: Parallel Sieve of Eratosthenes.

```
resource parallel_sieve()
   optype pipe(number : int)
   const N := 8
   var n : int := N; getarg(1, n)
   var debug : bool := false; getarg(2, debug)
   if n < 2 -> write("There are no prime numbers less than 2."); stop(1) fi
   op sieve[1:n] : pipe
   var seen_count[1:n] : int := ([n] 1)
   write("age()=", age(), "generating the first", n, "prime numbers")

   process filter(i := 1 to n)
      var prime, number : int
      receive sieve[i](prime)
      write("filter", i, "received prime", prime)
      if (i = n) -> write("age()=", age(), "done"); stop
      [] else ->
         do true ->
            receive sieve[i](number)
            seen_count[i]++
            if number % prime != 0 -> send /* don't call */ sieve[i+1](number)
            [] debug ->
               write("      *debug* filter", i, "discarding", number,
                  "(divisible by", prime)
            fi
         od
      fi
   end filter

   var max : int := n*n /* there is probably a better lower bound */
   fa number := 3 to max by 2 ->
      call /* better than send */ sieve[1](number)
      if debug -> write("      *debug* driver sent", number, "to filter 1")
      fi
   af
   write("all numbers 2 through", max, "sent to first filter")

   final
      write("the filters each saw the following counts of numbers")
      fa i := 1 to n -> writes(" ", seen_count[i]) af
      writes("\n")
   end final
end parallel_sieve
```

```
/* .............. Example compile and run(s)

% sr -o parallel_sieve parallel_sieve.sr
% ./parallel_sieve 8 true
age()= 18 generating the first 8 prime numbers
filter 1 received prime 3
      *debug* driver sent 3 to filter 1
      *debug* driver sent 5 to filter 1
filter 2 received prime 5
      *debug* driver sent 7 to filter 1
      *debug* filter 1 discarding 9 (divisible by 3
filter 3 received prime 7
      *debug* driver sent 9 to filter 1
      *debug* driver sent 11 to filter 1
filter 4 received prime 11
      *debug* driver sent 13 to filter 1
      *debug* filter 1 discarding 15 (divisible by 3
      *debug* driver sent 15 to filter 1
filter 5 received prime 13
      *debug* driver sent 17 to filter 1
filter 6 received prime 17
      *debug* driver sent 19 to filter 1
      *debug* filter 1 discarding 21 (divisible by 3
      *debug* driver sent 21 to filter 1
filter 7 received prime 19
      *debug* driver sent 23 to filter 1
filter 8 received prime 23
age()= 325 done
      *debug* driver sent 25 to filter 1
      *debug* filter 2 discarding 25 (divisible by 5
the filters each saw the following counts of numbers
 12 8 6 5 4 3 2 1
% ./parallel_sieve 50
age()= 61 generating the first 50 prime numbers
filter 1 received prime 3
filter 2 received prime 5
filter 3 received prime 7
filter 4 received prime 11
filter 5 received prime 13
filter 6 received prime 17
filter 7 received prime 19
filter 8 received prime 23
filter 9 received prime 29
filter 10 received prime 31
filter 11 received prime 37
filter 12 received prime 41
filter 13 received prime 43
filter 14 received prime 47
filter 15 received prime 53
filter 16 received prime 59
filter 17 received prime 61
filter 18 received prime 67
filter 19 received prime 71
filter 20 received prime 73
```

```
filter 21 received prime 79
filter 22 received prime 83
filter 23 received prime 89
filter 24 received prime 97
filter 25 received prime 101
filter 26 received prime 103
filter 27 received prime 107
filter 28 received prime 109
filter 29 received prime 113
filter 30 received prime 127
filter 31 received prime 131
filter 32 received prime 137
filter 33 received prime 139
filter 34 received prime 149
filter 35 received prime 151
filter 36 received prime 157
filter 37 received prime 163
filter 38 received prime 167
filter 39 received prime 173
filter 40 received prime 179
filter 41 received prime 181
filter 42 received prime 191
filter 43 received prime 193
filter 44 received prime 197
filter 45 received prime 199
filter 46 received prime 211
filter 47 received prime 223
filter 48 received prime 227
filter 49 received prime 229
filter 50 received prime 233
age()= 5377 done
the filters each saw the following counts of numbers
 117 78 62 53 48 45 44 43 42 41 40 39 38 37 36 35 34 33
 32 31 30 29 28 27 26 25 24 23 22 21 20 19 18 17 16 15
 14 13 12 11 10 9 8 7 6 5 4 3 2 1
                                            */
```

Program 6.4: Pipeline Sort.

```
resource pipeline_sort()
    op result(pos, value : int) {send}      # used to return results
    optype pipe(value : int) {send}         # used to send values


    # Worker receives m integers on mypipe from its predecessor.
    # It keeps smallest and sends others on to the next worker.
    # After seeing all m integers, worker sends smallest to sort,
    # together with the position (m) smallest is to be placed.
    procedure worker(m : int) returns p : cap pipe
        var candidate, smallest : int      # the smallest seen so far
        op mypipe : pipe
        p := mypipe
        write("worker started, will be receiving", m, "values")
        reply      # invoker now has a capability for mypipe
```

```
      receive mypipe(smallest)
      if m > 1 ->
         # create next instance of worker
         var next_worker : cap pipe     # pipe to next worker
         next_worker := worker(m-1)
         fa i := m-1 downto 1 ->
            receive mypipe(candidate)
            # save new value if it is smallest so far;
            # send other values on
            if candidate<smallest -> candidate :=: smallest fi
            send next_worker(candidate)
         af
      fi
      send result(m, smallest)       # return smallest to sort
   end

   # Sort array a into non-decreasing order
   procedure sort(ref a[1:*] : int)
      var pos, value : int
      if ub(a) = 0 -> return fi
      var first_worker : cap pipe
      # Call worker; get back a capability for its pipe operation,
      #     then use the pipe to send all values in a to the worker.
      first_worker := worker(ub(a))
      fa i := 1 to ub(a) -> send first_worker(a[i]) af
      # Gather the results and place them in the right place in a
      fa i := 1 to ub(a) ->
            receive result(pos, value)
            a[ub(a)-pos+1] := value
      af
   end

   # Print elements of array a
   procedure print_array(ref a[1:*] : int)
      fa i := 1 to ub(a) -> writes(" ", a[i]) af
      writes("\n")
   end

   var n : int
   writes("number of integers? "); read(n)
   var nums[1:n] : int
   write("input integers, separated by whitespace")
   fa i := 1 to n -> read(nums[i]) af
   write("original numbers")
   print_array(nums)
   sort(nums)
   write("sorted numbers")
   print_array(nums)
end pipeline_sort

/* ............. Example compile and run(s)

% sr -o pipeline_sort pipeline_sort.sr
% ./pipeline_sort
number of integers? 5
```

```
input integers, separated by whitespace
99 3 -44 98 -2
original numbers
 99 3 -44 98 -2
worker started, will be receiving 5 values
worker started, will be receiving 4 values
worker started, will be receiving 3 values
worker started, will be receiving 2 values
worker started, will be receiving 1 values
sorted numbers
 -44 -2 3 98 99
                                              */
```

6.2.2   Distributed Mutual Exclusion

The final message passing example is the distributed mutual exclusion algorithm, described in Chapter 11 of [6] and implemented in Program 6.5 (see also Section 18.2.2 of [20], page 555 of [21], and Section 11.2.2 of [24]).

A collection of processes that share memory can use the following for mutual exclusion and condition synchronization: the bakery algorithm of Section 3.8, semaphores, monitors, or message passing (messages can be sent through the shared memory). Suppose, though, that the processes do not share memory but have private memories and are connected to a local area network and suppose they still want to do condition synchronization to coordinate access to some shared resource. If all we have is message passing, can we implement some sort of "distributed mutual exclusion" algorithm? Suppose we also do not want to use a central server to avoid a bottleneck.

To recap, we want to solve the N-process mutual exclusion problem with an algorithm that works in a distributed environment, and does not involve a central server. We have N nodes connected by a network or point-to-point communication channels and we will assume

- error-free communication between all nodes, that is, no lost or garbled messages;

- but messages can arrive in a different order than they were sent; and

- nodes do not fail or halt, either inside or outside their critical sections.

In other words, nodes eventually respond to all request messages sent to them. The basic idea of the algorithm is:

do forever
        non-critical section code
        choose a sequence number
        send it to all other nodes
        wait for a reply message from all other nodes
        enter critical section
        post-protocol
  od

Each of the N nodes will consist of three processes executing concurrently (the three processes are executing on the CPU and memory of the node). One process does the above "do forever" loop. Another handles requests from other nodes. And the third waits for replies from all other nodes. A node, say node i, will send a reply or acknowledgement message to another node, say node j, that has sent node i a request message. Node i will send the reply immediately if node j has a lower sequence number (higher priority) or if node i is not trying to enter its critical section. Node i will defer the reply (until node i gets into then out of its critical section) if node j has a higher sequence number (lower priority). Ties are broken by node identifiers. A node chooses its sequence number by adding one to the highest sequence number it has seen so far in incoming messages from other nodes. Each node does the following.

> execute non-critical section code
>
> pre-protocol:
> > choose sequence number as highest seen so far + 1
> > send it to all other nodes
> > this represents request to enter critical section
>
> wait for replies
> while waiting,
> > reply to other nodes if their sequence number is lower
>
> enter critical section
>
> post-protocol:
> > reply to others (the deferreds)
> > if their sequence number was higher

This algorithm enforces mutual exclusion because a node does not enter its critical section until it receives replies to its request message from all other nodes. There is no deadlock since ties are broken by using node identifiers as shown in Program 6.5. There is no starvation in the absence contention since if none of the other nodes wants to enter its critical section, replies will be immediate. There is no starvation in the presence contention: after a node exits its critical section, it will choose a sequence number when it wants to enter again, and that number will be higher than those of other contending processes.

Program 6.5: Distributed Mutual Exclusion.

```
resource node
    op all_the_caps(node_cap[1:*] : cap node)
    op request_msg(number, id : int)
    op reply_msg(id : int)
body node(id, num_nodes, max_outside_time, max_inside_time : int)
    var node_cap[1:num_nodes] : cap node
    var number : int := 0
    var high_number : int := 0
    var requesting : bool := false
    var reply_count : int := 0
    sem s := 1
    sem wake_up := 0
    var deferred[1:num_nodes] : bool := ([num_nodes] false)

    procedure choose_number()
        P(s)
        requesting := true
        number := high_number + 1
```

```
      V(s)
  end choose_number

  procedure send_request()
      reply_count := 0
      fa j := 1 to num_nodes st j ~= id ->
          send node_cap[j].request_msg(number, id)
      af
  end send_request

  procedure wait_for_reply()
      P(wake_up)
  end wait_for_reply

  procedure reply_to_deferred_nodes()
      P(s)
      requesting := false
      V(s)
      fa j := 1 to num_nodes ->
          if deferred[j] ->
              deferred[j] := false
              send node_cap[j].reply_msg(id)
          fi
      af
  end reply_to_deferred_nodes

  procedure outside_cs(id : int)
      var napping : int
      napping := int(random(1000*max_outside_time))
      writes("age=", age(), ", node ", id,
          " outside critical section for ", napping, "ms\n")
      nap(napping)
  end outside_cs

  procedure inside_cs(id : int)
      var napping : int
      napping := int(random(1000*max_inside_time))
      writes("age=", age(), ", node ", id,
          " inside critical section for ", napping, "ms\n")
      nap(napping)
  end inside_cs

  write("node", id, "starting with max_outside_time of", max_outside_time,
      "and max_inside_time of", max_inside_time)
  reply

  process main
      receive all_the_caps(node_cap)
      write("node", id, "has all the node caps now")

      do true ->
          outside_cs(id)
          writes("age=", age(), ", node ", id,
              " wants to enter its critical section\n")
          choose_number()                    # PRE-PROTOCOL
```

```
                send_request()                    #       "
                wait_for_reply()                  #       "
                inside_cs(id)
                writes("age=", age(), ", node ", id,
                    " has now left its critical section\n")
                reply_to_deferred_nodes()     # POST-PROTOCOL
            od
        end main

    process handle_requests
        var received_number : int
        var received_id : int
        var decide_to_defer : bool

        do true ->
            receive request_msg(received_number, received_id)
            high_number := max(high_number, received_number)
            P(s)
            decide_to_defer := requesting and (number < received_number
                or (number = received_number and id < received_id))
            if decide_to_defer -> deferred[received_id] := true
            [] else -> send node_cap[received_id].reply_msg(id)
            fi
            V(s)
        od
    end handle_requests

    process handle_replies
        var received_id : int

        do true ->
            receive reply_msg(received_id)
            reply_count++
            if reply_count = num_nodes - 1 -> V(wake_up) fi
        od
    end handle_replies
end node

resource driver()
    import node
    var run_time : int := 30
    var max_outside_time : int := 8
    var max_inside_time : int := 2
    var stat : int
    var num_nodes : int
    var machine_name : string[64]
    var first_machine_name_position : int

    write("driver starting up")
    # First argument on command line is run time.
    first_machine_name_position := 1
    stat := getarg(first_machine_name_position, run_time)
    if stat = EOF ->     # first argument is nonexistent
        write("Some machine names needed!"); stop
    [] stat = 0 ->     # first argument is not a number but machine name
```

```
      write("Using default value of", run_time, "for run time.")
[] else -> first_machine_name_position++
fi
if run_time <= 1 ->
      write("run time =", run_time, "is too small."); stop
fi
# Second argument on command line is max_outside_time.
stat := getarg(first_machine_name_position, max_outside_time)
if stat = EOF ->    # second argument is nonexistent
      write("Some machine names needed!"); stop
[] stat = 0 ->     # second argument is not a number but machine name
      write("Using default value of", max_outside_time,
          "for max_outside_time.")
[] else -> first_machine_name_position++
fi
if max_outside_time <= 1 ->
      write("max_outside_time =", max_outside_time, "is too small."); stop
fi
# Third argument on command line is max_inside_time.
stat := getarg(first_machine_name_position, max_inside_time)
if stat = EOF ->    # second argument is nonexistent
      write("Some machine names needed!"); stop
[] stat = 0 ->     # second argument is not a number but machine name
      write("Using default value of", max_inside_time,
          "for max_inside_time.")
[] else -> first_machine_name_position++
fi
if max_inside_time <= 1 ->
      write("max_inside_time =", max_inside_time, "is too small."); stop
fi
num_nodes := numargs() - first_machine_name_position + 1
if num_nodes <= 0 ->
      write("Some machine names needed!"); stop
fi
# Subsequent arguments on command line are machine names.
var machine_cap[1:num_nodes] : cap vm
var node_cap[1:num_nodes] : cap node
fa i := 1 to num_nodes ->
      getarg(first_machine_name_position + i - 1, machine_name)
      machine_cap[i] := create vm() on machine_name
      if machine_cap[i] = null ->
          write("Cannot create vm on", machine_name, "so aborting."); stop
      fi
      writes("Virtual machine starting up on machine ",
          machine_name, ".\n")
af

write(num_nodes, "nodes to run for", run_time, "seconds")
fa j := 1 to num_nodes ->
      node_cap[j] :=
          create node(j, num_nodes, max_outside_time, max_inside_time)
          on machine_cap[j]
af
fa j := 1 to num_nodes -> call node_cap[j].all_the_caps(node_cap) af
write("all nodes started")
```

```
    nap(1000*run_time); write("must stop now"); stop
end driver

/* .............. Example compile and run(s)

% sr -o distr_mutual_excl distr_mutual_excl.sr
% ./distr_mutual_excl 10 4 2 king queen lily rose violet
driver starting up
Virtual machine starting up on machine king.
Virtual machine starting up on machine queen.
Virtual machine starting up on machine lily.
Virtual machine starting up on machine rose.
Virtual machine starting up on machine violet.
5 nodes to run for 10 seconds
node 1 starting with max_outside_time of 4 and max_inside_time of 2
node 2 starting with max_outside_time of 4 and max_inside_time of 2
node 3 starting with max_outside_time of 4 and max_inside_time of 2
node 4 starting with max_outside_time of 4 and max_inside_time of 2
node 5 starting with max_outside_time of 4 and max_inside_time of 2
node 1 has all the node caps now
node 2 has all the node caps now
age=8576, node 1 outside critical section for 752ms
age=6959, node 2 outside critical section for 785ms
node 3 has all the node caps now
node 4 has all the node caps now
node 5 has all the node caps now
all nodes started
age=810, node 5 outside critical section for 1431ms
age=2540, node 4 outside critical section for 1233ms
age=4550, node 3 outside critical section for 356ms
age=4920, node 3 wants to enter its critical section
age=5080, node 3 inside critical section for 1836ms
age=9341, node 1 wants to enter its critical section
age=7762, node 2 wants to enter its critical section
age=3780, node 4 wants to enter its critical section
age=2250, node 5 wants to enter its critical section
age=6920, node 3 has now left its critical section
age=6930, node 3 outside critical section for 1756ms
age=11024, node 1 inside critical section for 545ms
age=11588, node 1 has now left its critical section
age=9966, node 2 inside critical section for 209ms
age=11613, node 1 outside critical section for 1061ms
age=10182, node 2 has now left its critical section
age=5730, node 4 inside critical section for 1966ms
age=10184, node 2 outside critical section for 962ms
age=12697, node 1 wants to enter its critical section
age=8690, node 3 wants to enter its critical section
age=11152, node 2 wants to enter its critical section
age=5940, node 5 inside critical section for 756ms
age=7710, node 4 has now left its critical section
age=7710, node 4 outside critical section for 267ms
age=7990, node 4 wants to enter its critical section
age=6700, node 5 has now left its critical section
age=14583, node 1 inside critical section for 1822ms
age=6700, node 5 outside critical section for 3716ms
```

```
age=16419, node 1 has now left its critical section
age=12400, node 3 inside critical section for 1699ms
age=16462, node 1 outside critical section for 728ms
age=17203, node 1 wants to enter its critical section
age=14110, node 3 has now left its critical section
age=14110, node 3 outside critical section for 2778ms
age=16553, node 2 inside critical section for 989ms
age=10430, node 5 wants to enter its critical section
must stop now
                                                         */
```

6.2.3   Miscellaneous Examples

Program 6.6 shows that the SR runtime system buffers, in (virtual) memory that is allocated dynamically, messages that have been sent but not yet received. The output of the ps command in the sample run shows that the memory allocated to the process has grown tremendously, from a few hundred kilobytes (not shown) to 37 megabytes, since the messages are not being received.

Program 6.7 shows that the SR runtime system's process (thread) table is dynamically allocated. Each time a message (consisting of the value of i) is sent asynchronously (with send) to the proc create_a_thread, a new SR process is created to execute the code in the proc. This is an example of *dynamic process creation*. Memory for a stack for the variables of the process must be allocated. The output of the ps command in the sample run shows that the process has grown to almost 19 megabytes.

Program 6.6: Buffers for Unreceived Messages are Allocated Dynamically.

```
resource chicken
    import fox
    op cluck(d : string[*])
body chicken(foxy : cap fox)
    var s : string[64]
    write("chicken is alive")
    reply
    nap(1000000)                        #### don't receive the messages
    receive cluck(s)
    write("chicken receive cluck, s=", s)
    send foxy.quick(true)
end chicken

resource fox
    import chicken
    op quick(e : bool)
body fox()
    var chick : cap chicken
    var y : bool
    write("fox is alive")
    chick := create chicken(myresource())
    do true ->
        send chick.cluck("non-blocking")    #### send lots of messages
    od
```

```
  receive quick(y)
  write("fox receive quick, y=", y)
end fox

/* .............. Example compile and run(s)

% sr -o test_OS_buffer test_OS_buffer.sr
% ./test_OS_buffer
fox is alive
chicken is alive
^Z
Stopped
% ps uxww
USER         PID %CPU %MEM   SZ  RSS TT STAT START  TIME COMMAND
shartley 17491 76.3 73.13700822576 pe R   11:12   0:22 test_OS_buffer
% fg
./test_OS_buffer
^C
                                                */
```

Program 6.7: SR's Process Table is Allocated Dynamically.

```
# This shows that there is no fixed size process (thread) table
# since with an argument of 10000 this started to fill up megabytes
# of memory.
#
resource dyna_proc_alloc()

    op create_a_thread(i : int)

    proc create_a_thread(i)
       write("at age=", age(), "thread", i, "is alive")
       do true ->
          nap(300000)
          write("at age=", age(), "thread", i, "is still alive")
       od
    end create_a_thread

    var num_to_create : int := 10
    getarg(1, num_to_create)
    write("at age=", age(), "dyna_proc_alloc is alive")
    fa i := 1 to num_to_create -> send create_a_thread(i) af
end dyna_proc_alloc

/* .............. Example compile and run(s)

% sr -o dyna_proc_alloc dyna_proc_alloc.sr
% ./dyna_proc_alloc
at age= 9 dyna_proc_alloc is alive
at age= 78 thread 1 is alive
at age= 89 thread 2 is alive
at age= 96 thread 3 is alive
at age= 109 thread 4 is alive
```

```
at age= 115 thread 5 is alive
at age= 126 thread 6 is alive
at age= 133 thread 7 is alive
at age= 142 thread 8 is alive
at age= 150 thread 9 is alive
at age= 160 thread 10 is alive
^C
% ./dyna_proc_alloc 10000 >&/dev/null&
[1] 12828
% ps uxww
USER       PID %CPU %MEM   SZ  RSS TT STAT START   TIME COMMAND
shartley 12828 67.5 28.9 8592 8936 p1 R    08:05   0:01 dyna_proc_alloc 10000
shartley 12783  0.0  1.8  120  544 p1 S    08:04   0:00 -h -i (csh)
shartley 11433  0.0  0.0  176    0 p3 IW   07:01   0:03 -csh (csh)
shartley 12782  0.0  0.8   56  232 p3 S    08:04   0:00 script
shartley 12781  0.0  0.7   40  216 p3 S    08:04   0:00 script
shartley 12829  0.0  1.8  216  544 p1 R    08:05   0:00 ps uxww
% ps uxww
USER       PID %CPU %MEM   SZ  RSS TT STAT START   TIME COMMAND
shartley 12828 45.2 48.21897614896 p1 R    08:05   0:04 dyna_proc_alloc 10000
shartley 12783  0.0  1.7  120  520 p1 S    08:04   0:00 -h -i (csh)
shartley 11433  0.0  0.0  176    0 p3 IW   07:01   0:03 -csh (csh)
shartley 12782  0.0  0.8   56  232 p3 S    08:04   0:00 script
shartley 12781  0.0  0.7   40  216 p3 S    08:04   0:00 script
shartley 12830  0.0  1.7  216  528 p1 R    08:05   0:00 ps uxww
% kill %1
[1]    Terminated          ./dyna_proc_alloc 10000 >& /dev/null
                                    */
```

6.3   Lab: Message Passing

Objectives

To learn about message passing in SR.

Preparation Before Lab

Read Section 6.1 on message passing. Look at Programs 6.2 and 6.4. No semaphores or monitors are allowed in any of these assignments.

6.3.1   Assignment: Merge Sort

Write an SR program that implements the merge sort using message passing, that is using only **send** and **receive**. An array to be sorted is split in half and given to two processes. Each process sorts its half of the array and then sends, one at a time and in sorted order, its part of the array to a merge process. The merge process takes the smaller of the two numbers (or the next number available if one of the two sorts has had all its numbers read) and places it into the next available slot of the final sorted array.

Create three processes: two sorts and a merge. To one sort, pass the first half of the unsorted array; to the other sort, pass the other half. As the sorts progress in parallel, they will send to the merge process the sorted elements of their half of the array one-by-one as they are determined. In parallel with the sorts, the merge will receive the next element from the appropriate sort and place it into the final sorted array.

You have two choices for input data. You can read the size of the array and the unsorted array elements from the terminal, or you can get the array size from the command line and generate that many random numbers for the unsorted array.

Make sure you test your program on a set of numbers that is already sorted and on another that is in reverse sorted order. You should also make sure your program handles requests to sort arrays of length two, length one, length zero, and illegal negative length.

The following array of channel construction technique may be useful.

```
resource sort
    import merge
body sort(id : int; merge_cap : cap merge)
    var item : int := id
        #...
    send merge_cap.channel[id](item)
        #...
end sort

resource merge
    import sort
    op channel[1:2](item : int)
body merge()
    var value : int
        #...
    fa i := 1 to 2 -> create sort(i, myresource()) af
        #...
    fa i := 1 to 2 ->
        receive channel[i](value)
        write("merge received value", value, "on channel", i)
    af
        #...
end merge

/* ............... Example compile and run(s)

% sr -o ms merge_sort_skeleton.sr
% ./ms
merge received value 1 on channel 1
merge received value 2 on channel 2
                                            */
```

6.3.2 Assignment: Pipeline Sieve of Eratosthenes

Write an SR program, patterned after the one in Program 6.4, that uses asynchronous message passing (send and receive) to implement the pipeline Sieve of Eratosthenes.

Create a process filter(2) that will filter out all multiples of 2. To the filter(2) process, send all integers from 2 up to MAX_NUM (default value 1000).

The filter(2) process will create another process, filter(3), that will filter out all multiples of 3. The filter(2) process will then send to the filter(3) process the integers that were sent to filter(2) that are not multiples of 2, i.e., 3, 5, 7, 9, 11, 13, 15, ...

The filter(3) process will create another process, filter(5), that will filter out all multiples of 5. The filter(3) process will then send to the filter(5) process the integers that were sent to filter(3) that are not multiples of 3, i.e., 5, 7, 11, 13, 17, 19, ...

The `filter(5)` process will create another process, `filter(7)`, that will filter out all multiples of 7. The `filter(5)` process will then send to the `filter(7)` process the integers that were sent to `filter(5)` that are not multiples of 5, i.e., 7, 11, 13, 17, 19, 23, ... Etc.

Design the program so that it prints out all prime numbers less than or equal to `MAX_NUM`. Note that the smallest number each filter process gets is prime. Think about how and when to stop creating filter processes, and about the minimum number of filter processes necessary to print out all prime numbers less than or equal to `MAX_NUM`.

6.3.3   Assignment: Compare/Exchange Sort

Use asynchronous message passing to implement the compare/exchange sort. To sort N numbers (where for simplicity we assume N is even), distribute pairs of the numbers (using asynchronous message passing) to N/2 worker processes, i.e., the numbers are split up into N/2 pairs and each of the N/2 worker processes is given one of the pairs. The worker processes are laid out in a line; each worker process should communicate only with its two neighbors (except the two worker processes on the two ends, which have only one neighbor each). There are N/2 iterations of the algorithm. On each iteration, each worker sends its smaller number of the pair to the left and the larger of the pair to the right. After all the iterations, the workers send the final pair they end up with back to the main driver resource.

Here is a skeleton of the program (setting up the neighbor communication links between the workers is a little complicated in SR).

```
global Types
    optype channel(num: real)
    optype result_back(num: real; pos: int)
end Types

resource worker
    import Types, compare_exchange
    op left_in, right_in: channel
    op links(left_out, right_out: cap channel)
body worker(i, num_workers: int; ce_cap: cap compare_exchange)
    var left_out, right_out: cap channel
    var a, b, c, d : real
    write("worker", i, "alive, num_workers =", num_workers)
    reply
    receive left_in(a)
    receive right_in(b)
    receive links(left_out, right_out)    # now workers are released
    write("worker", i, "received", a, "and", b)

    # You put code for num_workers iterations of the compare-exchange here.

    write("worker", i, "now has", a, "and", b)
    send ce_cap.left_result(a, i)
    send ce_cap.right_result(b, i)
end worker

resource compare_exchange
    import Types, worker
    op left_result, right_result : result_back
body compare_exchange()
```

```
   procedure print_array(ref a[1:*] : real)
      fa i := lb(a) to ub(a) -> writes(" ", a[i]) af
      writes("\n")
   end print_array

   write("compare_exchange is alive")
   seed(42.0)
   var N : int := 10
   if getarg(1, N) = 0 -> write("bad argument for number to sort"); stop fi
   if N <= 0 or N % 2 != 0 ->
      write("number to sort must be positive even"); stop
   [] else -> write("N =", N)
   fi
   var number[1: N] : real
   var num_workers : int
   num_workers := N/2
   var worker_cap[1: num_workers] : cap worker
   var left_out, right_out : cap channel
   var ce_cap : cap compare_exchange
   var a_number : real
   var position : int
   fa i := 1 to N ->
      number[i] := random(-N, N)
   af
   writes("original array to sort=")
   print_array(number)
   ce_cap := myresource()
   fa i := 1 to num_workers ->
      worker_cap[i] := create worker(i, num_workers, ce_cap)
   af
   fa i := 1 to num_workers ->  # make sure all the workers have their
      send worker_cap[i].left_in(number[2*i-1])  # original pair before
      send worker_cap[i].right_in(number[2*i])   # they start sending
   af                                            # to each other
   fa i := 1 to num_workers ->
      if i = 1 -> left_out := worker_cap[i].left_in
      [] else -> left_out := worker_cap[i-1].right_in
      fi
      if i = num_workers -> right_out := worker_cap[i].right_in
      [] else -> right_out := worker_cap[i+1].left_in
      fi
      send worker_cap[i].links(left_out, right_out)  # worker released
   af                                                # to send to neighbors
   fa i := 1 to num_workers ->
      receive left_result(a_number, position)
      number[2*position-1] := a_number
      receive right_result(a_number, position)
      number[2*position] := a_number
   af
   writes("sorted array=")
   print_array(number)
end compare_exchange

/* .............. Example compile and run(s)
```

```
% sr -o cmpx cmpx_skeleton.sr
% ./cmpx 10
compare_exchange is alive
N = 10
original array to sort= -7.05816 -2.57207 -8.59442 -4.62885 -4.10069
-5.57617 2.30808 -6.23539 -0.763679 -5.77443
worker 1 alive, num_workers = 5
worker 2 alive, num_workers = 5
worker 3 alive, num_workers = 5
worker 4 alive, num_workers = 5
worker 5 alive, num_workers = 5
worker 1 received -7.05816 and -2.57207
worker 1 now has -7.05816 and -2.57207
worker 2 received -8.59442 and -4.62885
worker 2 now has -8.59442 and -4.62885
worker 3 received -4.10069 and -5.57617
worker 3 now has -4.10069 and -5.57617
worker 4 received 2.30808 and -6.23539
worker 4 now has 2.30808 and -6.23539
worker 5 received -0.763679 and -5.77443
worker 5 now has -0.763679 and -5.77443
sorted array= -7.05816 -2.57207 -8.59442 -4.62885 -4.10069 -5.57617
2.30808 -6.23539 -0.763679 -5.77443
                                    */
```

6.3.4 Assignment: Speedup

On a shared-memory multiprocessor, time Program 6.3 using various numbers of CPUs. What conclusions can you draw?

6.3.5 Assignment: Algorithm Animation

Animate one of the programs you have written for this lab.

6.3.6 Assignment: Distributed Mutual Exclusion

After reading Section 6.2.2, answer the following questions (from page 123 of [6]):

1. There is a binary semaphore s in Program 6.5, local to each node. Show that it is necessary.

2. Suppose the binary semaphore s is deleted from procedure `reply_to_deferred_nodes`, and suppose that the `V(s)` in process `handle_requests` is moved up to before the `if` statement. Show that deadlock is possible.

3. Suppose node m decides to enter its critical section and sends a request message to node n. Node n sends a reply message to node m indicating that node n does not want to enter its critical section. Suppose further that node n later decides to enter its critical section and sends a request message to node m (and to all the other nodes). What happens if node n's request message is received by node m before the earlier-sent reply message of node n to node m?

```
in name1(a, b, c) returns d st condition1 ->
   d := a + b - c
[] name2(x, y) st condition2 ->
   save := x * y
[] name3(z) returns q ->
   q := compute(z)
ni
```

Figure 6.2: Rendezvous with **in** Statement.

6.4 Rendezvous

Synchronous message passing is an example of the *rendezvous*: two processes both reaching some point in their code at the same time to exchange information. In synchronous message passing, the information flows in one direction only, from sender to receiver. In the full-fledged *general* or *extended* rendezvous, the information flow is two-way.

The extended rendezvous is implemented with the **in** statement in SR. An example of the **in** statement is shown in Figure 6.2. A process executing an **in** statement will block until some other process invokes one of the operations (**name1**, **name2**, or **name3** in Figure 6.2) in the **in** statement with **call** or **send**. The **in** statement will accept an invocation of one of the names if there is no guard on the name or if the guard on the name is true. A guard is constructed using the **st** *such that* followed by a boolean expression representing the condition for accepting an invocation of the name. If there are no invocations or no invocations with true guards, the **in** statement blocks. Otherwise it accepts the oldest invocation with a true guard. An else clause [] **else** ->··· can be added to an **in** statement. The else clause is executed if the **in** statement would have blocked without the else clause.

6.4.1 Classical Problems Using Rendezvous

Program 6.8 shows the bounded buffer resource of Program 4.2 implemented with an **in** statement. To run the program, replace the **bounded_buffer** resource in Program 4.2 with the one in Program 6.8. The **in** statement accepts only one invocation at a time so the buffer is never corrupted by race conditions.

A **reply** in the **in** statement in Program 6.8 could be added as shown in Figure 6.3 to increase concurrency slightly: the producer or consumer is released by the **reply** so it continues in parallel with the buffer process doing its slot index arithmetic.

Program 6.9 can be used to implement the dining philosophers problem with an **in** statement. To run the program, replace the **dining_server** resource in Program 4.5 with the one in Program 6.9.

Program 6.10 shows how to solve the readers and writers problem with an **in** statement.

Program 6.8: Bounded Buffer Using Rendezvous.

```
resource bounded_buffer
    op deposit(item : real)
    op fetch() returns item : real
body bounded_buffer(size : int)
    var buf[0:size-1] : real
    var count := 0
```

```
in deposit(item) st count < size ->
    buf[put_in] := item
    reply                               # for more concurrency
    put_in := (put_in + 1) % size
    count++
[] fetch() returns item st count > 0 ->
    item := buf[take_out]
    reply                               # for more concurrency
    take_out := (take_out + 1) % size
    count--
ni
```

Figure 6.3: A reply in an in Statement.

```
    var take_out := 0
    var put_in := 0
    write("bounded buffer resource with", size, "slots is alive")
    reply
    do true ->
        in deposit(item) st count < size ->
            buf[put_in] := item
            put_in := (put_in + 1) % size
            count++
        [] fetch() returns item st count > 0 ->
            item := buf[take_out]
            take_out := (take_out + 1) % size
            count--
        ni
    od
end bounded_buffer
```

Program 6.9: Dining Philosophers Using Rendezvous.

```
resource dining_server
    op take_forks(i : int), put_forks(i : int)
body dining_server(num_phil : int)
    write("dining server for", num_phil, "philosophers is alive")
    reply
    type states = enum(thinking, hungry, eating)
    var state[1:num_phil] : states := ([num_phil] thinking)

    procedure left(i : int) returns lft : int
        if i=1 -> lft := num_phil [] else -> lft := i-1 fi
    end left

    procedure right(i : int) returns rgh : int
        if i=num_phil -> rgh := 1 [] else -> rgh := i+1 fi
    end right
```

```
    do true ->    # no explicit hungry state
       in take_forks(i) st state[left(i)] ~= eating
             and state[right(i)] ~= eating ->
          state[i] := eating
       [] put_forks(i) -> state[i] := thinking
       ni
    od
end dining_server
```

Program 6.10: Readers and Writers Using Rendezvous.

```
resource server
    op Start_Read(i : int), End_Read(i : int)
    op Start_Write(i : int), End_Write(i : int)
body server()
    write("readers and writers server is alive")
    reply
    var Readers : int := 0
    var nobody_writing : bool := true

    do true ->
       in Start_Read(i) st nobody_writing ->
          Readers++
          write("   age=",age(),"reader",i,"has begun reading, readers=",
             Readers)
       [] End_Read(i) ->
          Readers--
          write("   age=",age(),"reader",i,"finished reading, readers=",
             Readers)
       [] Start_Write(i) st nobody_writing and Readers = 0 ->
          nobody_writing := false
          write("   age=",age(),"WRITER",i,"has begun WRITING")
       [] End_Write(i) ->
          nobody_writing := true
          write("   age=",age(),"WRITER",i,"has finished WRITING")
       ni
    od
end server
```

6.4.2 Nested in Statements

The example in Program 6.11 show a simulation of some processes that deposit to (incre
ment) or withdraw from (decrement) a bank account. Bank rules prohibit the account from
falling below $100 dollars. The example shows that in statements can be nested and that the
same operation (op) name can be implemented in two different in statements (**increment**
in the Figure). Also, the same operation name can be in more than one branch of the same
in statement, as **increment** does here.

If instead of a nested in we used

```
       [] decrement(amount) st value - amount >= 100 ->
```

to enforce the $100 minimum balance rule, then attempts to withdraw large amounts may end up waiting while small withdrawals succeed, an example of starvation. The nested **in** prevents this form of starvation.

Program 6.11 also shows that the **in** statement can have an **else** clause, similar to the **else** clause on the **if** statement. If there are no outstanding invocations of any operations in the **in** statement when it is executed, then rather than block as it would without an **else**, the **else** clause is executed.

SR has a useful built-in function ? that can be used with the **in** statement. When ? is applied to an operation name, it returns the number of outstanding (unserviced) invocations of that operation. This can be used in such-that (**st**) clauses on the operation names implemented in the **in** statement to give priority to one name over another. For example we could modify the outer **in** statement in Program 6.11 to be

```
# priority to servicing invocations of increment over decrement
in increment(amount) ->
   ...
[] decrement(amount) st ?increment = 0 ->
   ...
ni
```

Then an **increment** would be given priority since no **decrement** could be accepted if there were an outstanding **increment** invocation.

The following excerpt from pages 17-19 of [2] gives some technical details.

The **call** and **send** statements generate a new invocation of the denoted operation.

An invocation statement is executed by first evaluating the argument expressions; these must agree in number and type with the corresponding formal parameters. If the denoted operation is implemented by a **proc**, a new process is then created to execute the operation. If the denoted operation is implemented by one or more input (**in**) statements, the argument expressions are placed on the queue associated with the operation. Invocations of the same operation by the same invoking process are queued in the order they are invoked.

A **call** statement terminates when the operation has been serviced and results (if any) have been returned. A **send** statement terminates when a service process has been created or when the arguments have been queued, depending on how the operation is implemented. Execution of **call** is thus *synchronous* — the caller waits for the operation to be executed. In contrast, **send** is *asynchronous* — the sender waits only until the operation has been started or queued. Note that the keyword **call** is optional in a **call** statement.

An input statement delays the executing process until some invocation is selectable. An invocation is *selectable* if the boolean-valued synchronization expression in the corresponding operation guard is true. The synchronization expression is optional; if omitted it is implicitly true. When an input statement contains an **else** command, that command is selected if no invocation is selectable.

In general, the oldest selectable invocation is serviced. An invocation is serviced by executing the block in the corresponding operation command, with the formal identifiers bound to the arguments of the invocation. Synchronization expressions can reference invocation arguments since they are in the scope of the formal identifiers in an operation command. Hence selection can be based on invocation arguments in addition to other variables and parameters.

An input statement terminates when the selected block terminates or when a **return** statement is executed. Executing **exit** or **next** also terminates execution of an input statement that is within an iterative statement. If the invocation serviced by an input statement was called, results are returned to the caller when the input statement terminates.

A **receive** statement is an abbreviation for an input statement that merely waits for the next invocation of the named operation, then assigns the contents of the received message to the denoted variables (if the received operation has parameters). In particular,

```
receive operid(v1, ...,vN)
```

is an abbreviation for

```
in operid(f1, ...,fN) -> v1 := f1; ...; vN := fN ni
```

where the **f**'s are identifiers different from the **v**'s.

Executing a **return** or **reply** statement causes the invocation being serviced by the smallest enclosing **proc** or operation command to terminate, if it was called. Executing **return** also causes the smallest enclosing **proc** or operation command to terminate. In contrast, a process that executes **reply** continues executing with the statement following **reply**. Such a process may continue to reference the formals until it leaves their scope; however, no subsequent change to formal parameters or to the return value is reflected back to the caller. A **reply** to an invocation for which a **reply** has already been executed has no effect.

Program 6.11: Nested **in** Statements.

```
resource nested_in_example()
    op increment(amount : int), decrement(amount : int)
    var num_incs : int := 10, num_decs : int := 10
    getarg(1, num_incs);  getarg(2, num_decs)

    process inc(i := 1 to num_incs)
        var amount : int
        do true ->
            nap(int(random(i*1000)))
            amount := int(random(i*10))
            write("inc", i, "wants to inc by", amount)
            increment(amount)
        od
    end inc

    process dec(j := 1 to num_decs)
        var amount : int
        do true ->
            nap(int(random(j*1000)))
            amount := int(random(j*10))
            write("dec", j, "wants to dec by", amount)
            decrement(amount)
        od
    end dec

    var value : int := 110;  getarg(3, value)
```

```
    var run_time : int := 60;  getarg(4, run_time)
    write("simulation starting with", num_incs, "incs,", num_decs, "decs,",
        value, "value, and", run_time, "run_time")

  process server
      do true ->
          in increment(amount) st amount > 50 ->  # put this branch first, else
              value +:= amount                     # next branch always gets it
              write("WOW! Parents! value +:=", amount, "is", value)
          [] increment(amount) ->
              value +:= amount
              write("value +:=", amount, "is", value)
          [] decrement(amount) ->
              # never let value be decremented below 100
              do value - amount < 100 ->
                  in increment(amount2) -> value +:= amount2 + 10
                      write("value +:=", amount2, "+ 10 bonus is", value)
                  ni
              od
              value -:= amount
              write("value -:=", amount, "is", value)
          [] else -> write("server is idle so nap..."); nap(1000)
          ni
      od
    end server

  nap(1000*run_time); write("must stop now"); stop
end nested_in_example

/* .............. Example compile and run(s)

% sr -o nested_ins nested_ins.sr
% ./nested_ins 10 10 110 5
simulation starting with 10 incs, 10 decs, 110 value, and 5 run_time
server is idle so nap...
inc 6 wants to inc by 11
dec 1 wants to dec by 3
dec 5 wants to dec by 24
inc 1 wants to inc by 0
dec 3 wants to dec by 20
dec 2 wants to dec by 16
inc 4 wants to inc by 18
value +:= 11 is 121
value -:= 3 is 118
value +:= 0 + 10 bonus is 128
value -:= 24 is 104
value +:= 18 + 10 bonus is 132
value -:= 20 is 112
dec 1 wants to dec by 2
inc 2 wants to inc by 17
value +:= 17 + 10 bonus is 139
value -:= 16 is 123
value -:= 2 is 121
server is idle so nap...
inc 3 wants to inc by 1
```

```
dec 1 wants to dec by 8
inc 2 wants to inc by 18
inc 1 wants to inc by 3
inc 5 wants to inc by 0
value +:= 1 is 122
value -:= 8 is 114
value +:= 18 is 132
value +:= 3 is 135
value +:= 0 is 135
server is idle so nap...
dec 1 wants to dec by 9
dec 7 wants to dec by 50
inc 2 wants to inc by 19
dec 3 wants to dec by 29
inc 1 wants to inc by 9
dec 2 wants to dec by 9
inc 6 wants to inc by 43
dec 6 wants to dec by 41
value -:= 9 is 126
value +:= 19 + 10 bonus is 155
value -:= 50 is 105
value +:= 9 + 10 bonus is 124
value +:= 43 + 10 bonus is 177
value -:= 29 is 148
value -:= 9 is 139
dec 1 wants to dec by 1
dec 4 wants to dec by 17
dec 3 wants to dec by 24
inc 1 wants to inc by 2
value +:= 2 + 10 bonus is 151
value -:= 41 is 110
value -:= 1 is 109
inc 10 wants to inc by 95
value +:= 95 + 10 bonus is 214
value -:= 17 is 197
value -:= 24 is 173
server is idle so nap...
inc 2 wants to inc by 19
inc 8 wants to inc by 17
inc 1 wants to inc by 3
inc 4 wants to inc by 0
dec 2 wants to dec by 5
inc 6 wants to inc by 58
inc 3 wants to inc by 23
dec 1 wants to dec by 2
inc 7 wants to inc by 69
value +:= 19 is 192
value +:= 17 is 209
value +:= 3 is 212
value +:= 0 is 212
value -:= 5 is 207
WOW! Parents! value +:= 58 is 265
value +:= 23 is 288
value -:= 2 is 286
WOW! Parents! value +:= 69 is 355
```

```
server is idle so nap...
dec 1 wants to dec by 9
inc 3 wants to inc by 7
must stop now
                                            */
```

6.4.3   A Lock Resource

The next example uses the in statement to implement the strict binary semaphore (lock) that was discussed in Section 4.4. Program 6.12 uses a rendezvous in an infinite loop to implement a lock, one lock for each instance of the lockd resource created. A process that tries to lock an already locked lock will block. Program 6.13 implements general counting semaphores using binary semaphores or locks, as seen in Section 4.4. Program 6.14 tests the implementation. As can be seen in the example run, a process doing a **down** on the semaphore S will block if the value of the semaphore is zero. Also note that in Program 6.13, the lock serial prevents the value of the variable count from ever going below −1.

Program 6.12: A Lock Resource.

```
# This resource implements a different lock for each time it
# is created.  A lock is equivalent to a strict binary semaphore.
#
resource lockd
    op lock(), unlock()
body lockd(name : string[64]; initially_locked : bool)
    var locked : bool := initially_locked
    write("lockd: a lock named", name,
        "has been created, initially locked?", locked)
    reply

    do true ->
        in lock() st not locked ->
            write("DEBUG lockd: lock(", name, ")")
            locked := true
        [] unlock() ->
            write("DEBUG lockd: unlock(", name, ")")
            if locked -> locked := false
            [] else -> write("DEBUG unlock(", name, ") in lockd: not locked")
            fi
        ni
    od
end lockd
```

Program 6.13: A General Semaphore Resource Implemented with Locks.

```
resource general_semaphore
    import lockd
    op down(), up()
body general_semaphore(name : string[64]; n : int)
```

```
      var mutex, blocked, serial : cap lockd
      mutex := create lockd("mutex", false)
      blocked := create lockd("blocked", true)
      serial := create lockd("serial", false)
      var count : int := n   /* whatever the initial value of S is to be */
      write("a general semaphore named", name,
         "with initial value", n, "has been created")
      reply

   proc down()
      serial.lock()
      mutex.lock()
      count--
      write("DEBUG down: for", name, "count now is", count)
      if count < 0 ->
         mutex.unlock()
         blocked.lock()
      [] else ->
         mutex.unlock()
      fi
      serial.unlock()
   end down

   proc up()
      mutex.lock()
      count++
      write("DEBUG up: for", name, "count now is", count)
      if count <= 0 ->
         blocked.unlock()
      fi
      mutex.unlock()
   end up
end general_semaphore
```

Program 6.14: Testing the General Semaphore Resource.

```
resource users()
   import general_semaphore
   var S : cap general_semaphore
   S := create general_semaphore("S", 3)
   var num_users : int := 5, nap_time : int := 4, run_time : int := 60
   getarg(1, num_users); getarg(2, nap_time); getarg(3, run_time)
   write(num_users, "users with nap_time=", nap_time, "and run_time=", run_time)

   process a_user(i := 1 to num_users)
      var napping : int
      do true ->
         napping := int(random(1000*nap_time))
         write("age()=", age(), "user", i, "napping for", napping)
         napping := int(random(1000*nap_time))
         nap(napping)
         write("age()=", age(), "user", i, "doing a down")
         S.down()
```

```
          write("age()=", age(), "after down, user", i, "napping for", napping)
          napping := int(random(1000*nap_time))
          nap(napping)
          write("age()=", age(), "user", i, "doing an up")
          S.up()
      od
   end a_user

   nap(1000*run_time); write("must stop now"); stop
end users

/* .............. Example compile and run(s)

% sr -o semaphores lock.sr general_semaphore.sr users.sr
lock.sr:
general_semaphore.sr:
users.sr:
lock.sr:
general_semaphore.sr:
users.sr:
linking:
% ./semaphores 5 4 10
lockd: a lock named mutex has been created, initially locked? false
lockd: a lock named blocked has been created, initially locked? true
lockd: a lock named serial has been created, initially locked? false
a general semaphore named S with initial value 3 has been created
5 users with nap_time= 4 and run_time= 10
age()= 84 user 1 napping for 2032
age()= 87 user 2 napping for 2302
age()= 91 user 3 napping for 1400
age()= 94 user 4 napping for 3271
age()= 97 user 5 napping for 3924
age()= 986 user 3 doing a down
DEBUG lockd: lock( serial )
DEBUG lockd: lock( mutex )
DEBUG down: for S count now is 2
DEBUG lockd: unlock( mutex )
DEBUG lockd: unlock( serial )
age()= 997 after down, user 3 napping for 886
age()= 1086 user 1 doing a down
DEBUG lockd: lock( serial )
DEBUG lockd: lock( mutex )
DEBUG down: for S count now is 1
DEBUG lockd: unlock( mutex )
DEBUG lockd: unlock( serial )
age()= 1095 after down, user 1 napping for 999
age()= 1616 user 1 doing an up
DEBUG lockd: lock( mutex )
DEBUG up: for S count now is 2
DEBUG lockd: unlock( mutex )
age()= 1629 user 1 napping for 1088
age()= 1986 user 5 doing a down
DEBUG lockd: lock( serial )
DEBUG lockd: lock( mutex )
DEBUG down: for S count now is 1
```

```
DEBUG lockd: unlock( mutex )
DEBUG lockd: unlock( serial )
age()= 2000 after down, user 5 napping for 1879
age()= 3511 user 4 doing a down
age()= 3515 user 2 doing a down
DEBUG lockd: lock( serial )
DEBUG lockd: lock( mutex )
DEBUG down: for S count now is 0
DEBUG lockd: unlock( mutex )
DEBUG lockd: unlock( serial )
DEBUG lockd: lock( serial )
age()= 3523 after down, user 4 napping for 3394
DEBUG lockd: lock( mutex )
DEBUG down: for S count now is -1
DEBUG lockd: unlock( mutex )
age()= 4506 user 3 doing an up
DEBUG lockd: lock( mutex )
DEBUG up: for S count now is 0
DEBUG lockd: unlock( blocked )
DEBUG lockd: lock( blocked )
DEBUG lockd: unlock( mutex )
DEBUG lockd: unlock( serial )
age()= 4528 user 3 napping for 3549
age()= 4530 after down, user 2 napping for 3402
age()= 4531 user 5 doing an up
DEBUG lockd: lock( mutex )
DEBUG up: for S count now is 1
DEBUG lockd: unlock( mutex )
age()= 4536 user 5 napping for 3680
age()= 5356 user 1 doing a down
DEBUG lockd: lock( serial )
DEBUG lockd: lock( mutex )
DEBUG down: for S count now is 0
DEBUG lockd: unlock( mutex )
DEBUG lockd: unlock( serial )
age()= 5365 after down, user 1 napping for 3724
age()= 5386 user 1 doing an up
DEBUG lockd: lock( mutex )
DEBUG up: for S count now is 1
DEBUG lockd: unlock( mutex )
age()= 5392 user 1 napping for 2144
age()= 5597 user 1 doing a down
DEBUG lockd: lock( serial )
DEBUG lockd: lock( mutex )
DEBUG down: for S count now is 0
DEBUG lockd: unlock( mutex )
DEBUG lockd: unlock( serial )
age()= 5609 after down, user 1 napping for 200
age()= 6736 user 4 doing an up
DEBUG lockd: lock( mutex )
DEBUG up: for S count now is 1
DEBUG lockd: unlock( mutex )
age()= 6743 user 4 napping for 114
age()= 6776 user 4 doing a down
DEBUG lockd: lock( serial )
```

```
DEBUG lockd: lock( mutex )
DEBUG down: for S count now is 0
DEBUG lockd: unlock( mutex )
DEBUG lockd: unlock( serial )
age()= 6784 after down, user 4 napping for 31
age()= 6916 user 2 doing an up
DEBUG lockd: lock( mutex )
DEBUG up: for S count now is 1
DEBUG lockd: unlock( mutex )
age()= 6922 user 2 napping for 2058
age()= 7496 user 3 doing a down
DEBUG lockd: lock( serial )
DEBUG lockd: lock( mutex )
DEBUG down: for S count now is 0
DEBUG lockd: unlock( mutex )
DEBUG lockd: unlock( serial )
age()= 7505 after down, user 3 napping for 2961
age()= 7736 user 2 doing a down
DEBUG lockd: lock( serial )
DEBUG lockd: lock( mutex )
DEBUG down: for S count now is -1
DEBUG lockd: unlock( mutex )
age()= 8326 user 5 doing a down
age()= 9366 user 1 doing an up
DEBUG lockd: lock( mutex )
DEBUG up: for S count now is 0
DEBUG lockd: unlock( blocked )
DEBUG lockd: lock( blocked )
DEBUG lockd: unlock( mutex )
DEBUG lockd: unlock( serial )
DEBUG lockd: lock( serial )
age()= 9382 user 1 napping for 2121
age()= 9383 after down, user 2 napping for 805
DEBUG lockd: lock( mutex )
DEBUG down: for S count now is -1
DEBUG lockd: unlock( mutex )
must stop now
                                          */
```

6.4.4 The Distributed Dining Philosophers

The next example in this section, Program 6.15, uses both message passing (asynchronous) and the extended rendezvous (SR in statement). It is a solution from the SR software distribution to the distributed dining philosophers problem: implement the dining philosophers without a central server process. In other words, each philosopher is to communicate only with its two neighbors and negotiate the use of a fork with the neighbor that shares that fork. Each philosopher has a servant process that does the fork negotiation. This lets each philosopher devote maximal time to philosophizing. In the central server version, the central server keeps track of the forks and hands them out to a hungry philosopher when both its forks are not in use.

Starvation is prevented by requiring a philosopher to give up a fork it holds that is "dirty," i.e., that it was the last one to use. Deadlock is prevented by distributing the forks initially in an asymmetric pattern: philosopher 1 gets both forks in the dirty state, philosophers 2 through $n-1$ get one clean fork (the right one) each, and the last philosopher gets no forks. In general, if philosopher p is the most recent philosopher to eat, then it will possess both forks in the dirty state. If a circular chain starts to develop around the table, the chain will be broken when it tries to pass through philosopher p. Either philosopher $p-1$ or $p+1$ will get to eat and deadlock will not occur.

Program 6.15: Distributed Dining Philosophers.

```
resource Philosopher
    import Servant
body Philosopher(myservant : cap Servant; id, thinking, eating: int)
    process phil
        do true ->
            nap(int(random(thinking)))
            write(age(), "philosopher", id, "is hungry")
            myservant.getforks()
            nap(int(random(eating)))
            myservant.relforks()
        od
    end phil
end Philosopher

resource Servant
    op getforks(), relforks()
    op needL(), needR(), passL(), passR()
    op links(l, r : cap Servant)
    op forks(haveL, dirtyL, haveR, dirtyR : bool)
body Servant(id : int)
    var l, r : cap Servant
    var haveL, dirtyL, haveR, dirtyR : bool
    op hungry(), eat()

    proc getforks()
        send hungry(); receive eat()
    end

    process server
        receive links(l, r)
        receive forks(haveL, dirtyL, haveR, dirtyR)
        do true->
            in hungry() ->
                if ~haveR -> send r.needL()
                [] else -> write(age(), "philosopher", id, "has right fork")
                fi
                if ~haveL -> send l.needR()
                [] else -> write(age(), "philosopher", id, "has left fork")
                fi
                do ~(haveL & haveR) ->
                    in passL() -> haveL := true; dirtyL := false
                        write(age(), "philosopher", id, "got left fork")
                    [] passR() -> haveR := true; dirtyR := false
                        write(age(), "philosopher", id, "got right fork")
                    [] needR() st dirtyR -> haveR := false; dirtyR := false
```

```
                     send r.passL(); send r.needL()
                     write(age(), "philosopher", id, "sends dirty right fork")
                 [] needL() st dirtyL -> haveL := false; dirtyL := false
                     send l.passR(); send l.needR()
                     write(age(), "philosopher", id, "sends dirty left fork")
                 ni
            od
            write(age(), "philosopher", id, "has both forks")
            send eat(); dirtyL := true; dirtyR := true
            receive relforks()
            write(age(), "philosopher", id, "is finished eating")
        [] needR() -> haveR := false; dirtyR := false; send r.passL()
            write(age(), "philosopher", id, "sends right fork")
        [] needL() -> haveL := false; dirtyL := false; send l.passR()
            write(age(), "philosopher", id, "sends left fork")
        ni
      od
   end server
end Servant

resource Main()
   import Philosopher, Servant
   var num_phil := 5; getarg(1, num_phil)
   var run_time : int := 60; getarg(2, run_time)
   var s[1:num_phil] : cap Servant, p[1:num_phil] : cap Philosopher
   var think[1:num_phil] : int := ([num_phil] 5)
   var eat[1:num_phil] : int := ([num_phil] 2)
   fa i := 1 to num_phil -> getarg(2*i+1, think[i]); getarg(2*i+2, eat[i]) af
   fa i := 1 to num_phil -> s[i] := create Servant(i)
      create Philosopher(s[i], i, 1000*think[i], 1000*eat[i])
   af
   printf("%4d philosophers created; think, eat times in seconds:\n", num_phil)
   fa i := 1 to num_phil -> printf("%4d", think[i]) af; printf("\n")
   fa i := 1 to num_phil -> printf("%4d",   eat[i]) af; printf("\n")
   fa i := 1 to num_phil ->
      send s[i].links(s[((i-2) mod num_phil)+1], s[(i mod num_phil)+1])
   af
   send s[1].forks(true, true, true, true)
   fa i := 2 to num_phil-1 ->
      send s[i].forks(false, false, true, false)
   af
   send s[num_phil].forks(false, false, false, false)
   nap(1000*run_time); write("must stop now"); stop
end Main

/* ............... Example compile and run(s)

% sr -o didp didp.sr
% ./didp 5 10
   5 philosophers created; think, eat times in seconds:
   5    5    5    5    5
   2    2    2    2    2
622 philosopher 2 is hungry
626 philosopher 2 has right fork
629 philosopher 1 sends right fork
```

```
 632 philosopher 2 got left fork
 635 philosopher 2 has both forks
 652 philosopher 4 is hungry
 655 philosopher 4 has right fork
 663 philosopher 3 sends right fork
 671 philosopher 4 got left fork
 674 philosopher 4 has both forks
1653 philosopher 2 is finished eating
1893 philosopher 4 is finished eating
3312 philosopher 2 is hungry
3317 philosopher 2 has right fork
3318 philosopher 2 has left fork
3319 philosopher 2 has both forks
3442 philosopher 5 is hungry
3445 philosopher 1 sends left fork
3447 philosopher 4 sends right fork
3448 philosopher 5 got right fork
3449 philosopher 5 got left fork
3450 philosopher 5 has both forks
3592 philosopher 3 is hungry
3595 philosopher 4 sends left fork
3597 philosopher 3 got right fork
3922 philosopher 1 is hungry
4143 philosopher 5 is finished eating
4146 philosopher 5 sends right fork
4147 philosopher 1 got left fork
4913 philosopher 2 is finished eating
4916 philosopher 2 sends right fork
4917 philosopher 2 sends left fork
4919 philosopher 3 got left fork
4920 philosopher 3 has both forks
4921 philosopher 1 got right fork
4922 philosopher 1 has both forks
5382 philosopher 4 is hungry
5386 philosopher 5 sends left fork
5388 philosopher 4 got right fork
5842 philosopher 1 is finished eating
5912 philosopher 3 is finished eating
5915 philosopher 3 sends right fork
5917 philosopher 4 got left fork
5918 philosopher 4 has both forks
6452 philosopher 5 is hungry
6456 philosopher 1 sends left fork
6458 philosopher 5 got right fork
6979 philosopher 4 is finished eating
6990 philosopher 4 sends right fork
6992 philosopher 5 got left fork
6994 philosopher 5 has both forks
7123 philosopher 4 is hungry
7133 philosopher 4 has left fork
8143 philosopher 3 is hungry
8147 philosopher 5 is finished eating
8148 philosopher 5 sends left fork
8149 philosopher 3 has left fork
8151 philosopher 4 got right fork
```

```
8152 philosopher 4 has both forks
9372 philosopher 2 is hungry
9376 philosopher 3 sends dirty left fork
9378 philosopher 1 sends right fork
9379 philosopher 2 got right fork
9380 philosopher 2 got left fork
9381 philosopher 2 has both forks
9432 philosopher 2 is finished eating
9436 philosopher 2 sends right fork
9438 philosopher 3 got left fork
9592 philosopher 4 is finished eating
9595 philosopher 4 sends left fork
9597 philosopher 3 got right fork
9598 philosopher 3 has both forks
9783 philosopher 3 is finished eating
must stop now
                                              */
```

6.5   RPC and Client-Server Programming

Program 6.16 shows a template for coding services performed on behalf of client processes by a server process. Clients make remote procedure calls, described in Section 6.1, to a server process, requesting that a service be performed and a value returned. The server process can be running on the same machine, or on a different machine that is better suited in terms of architecture or computing load for performing the service. The server process uses an **in** statement to wait for invocations from the clients for services. The server can use the **forward** statement to perform the service for the client asynchronously in a new process while the server waits for and accepts new requests for service from clients. Or the server can perform the service synchronously for the client while newly arriving requests for service wait.

Program 6.16: Client-Server Programming Using **forward**.

```
resource server
   optype serve = (client_id, want_done, service_time: int) returns value : real
   op service : serve
body server()
   op do_service : serve

   write("server is alive")
   reply

   do true ->
      in service(client_id, want_done, service_time) returns value ->
         if want_done = 1 or want_done = 3 ->
            write("age=", age(), "service", want_done,
               "forwarded for client", client_id, "for", service_time, "ms")
            forward do_service(client_id, want_done, service_time)
         [] want_done = 2 ->
            write("age=", age(), "service", want_done,
               "starting for client", client_id, "for", service_time, "ms")
```

```
                value := do_service(client_id, want_done, service_time)
            [] else ->
                write("age=", age(), "service", want_done,
                    "not implemented, client=", client_id)
                value := -1
            fi
        ni
    od

    proc do_service(client_id, want_done, service_time) returns value
        nap(service_time)
        value := random()*want_done
        write("age=", age(), "service", want_done,
            "completed for client", client_id, "value=", value)
      end do_service
end server

resource client
    import server
body client(client_id : int; server_cap : cap server; num_services : int;
        max_nap_time, max_service_time : int)
    write("client", client_id, "is alive, num_services=", num_services,
        "max_nap_time=", max_nap_time, "max_service_time=", max_service_time)
    reply

    var napping, service_time, want_done : int
    var value : real
    do true ->
        napping:=int(random(1000*max_nap_time))
        write("age=", age(), "client", client_id, "napping for", napping, "ms")
        nap(napping)
        service_time := int(random(1000*max_service_time))
        want_done := int(random(num_services)) + 1
        write("age=", age(), "client", client_id, "wants service", want_done,
            "for", service_time, "ms")
        value := server_cap.service(client_id, want_done, service_time)
        write("age=", age(), "client", client_id, "value returned=", value)
    od
end client

resource client_server()
    import server, client
    var server_cap : cap server
    var num_clients : int := 20,  num_services : int := 5
    var max_nap_time : int := 10, max_service_time : int :=  3
    var run_time : int := 60

    getarg(1, num_clients);  getarg(2, num_services)
    getarg(3, max_nap_time); getarg(4, max_service_time)
    getarg(5, run_time)
    server_cap := create server()
    write(num_clients, "clients and", num_services,
        "services starting with max nap time of", max_nap_time,
        "and max service time of", max_service_time)
    fa i := 1 to num_clients ->
```

```
        create client(i, server_cap, num_services, max_nap_time,
            max_service_time)
   af
   nap(1000*run_time); write("must stop now"); stop
end client_server

/* .............. Example compile and run(s)

% sr -o client_server client_server.sr
% ./client_server 10 5 5 3 5
server is alive
10 clients and 5 services starting with max nap time of 5
  and max service time of 3
client 1 is alive, num_services= 5 max_nap_time= 5 max_service_time= 3
age= 29 client 1 napping for 3463 ms
client 2 is alive, num_services= 5 max_nap_time= 5 max_service_time= 3
age= 407 client 2 napping for 3935 ms
client 3 is alive, num_services= 5 max_nap_time= 5 max_service_time= 3
age= 477 client 3 napping for 3864 ms
client 4 is alive, num_services= 5 max_nap_time= 5 max_service_time= 3
age= 493 client 4 napping for 1062 ms
client 5 is alive, num_services= 5 max_nap_time= 5 max_service_time= 3
age= 506 client 5 napping for 4224 ms
client 6 is alive, num_services= 5 max_nap_time= 5 max_service_time= 3
age= 521 client 6 napping for 468 ms
client 7 is alive, num_services= 5 max_nap_time= 5 max_service_time= 3
age= 538 client 7 napping for 1924 ms
client 8 is alive, num_services= 5 max_nap_time= 5 max_service_time= 3
age= 552 client 8 napping for 3574 ms
client 9 is alive, num_services= 5 max_nap_time= 5 max_service_time= 3
age= 575 client 9 napping for 3217 ms
client 10 is alive, num_services= 5 max_nap_time= 5 max_service_time= 3
age= 588 client 10 napping for 773 ms
age= 1000 client 6 wants service 3 for 1672 ms
age= 1005 service 3 forwarded for client 6 for 1672 ms
age= 1370 client 10 wants service 5 for 891 ms
age= 1374 service 5 not implemented, client= 10
age= 1377 client 10 value returned= -1.00000
age= 1384 client 10 napping for 517 ms
age= 1561 client 4 wants service 3 for 1889 ms
age= 1565 service 3 forwarded for client 4 for 1889 ms
age= 1910 client 10 wants service 4 for 2320 ms
age= 1915 service 4 not implemented, client= 10
age= 1918 client 10 value returned= -1.00000
age= 1921 client 10 napping for 3203 ms
age= 2470 client 7 wants service 3 for 157 ms
age= 2475 service 3 forwarded for client 7 for 157 ms
age= 2652 service 3 completed for client 7 value= 1.25272
age= 2658 client 7 value returned= 1.25272
age= 2662 client 7 napping for 1076 ms
age= 2690 service 3 completed for client 6 value= 1.01472
age= 2695 client 6 value returned= 1.01472
age= 2698 client 6 napping for 3029 ms
age= 3471 service 3 completed for client 4 value= 1.68025
age= 3476 client 4 value returned= 1.68025
```

```
age= 3478 client 4 napping for 436 ms
age= 3711 client 1 wants service 3 for 2273 ms
age= 3715 service 3 forwarded for client 1 for 2273 ms
age= 3751 client 7 wants service 3 for 518 ms
age= 3754 service 3 forwarded for client 7 for 518 ms
age= 3800 client 9 wants service 1 for 2632 ms
age= 3804 service 1 forwarded for client 9 for 2632 ms
age= 3920 client 4 wants service 3 for 12 ms
age= 3924 service 3 forwarded for client 4 for 12 ms
age= 3970 service 3 completed for client 4 value= 0.484111
age= 4063 client 4 value returned= 0.484111
age= 4067 client 4 napping for 4859 ms
age= 4130 client 8 wants service 2 for 2637 ms
age= 4134 service 2 starting for client 8 for 2637 ms
age= 4280 service 3 completed for client 7 value= 0.390791
age= 4285 client 7 value returned= 0.390791
age= 4287 client 7 napping for 721 ms
age= 4350 client 3 wants service 1 for 1175 ms
age= 4400 client 2 wants service 3 for 2469 ms
age= 4740 client 5 wants service 3 for 1235 ms
age= 5033 client 7 wants service 3 for 176 ms
age= 5130 client 10 wants service 1 for 1881 ms
must stop now
                                            */
```

6.6   Summary of Operations and Invocations

As shown above, SR supports a number of different operations and their invocations, which are summarized in this section.

- Each SR program has one main resource, which is created automatically when the program is run. It is the resource that is imported by no other resources and is usually the last resource in the file (or last file) containing the program source code.

- This resource may then create or "enliven" other resources declared and compiled with the main one.

- A resource may contain procedures that can be referenced from within the resource or from other resources.

- A resource may contain one or more processes.

- A process can call a procedure (a proc or procedure) in the same resource, analogous to procedure calling in a sequential high-level language.

- A process can call a procedure (a proc) in a different resource. This is a *remote procedure call*. A process wanting to call a procedure in another resource needs a *capability* for that resource. The process can be given that capability when the process is created, e.g., create Strangelove(pc) in Program 2.15, or when the resource containing the called procedure is created, e.g., fac_cap := create factorial() in Program 2.13.

- SR provides facilities for processes to communicate: the **send** and **receive** statements. The latter is a special form of the **in** statement. All **receives**, and **ins** without an **else**, are blocking. The **send** invocation is non-blocking, giving us (asynchronous) *message passing.*

- To *rendezvous* with another process, use **call** instead of **send**.

- A process can **send** to a **proc** in the same resource or in another resource, performing *dynamic process creation* (see Program 6.7). The **send** does not block while the code in the **proc** is executed in the context of a new process (a **call** would block while the **proc** is executed by the new process).

- **receive name(a, b, ..., c)** is an abbreviation for

    ```
    in name(x, y, ..., z) ->
        a := x
        b := y
        ...
        c := z
    ni
    ```

- General counting *semaphores* are implemented using an operation, and **send** and **receive**: V is a **send** and P is a **receive**.

- There are three kinds of *operation invocation*:

    1.   send rcap.$name_1$(...)
    2.   call rcap.$name_2$(...)
    3.   x = rcap.$name_3$(...)

- The **rcap** capability above is only needed to **call** or **send** from one resource to another.

- There are three kinds of *operation implementation*:

    1.   proc $name_4$(...) /* if function */ returns ...
          ...
          end $name_4$
    2.   receive $name_5$(...)
    3.   in $name_6$(...) st *condition* ->
          ...
          [] $name_7$(...) returns ... ->
          ...
          [] $name_8$(...) returns ... st *condition* ->
          ...
          [] ...
          ...
          [] else ... # optional
          ni

- If $name_2$ or $name_3$ are the same identifier as $name_4$ above, then we have a (possibly *remote*) *procedure* or function *call.*

- If $name_1$ is the same identifier as $name_4$, then we have *dynamic process creation.*

- If $name_1$ is the same identifier as $name_5$, then we have *asynchronous message passing.*

- If $name_2$ is the same identifier as $name_5$, then we have *synchronous message passing*.

- If $name_2$ or $name_3$ is the same identifier as one of $name_6$, $name_7$, or $name_8$, then we have the Ada *rendezvous*. The **in** in SR is like the Ada **accept** and the SR **st** *condition* is like the Ada **select**.

6.7 Lab: Rendezvous

Objectives

To learn about SR's **in** statement, which implements the rendezvous principle.

Preparation Before Lab

Read Section 6.4 on the rendezvous and the **in** statement. Look at Programs 6.8, 6.9, and 6.10. No semaphores or monitors are allowed in any of these assignments.

6.7.1 Assignment: Fair Baboons

Write a rendezvous version of the fair baboons program done in Lab 4.5.

6.7.2 Assignment: Sleeping Barber

Write a rendezvous version of the sleeping barber program done in Lab 4.5.

Also generalize the program so that there can be any number of barbers, each with its own room and barber chair. There is still just one common waiting waiting room with n chairs for all the customers. There are m customers, $m > n + k$, where k is the number of barbers.

Have the program take values from the command line to override default values for the number of customers, the number of chairs in the shop, the number of barbers, and the maximum delay grow (walk around) and cut times for each customer. In other words, to use default values internal to the program, it is run as **slba**, but to override all defaults, the program is run as

```
sr -o slba slba.sr
slba m n k g c
```

where m is the number of customers, n the number of waiting room chairs, k the number of barbers, and g and c the maximum grow and cut times for a customer, respectively.

6.7.3 Assignment: Fair Readers and Writers

Write a rendezvous version of the fair readers and writers program done in Lab 4.5. See the monitor version in Program 5.6 and note that the SR built-in function ? corresponds to **_empty**.

In other words, rewrite the SR version of the readers and writers program, Programs 4.8 and 6.10, so that it uses the **in** statement, and so that it is fair to both readers and writers, that is, neither readers nor writers can starve.

Note the following. First, you should take the version that allows starvation, Figure 6.10, seed the random number generator with a non-zero constant, and set up numbers for the command line that show starvation of writers occurring. You will have to add new variables like **read_nap_time** and **write_nap_time** to the program with default values overridden from the command line. With the random number generator seeded and the random numbers reproducible, you will have an easier time debugging. Then modify the code to prevent starvation of both readers and writers.

Remember the ? operator described in Section 6.4.2. You may find this extremely useful in converting the readers-writers program (**in** statement version) to be free of starvation of both readers and writers.

You must turn in three outputs, one showing starvation in the original version of the program, then two more: one showing that readers cannot starve in your version of the program and the other that writers cannot starve in your version of the program. You must highlight with yellow or other color where starvation is occurring and where it is prevented, as described in **For Every Lab** in Lab 2.3.

6.7.4   Assignment: Fair Dining Philosophers

Write a rendezvous version of the fair dining philosophers program done in Lab 4.5.

To make the central server **in** statement version of the dining philosophers starvation free, note the following. First, you should take the version that allows starvation, Programs 4.5 and 6.9, seed the random number generator with a constant, and set up numbers for the command line that show starvation of a philosopher occurring. With the random number generator seeded, you will have an easier time debugging. Then hack away at the code to prevent starvation of a philosopher.

Read Lab 2.3 **For Every Lab** again, paying attention to what it says about starvation. You must turn in two outputs, one showing starvation, the other one showing it prevented. You must highlight with yellow or other color where starvation is occurring and where it is prevented, as described in **For Every Lab** in Lab 2.3.

6.7.5   Assignment: Fraternity Party

Write a rendezvous version of the fraternity party program done in Lab 4.5.

6.7.6   Assignment: Bakery

Write a rendezvous version of the bakery program done in Lab 4.5.

6.7.7   Assignment: Banker's Algorithm

Write an SR program that simulates a computing system in which there are n resource types and $E = (e_1, e_2, \ldots, e_n)$ existing resources of each type. There are m processes in the system. To apply the Banker's Algorithm (see Section 6.8 in [8], Section 7.5 in [20], Section 4.5 in [21], or Section 6.5 in [24]), we must know the total demands of the processes in advance, and this information is in the m by n matrix T. Your program will simulate the processes requesting and returning resources from a central server process. In order to avoid deadlock, your program will need to compute (using the Banker's Algorithm) if granting the request will keep the system in a safe state. Use SR's message passing and/or rendezvous (**in** statement).

When a process submits a request for resources, $R = (r_1, r_2, \ldots, r_n)$, i.e., it wants r_i units of type i, the central server will satisfy the request atomically, that is, the central server will allocate either all or none of the requested resources to the process, depending on whether or not the resulting state is safe. If the state would be unsafe, the process blocks and the central server remembers the request. Also, a request by a process for more resources than are currently available must be queued by the central server (the process must block). Requests by a process for more resources than exist or for more resources than its maximum demand will abort the process.

Processes may also release resources. If there are blocked processes with outstanding requests, then the freed resources may be used to satisfy outstanding requests, but only if the resulting state is safe.

Note that starvation is possible in this program. It could happen like this. You are keeping a FCFS queue of processes whose requests could not be granted because the resulting state would be unsafe or the resources are currently not available. As other processes release resources, the central server scans the queue of blocked processes and grants resources to those for which it is safe. The problem is that processes could possibly starve if they are repeatedly passed over as the central server scans the queue.

If, while trying to decide if a state is safe or not, you finish off as many processes as possible one-by-one, and there are some left, you do not have to backtrack and try a different order. In other words, one order of finishing off processes is good enough: either they all finish and the state is safe, or you end up with some potentially deadlocked ones, and the state is unsafe.

In order to test your program thoroughly, you will need to drive the processes with input scripts. Use reasonable values for m, n, E, and T. Each process will have its own input file. The input data for each process will consist of lines of the following form:

nap_time   request_release_flag $r_1 r_2 \ldots r_n$

A process will read lines from its input file and first nap for the napping time input, then send a request or release to the central server (Banker) of the resources ($r_1, r_2, \ldots, r_n$). The process will then block until its request has been granted (no need to block for a release of resources).

6.7.8   Assignment: Distributed Dining Philosophers

After reading Section 6.4.4, answer the following questions:

1. Does the solution to the dining philosophers shown in Program 6.15 have the desirable "maximal parallelism" property?

2. Show that deadlock is possible if philosopher 1 is initially given both forks in the clean state (that is, all forks are handed out initially clean).

3. Show that deadlock is possible if the other philosophers are given dirty forks initially, in addition to the two given initially to philosopher 1 (that is, all forks are handed out initially dirty).

6.8   More Animation with XTANGO

Program 6.17 is an enhanced version of Program 6.15 with additional print statements to drive the animation interpreter. The philosophers are represented by small circles equally spaced around a large circle representing the table. Forks are represented with very small circles. The state of each philosopher is represented by a different color: green for hungry and blue for eating. Dirty forks are orange. See the comments in the program for an explanation of the animation `printf` statements. Figure 6.4 shows a snapshot of the window during the animation.

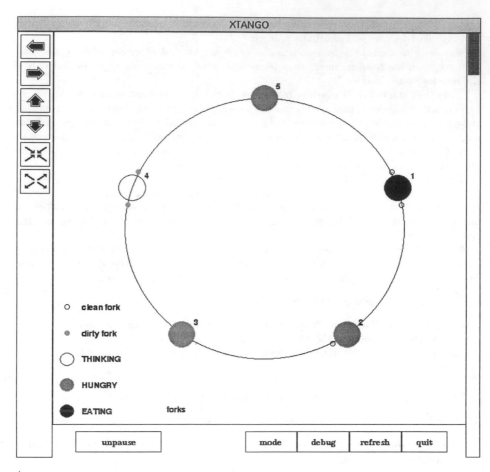

Figure 6.4: Animation Snapshot of the Distributed Dining Philosophers.

Program 6.17: Animation of Distributed Dining Philosophers.

```
# Distributed Dining Philosophers.  Based on the example in Section 13.3 of
# "The SR Programming Language: Concurrency in Practice", by Greg Andrews and
# Ron Olsson, Benjamin/Cummings, 1993.  The algorithm is from Chandy and Misra,
# "Drinking Philosophers Problem", ACM TOPLAS v 6, n 4, Oct 1984, pp 632-646.
# Usage:  a.out [n secs t_secs e_secs t_secs e_secs ...]
# (for n philosophers, secs seconds running time, t_secs max thinking seconds,
# e_secs max eating seconds for each philosopher)
#
# Modified for xtango's animator interpreter.  All normal SR simulation output
# is done with write, and all xtango animator commands are output with printf.
#
resource Philosopher
    import Servant
body Philosopher(myservant : cap Servant; id, thinking, eating: int)
```

```
    process phil
        do true ->
            nap(int(random(thinking)))
            printf("comment "); write(age(), "philosopher", id, "is hungry")

##### animator #####v
# Change a hungry philosopher's symbol to be solid green.
            printf("color %d green\n", id); printf("fill %d solid\n", id)
##### animator #####^

            myservant.getforks()

##### animator #####v
# Change an eating philosopher's symbol to be solid blue.
            printf("color %d blue\n", id)
##### animator #####^

            nap(int(random(eating)))

##### animator #####v
# Change a thinking philosopher's symbol to an outline black circle.
            printf("fill %d outline\n", id); printf("color %d black\n", id)
##### animator #####^

            myservant.relforks()
        od
    end phil
end Philosopher

resource Servant
    op getforks(), relforks()
    op needR(), needL(), passR(), passL()
    op links(r, l : cap Servant)
    op forks(haveR, dirtyR, haveL, dirtyL : bool)

##### animator #####v
# This op and the variables below are used to hold the symbol id numbers of
# the left and right fork symbols and where the left and right forks are
# placed next to the philosopher when it possesses them.
    op fork_ids(forkR, forkL, holderR, holderL : int)
##### animator #####^

body Servant(id : int)
    op hungry(), eat()
    var r, l : cap Servant
    var haveR, dirtyR, haveL, dirtyL : bool

##### animator #####v
    var forkR, forkL, holderR, holderL : int
##### animator #####^

    proc getforks()
        send hungry(); receive eat()
    end
```

```
    process server
       receive links(r, l)
       receive forks(haveR, dirtyR, haveL, dirtyL)


##### animator #####v
# Move a left or right fork initially given to this philosopher to be next
# to the philosopher.
       receive fork_ids(forkR, forkL, holderR, holderL)
       if haveR -> printf("jumpto %d %d\n", forkR, holderR) fi
       if haveL -> printf("jumpto %d %d\n", forkL, holderL) fi
       if dirtyR -> printf("color %d orange\n", forkR)
                    printf("fill  %d  solid\n", forkR) fi
       if dirtyL -> printf("color %d orange\n", forkL)
                    printf("fill  %d  solid\n", forkL) fi
##### animator #####^

       do true->
          in hungry() ->
             if ~haveR -> send r.needL()
             [] else ->
                printf("comment ")
                write(age(), "philosopher", id, "has right fork")
             fi
             if ~haveL -> send l.needR()
             [] else ->
                printf("comment ")
                write(age(), "philosopher", id, "has left fork")
             fi
             do ~(haveR & haveL) ->
                in passR() -> haveR := true; dirtyR := false
                   printf("comment ")
                   write(age(), "philosopher", id, "got right fork")


##### animator #####v
# Move the fork from where it was to be next to this philosopher and then
# change its symbol to be a black outline circle i.e. not dirty.  Also raise
# the fork's symbol to the closest viewing plane to make it more visible.
                   printf("moveto %d %d\n", forkR, holderR)
                   printf("fill  %d  outline\n", forkR)
                   printf("color %d black\n", forkR)
                   printf("raise %d\n", forkR)
##### animator #####^

                [] passL() -> haveL := true; dirtyL := false
                   printf("comment ")
                   write(age(), "philosopher", id, "got left fork")


##### animator #####v
# Ditto.
                   printf("moveto %d %d\n", forkL, holderL)
                   printf("fill  %d  outline\n", forkL)
                   printf("color %d black\n", forkL)
                   printf("raise %d\n", forkL)
##### animator #####^
```

```
                   [] needR() st dirtyR -> haveR := false; dirtyR := false
                      send r.passL(); send r.needL()
                      printf("comment ")
                      write(age(), "philosopher", id, "sends dirty right fork")
                   [] needL() st dirtyL -> haveL := false; dirtyL := false
                      send l.passR(); send l.needR()
                      printf("comment ")
                      write(age(), "philosopher", id, "sends dirty left fork")
                   ni
                od
                printf("comment ")
                write(age(), "philosopher", id, "has both forks")
                send eat(); dirtyR := true; dirtyL := true
                receive relforks()
                printf("comment ")
                write(age(), "philosopher", id, "is finished eating")

##### animator #####v
# Now that the philosopher has finished eating, its forks are dirty so
# change their symbols to be solid orange circles.
                printf("color %d orange\n", forkL)
                printf("fill %d  solid\n", forkL)
                printf("color %d orange\n", forkR)
                printf("fill %d  solid\n", forkR)
##### animator #####^

                [] needR() -> haveR := false; dirtyR := false; send r.passL()
                   printf("comment ")
                   write(age(), "philosopher", id, "sends right fork")
                [] needL() -> haveL := false; dirtyL := false; send l.passR()
                   printf("comment ")
                   write(age(), "philosopher", id, "sends left fork")
                ni
             od
          end server
    end Servant

resource Main()
    import Philosopher, Servant
    var n := 5; getarg(1, n); var runtime := 60; getarg(2, runtime)
    var s[1:n] : cap Servant; var p[1:n] : cap Philosopher
    var think[1:n] : int := ([n] 5); var eat[1:n] : int := ([n] 2)
    fa i := 1 to n -> getarg(2*i+1, think[i]); getarg(2*i+2, eat[i]) af
    printf("comment "); write(n, "philosophers; think, eat times in seconds:")
    printf("comment "); fa i := 1 to n -> writes(" ", think[i]) af; write()
    printf("comment "); fa i := 1 to n -> writes(" ",   eat[i]) af; write()

##### animator #####v
# Change coordinates so 0,0 is the center, then create a big black outline
# circle to be the table.
   printf("coords -1.5 -1.5 1.5 1.5\n")
   printf("circle 1000  0.0  0.0 1.0  black outline\n")
# Put some annotated symbols on the screen.
   printf("circle 1001 -1.4 -0.6 0.02 black outline\n")
```

```
    printf("text    1002 -1.3 -0.625 0  black clean fork\n")
    printf("circle 1003 -1.4 -0.8 0.02 orange solid\n")
    printf("text    1004 -1.3 -0.825 0  black dirty fork\n")
    printf("circle 1005 -1.4 -1.0 0.05 black outline\n")
    printf("text    1006 -1.3 -1.025 0  black THINKING\n")
    printf("circle 1007 -1.4 -1.2 0.05 green solid\n")
    printf("text    1008 -1.3 -1.225 0  black HUNGRY\n")
    printf("circle 1009 -1.4 -1.4 0.05 blue  solid\n")
    printf("text    1010 -1.3 -1.425 0  black EATING\n")
# Put a clean set of forks, small black outline circles, near the table.
    printf("text    1011 %7.2f -1.41 0  black forks\n", -1.0+0.05*(n+1))
    fa i := 1 to n ->
        printf("circle %d %7.2f -1.4 0.02 black outline\n",
            3000+i-1, -1.0+0.05*i)
    af
    const TWO_PI := 2.0*acos(-1.0)
    fa i := 1 to n ->
# Put the philosophers, black outline circles, around the table.
        printf("circle %d %7.2f %7.2f 0.1 black outline\n",
            i, sin(i*(TWO_PI/n)), cos(i*(TWO_PI/n)))
# Number the philosophers.
        printf("text %d %7.2f %7.2f 1 black %d\n",
            2000+i, sin(i*(TWO_PI/n))+0.1, cos(i*(TWO_PI/n))+0.1, i)
# Put nearly invisible circles (points) on the left and right side of each
# philosopher to be places the forks can be moved to when the philosopher
# gets possession of a fork.
        printf("circle %d %7.2f %7.2f 0.001 black outline\n",
            4000+2*i, sin(i*(TWO_PI/n)-0.12), cos(i*(TWO_PI/n)-0.13))
        printf("circle %d %7.2f %7.2f 0.001 black outline\n",
            4000+2*i+1, sin(i*(TWO_PI/n)+0.12), cos(i*(TWO_PI/n)+0.13))
    af
##### animator #####^

    fa i := 1 to n -> s[i] := create Servant(i)
        create Philosopher(s[i], i, 1000*think[i], 1000*eat[i])
    af
    fa i := 1 to n -> send s[i].links(s[((i-2) mod n)+1], s[(i mod n)+1]) af
    send s[1].forks(true, true, true, true)
    fa i := 2 to n-1 -> send s[i].forks(false, false, true, false) af
    send s[n].forks(false, false, false, false)


##### animator #####v
# Send to each philosopher the xtango animator symbol id's of the two forks
# the philosopher needs to eat and the places where possessed forks are to
# be moved next to the philosopher.
    fa i := 1 to n ->
        send s[i].fork_ids(3000+((i-1) mod n), 3000+(i mod n),
            4000+2*i, 4000+2*i+1)
    af
##### animator #####^

    nap(1000*runtime); printf("comment "); write("must stop now"); stop
end Main

/* .............. Example compile and run(s)
```

```
% sr -o didp didp.sr
% ./didp 5 10 | animator
Press RUN ANIMATION button to begin

XTANGO Version 1.52

 5 philosophers; think, eat times in seconds:
  5 5 5 5 5
  2 2 2 2 2
430 philosopher 1 is hungry
434 philosopher 1 has right fork
435 philosopher 1 has left fork
440 philosopher 1 has both forks
1352 philosopher 2 is hungry
1354 philosopher 2 has left fork
1562 philosopher 5 is hungry
1564 philosopher 4 sends left fork
1565 philosopher 5 got right fork
2012 philosopher 3 is hungry
2014 philosopher 3 has left fork
2223 philosopher 1 is finished eating
2226 philosopher 1 sends left fork
2227 philosopher 1 sends right fork
2228 philosopher 2 got right fork
2232 philosopher 2 has both forks
2233 philosopher 5 got left fork
2235 philosopher 5 has both forks
2355 philosopher 5 is finished eating
2692 philosopher 4 is hungry
2694 philosopher 5 sends right fork
2695 philosopher 4 got left fork
2993 philosopher 2 is finished eating
2995 philosopher 2 sends left fork
2997 philosopher 3 got right fork
2999 philosopher 3 has both forks
3272 philosopher 5 is hungry
3274 philosopher 5 has left fork
4924 philosopher 3 is finished eating
4926 philosopher 3 sends left fork
4927 philosopher 4 got right fork
7791 philosopher 4 has both forks
7792 philosopher 2 is hungry
7794 philosopher 1 is hungry
7796 philosopher 2 has right fork
7798 philosopher 3 sends right fork
7799 philosopher 5 sends dirty left fork
7800 philosopher 2 sends dirty right fork
7801 philosopher 2 got left fork
7803 philosopher 1 got right fork
7806 philosopher 1 got left fork
7808 philosopher 1 has both forks
8912 philosopher 3 is hungry
9123 philosopher 4 is finished eating
9125 philosopher 4 sends left fork
```

```
9126 philosopher 4 sends right fork
9127 philosopher 5 got right fork
9133 philosopher 3 got left fork
9453 philosopher 1 is finished eating
9455 philosopher 1 sends right fork
9456 philosopher 1 sends left fork
9458 philosopher 5 got left fork
9460 philosopher 5 has both forks
9461 philosopher 2 got right fork
9463 philosopher 2 has both forks
must stop now
                                        */
```

6.9   Lab: Algorithm Animation

Objectives

To get a better understanding of the rendezvous, particularly when used in programs that prevent starvation, through algorithm animation.

Preparation Before Lab

Read Sections 6.8. Study Program 6.17.

6.9.1   Assignment

Animate one of the programs you wrote for Lab 6.7.

Chapter 7

Parallel Computing

So far, most of our SR examples have been concerned with race conditions, critical sections, mutual exclusion, process synchronization, and interprocess communication in the context of an operating systems course. In this book, the term *concurrent programming* will be used to describe the types of programs we have looked at in the previous chapters. Although there are no standard definitions for concurrent programming and parallel computing, this book will use the latter to describe programs that perform numerically intensive computations and that have processes that communicate or need to synchronize relatively frequently. Specialized architectures, other than shared-memory multiprocessors and clusters of workstations on a local area network, may be involved.

The terms *coarse-grained* and *fine-grained* concurrency can be used to indicate the amount of synchronization relative to the amount of computation. Sometimes the term *medium-grained* concurrency is used as well. In a uniprocessor with multiple functional units (one for integer addition, another for floating-point multiplication, another for branch prediction, etc.), the concurrency is fine-grained because synchronization is needed at the individual instruction level: one unit may need to wait for the result produced by another unit. A vector unit in a Cray computer is another example. So is an SIMD (single instruction, multiple data) machine, such as the Connection Machine CM-2, where each instruction is executed by all the processors in lockstep.

A shared-memory multiprocessor running a collection of processes that use semaphores or locks for process synchronization can be either medium-grained or coarse-grained, depending on how frequently the semaphores and locks are accessed. A collection of workstations on a local area network cooperating to solve some problem is an example of coarse-grained parallelism. Since it is more expensive to communicate or synchronize over the network than through shared memory, it is more efficient and cost effective to do large amounts of computation between synchronization steps.

This chapter is a brief introduction to the parallel computing capabilities of SR. There are many books on parallel computer architectures and parallel programming. See, for example, [7, 16, 19].

We start with some examples of coarse-grained parallelism.

7.1 Coarse-Grained Concurrency in SR

Program 7.1 solves the N queens problem and is an example of coarse-grained parallelism. If fact, the processes in this program do not share any data and therefore do not need to be synchronized at all. For each different square in the first column on which a queen can be

Number of Calls	Array Size	Average Time (ms) Per Call		
		Local Call	Remote Call	Send/Receive
1000	1	0.055	0.119	0.574
1000	1000	3.404	4.703	6.205
1000	10000	35.405	52.837	59.879

Figure 7.1: Communication Times.

placed, a process is created to compute how many ways the rest of the board can be filled with mutually non-attacking queens. Each process produces a separate count.

If all the processes wanted to accumulate their counts into the same variable, then synchronization would be required to avoid race conditions. Program 7.2 shows each process using a semaphore to get exclusive access to the total count. When all processes have finished, a **final** block prints out the total count.

As described in Section 3.3, an SR program with multiple processes can run on a uniprocessor with the concurrency simulated. The sample output shown in Program 7.1 was produced on a uniprocessor workstation. Notice that using the **srl -L 1** compilation method to increase interleaving among the SR processes (1) starts all (8 by default) processes at about the same time, and (2) about doubles the total execution time due to the increased context switching overhead.

In a laboratory exercise, you will run the code in Program 7.1 on a shared-memory multiprocessor using just one of the CPUs (**setenv SR_PARALLEL 1**) and then run it again using all available CPUs (**setenv SR_PARALLEL 8**). You will be asked to observe and explain the differences in the output. This program could be easily modified to run on a cluster of workstations (see Program 3.5).

Program 7.3 is the semaphore version of the dining philosophers program with code added, as described in Section 3.3, to start each philosopher process running on a machine named on the command line. If **king**, **queen**, **violet**, **rose**, and **lily** are the names of machines on a local area network, all sharing a common disk partition of user files mounted with NFS, then the command

```
sr -o dpla dpla.sr
dpla runtime naptime king queen violet rose lily
```

would start five philosopher processes, one per physical machine. The program's command line parsing has been written so that *runtime* and *naptime* are optional arguments.

Only two changes must be made to the original semaphore version. The first is adding the block of code commented with **starts HERE** and **ends HERE**. This block parses the command line and reads in the machine names. The second change is adding **on machine_cap[i]** to the statement that creates each philosopher resource. This addition causes the resource and all its processes to run in the virtual machine on the other physical machine.

This is an example of coarse-grained parallelism since the philosophers only communicate with the central server process when they get hungry and when they are finished eating. Relative to the time the philosophers spend thinking and eating, this synchronization is infrequent.

How much does synchronization cost? How much time does it take? Program 7.4 compares the time it takes to call a procedure on the same machine with calling a procedure doing the same thing on a different machine. Also included is the time to send a message to a different machine and get a reply back. The procedures **proc_ping** and **local_ping** both take an integer array as a **var** (copy in, copy out) parameter and add one to each entry of the array. The program starts up an instance of resource **remote** on a different physical machine, then calls `local_ping` some number of times, e.g., 1000, and `proc_ping` the same number of times. The times in milliseconds are shown in Figure 7.1. Times for different sizes of the array are also shown.

The output of the program shows it takes about 5 to 6 milliseconds per 1000 integers to copy an array across a local area network (standard ethernet) using SR.

Program 7.1: N Queens Problem with Independent Helper Processes.

```
resource helper(c : int; board[1:*] : int)
   var N : int
   var solution : int := 0

   procedure safe(row, column: int; board[1:*]: int) returns answer: bool
      fa j := 1 to column-1 ->
         if board[column-j] = row
               or board[column-j] = row-j
               or board[column-j] = row+j ->
            answer := false
            return
         fi
      af
      answer := true
   end safe

   procedure place(column: int; board[1:*]: int)
      fa row := 1 to N ->
         board[column] := row
         if safe(row, column, board) ->
            if column = N -> solution++
            [] column<N -> place(column+1, board)
            fi
         fi
         board[column] := 0
      af
   end place

   process go
      N := ub(board)
      write("age=", age(), "Helper", board[1], "starting.")
      place(c, board)
      write("age=", age(), "There are", solution,
         "solutions with a 1st column queen in row", board[1])
   end go
end helper

resource EightQueens()
   import helper
   var N : int := 8
   getarg(1, N)
   var board[1:N]: int := ([N] 0)
   write("Solutions to the", N, "queens problem:")
   fa r := 1 to N ->
      board[1] := r
      create helper(2, board)
```

```
    af
end EightQueens

/* ............... Example compile and run(s)

% sr -o Nqueens Nqueens.sr
% ./Nqueens
Solutions to the 8 queens problem:
age= 43 Helper 1 starting.
age= 426 There are 4 solutions with a 1st column queen in row 1
age= 447 Helper 2 starting.
age= 1056 There are 8 solutions with a 1st column queen in row 2
age= 1068 Helper 3 starting.
age= 1754 There are 16 solutions with a 1st column queen in row 3
age= 1760 Helper 4 starting.
age= 2140 There are 18 solutions with a 1st column queen in row 4
age= 2145 Helper 5 starting.
age= 2549 There are 18 solutions with a 1st column queen in row 5
age= 2554 Helper 6 starting.
age= 2920 There are 16 solutions with a 1st column queen in row 6
age= 2925 Helper 7 starting.
age= 3314 There are 8 solutions with a 1st column queen in row 7
age= 3320 Helper 8 starting.
age= 3605 There are 4 solutions with a 1st column queen in row 8
% sr -c Nqueens.sr
% srl -L 1 -o Nqueens helper EightQueens
% ./Nqueens
Solutions to the 8 queens problem:
age= 35 Helper 1 starting.
age= 53 Helper 2 starting.
age= 65 Helper 3 starting.
age= 85 Helper 4 starting.
age= 102 Helper 5 starting.
age= 116 Helper 6 starting.
age= 135 Helper 7 starting.
age= 149 Helper 8 starting.
age= 8504 There are 4 solutions with a 1st column queen in row 1
age= 8532 There are 4 solutions with a 1st column queen in row 8
age= 9364 There are 16 solutions with a 1st column queen in row 3
age= 9376 There are 16 solutions with a 1st column queen in row 6
age= 9394 There are 18 solutions with a 1st column queen in row 4
age= 9399 There are 18 solutions with a 1st column queen in row 5
age= 9441 There are 8 solutions with a 1st column queen in row 2
age= 9447 There are 8 solutions with a 1st column queen in row 7
                                              */
```

Program 7.2: N Queens Problem with Shared Solution Count.

```
resource EightQueens()
    var N : int := 8

    procedure safe(row, column: int; board[1:*]: int) returns answer: bool
        fa j := 1 to column-1 ->
```

```
            if board[column-j] = row or board[column-j] = row-j
                or board[column-j] = row+j ->
              answer := false
              return
          fi
      af
      answer := true
    end safe

    procedure place(column: int; board[1:*]: int; ref num_found : int)
        fa row := 1 to N ->
          board[column] := row
          if safe(row, column, board) ->
              if column = N -> num_found++
              [] column < N -> place(column+1, board, num_found)
              fi
          fi
          board[column] := 0
        af
    end place

    var solution : int := 0
    sem mutex := 1
    getarg(1, N)
    write("Solutions to the", N, "queens problem:")

    process helper(r := 1 to N)
        var board[1:N]: int := ([N] 0)
        var num_found : int := 0
        board[1] := r
        place(2, board, num_found)
        write("There are", num_found,
            "solutions with a 1st column queen in row", r)
        P(mutex); solution +:= num_found; V(mutex)
    end helper

    final
        write("There are", solution, "solutions overall.")
    end final
end EightQueens

/* .............. Example compile and run(s)

% sr -o Nqueens Nqueens.sr
% ./Nqueens
Solutions to the 8 queens problem:
There are 4 solutions with a 1st column queen in row 1
There are 16 solutions with a 1st column queen in row 3
There are 18 solutions with a 1st column queen in row 5
There are 8 solutions with a 1st column queen in row 7
There are 8 solutions with a 1st column queen in row 2
There are 18 solutions with a 1st column queen in row 4
There are 4 solutions with a 1st column queen in row 8
There are 16 solutions with a 1st column queen in row 6
There are 92 solutions overall.
```

```
% sr -c Nqueens.sr
% srl -L 1 -o Nqueens EightQueens
% ./Nqueens
Solutions to the 8 queens problem:
There are 4 solutions with a 1st column queen in row 1
There are 4 solutions with a 1st column queen in row 8
There are 16 solutions with a 1st column queen in row 3
There are 16 solutions with a 1st column queen in row 6
There are 18 solutions with a 1st column queen in row 4
There are 18 solutions with a 1st column queen in row 5
There are 8 solutions with a 1st column queen in row 2
There are 8 solutions with a 1st column queen in row 7
There are 92 solutions overall.
                                             */
```

Program 7.3: Multi-Machine Dining Philosophers.

```
resource philosopher
    import dining_server
body philosopher(i : int; dcap : cap dining_server; nap_time: int)
    write("philosopher", i, "is alive, nap_time =", nap_time)
    reply

    procedure think()
       var napping : int
       napping := int(random(1000*nap_time))
       writes("age=",age(),", philosopher ",i," thinking for ",napping," ms\n")
       nap(napping)
    end think

    procedure eat()
       var napping : int
       napping := int(random(1000*nap_time))
       writes("age=",age(),", philosopher ",i," eating for ",napping," ms\n")
       nap(napping)
    end eat

    do true ->
       think()
       writes("age=", age(), ", philosopher ", i, " hungry\n")
       dcap.take_forks(i)
       writes("age=", age(), ", philosopher ", i, " taken forks\n")
       eat()
       dcap.put_forks(i)
       writes("age=", age(), ", philosopher ", i, " returned forks\n")
    od
end philosopher

resource dining_server
    op take_forks(i : int), put_forks(i : int)
body dining_server(num_phil : int)
    write("dining server for", num_phil, "philosophers is alive")
    sem mutex := 1
```

```
     type states = enum(thinking, hungry, eating)
     var state[1:num_phil] : states := ([num_phil] thinking)
     sem phil[1:num_phil] := ([num_phil] 0)

     procedure left(i : int) returns lft : int
        if i=1 -> lft := num_phil [] else -> lft := i-1 fi
     end left

     procedure right(i : int) returns rgh : int
        if i=num_phil -> rgh := 1 [] else -> rgh := i+1 fi
     end right

     procedure test(i : int)
        if state[i] = hungry and state[left(i)] ~= eating
              and state[right(i)] ~= eating ->
           state[i] := eating
           V(phil[i])
        fi
     end test

   proc take_forks(i)
      P(mutex)
      state[i] := hungry
      test(i)
      V(mutex)
      P(phil[i])
   end take_forks

   proc put_forks(i)
      P(mutex)
      state[i] := thinking
      test(left(i)); test(right(i))
      V(mutex)
   end put_forks
end dining_server

resource start()
   import philosopher, dining_server
   var nap_time : int := 3
   var run_time : int := 60

   var stat : int                 # added code starts HERE #####
   var num_machines : int
   var machine_name : string[64]
   var first_machine_name_position : int
   # First argument on command line is run time.
   first_machine_name_position := 1
   stat := getarg(first_machine_name_position, run_time)
   if stat = EOF ->      # first argument is nonexistent
      write("Some machine names needed!"); stop
   [] stat = 0 ->    # first argument is not a number but machine name
      write("Using default value of", run_time, "for run time.")
   [] else -> first_machine_name_position++
   fi
   if run_time <= 1 ->
```

```
      write("run time =", run_time, "is too small."); stop
   fi
   # Second argument on command line is nap time.
   stat := getarg(first_machine_name_position, nap_time)
   if stat = EOF ->    # second argument is nonexistent
      write("Some machine names needed!"); stop
   [] stat = 0 ->     # second argument is not a number but machine name
      write("Using default value of", nap_time, "for nap time.")
   [] else -> first_machine_name_position++
   fi
   if nap_time <= 1 ->
      write("nap time =", nap_time, "is too small."); stop
   fi
   num_machines := numargs() - first_machine_name_position + 1
   if num_machines <= 0 ->
      write("Some machine names needed!"); stop
   fi
   # Subsequent arguments on command line are machine names.
   var machine_cap[1:num_machines] : cap vm
   fa i := 1 to num_machines ->
      getarg(first_machine_name_position + i - 1, machine_name)
      machine_cap[i] := create vm() on machine_name
      if machine_cap[i] = null ->
         write("Cannot create vm on", machine_name, "so aborting."); stop
      fi
      write("Virtual machine starting up on machine", machine_name)
   af                            # added code ends HERE except ...

   var num_phil : int
   num_phil := num_machines        # ... for this line HERE ...
   var dcap : cap dining_server
   dcap := create dining_server(num_phil)
   write(num_phil, "dining philosophers starting with run time",
      run_time, "and nap time", nap_time)
   fa i := 1 to num_phil ->
      create philosopher(i, dcap, nap_time)
         on machine_cap[i]        # ... and for this line HERE
   af
   write("all philosophers started")
   nap(1000*run_time); write("must stop now"); stop
end start

/* .............. Example compile and run(s)

% sr -o dphiLAN dphiLAN.sr
% ./dphiLAN 10 2 king queen lily rose violet
Virtual machine starting up on machine king
Virtual machine starting up on machine queen
Virtual machine starting up on machine lily
Virtual machine starting up on machine rose
Virtual machine starting up on machine violet
dining server for 5 philosophers is alive
5 dining philosophers starting with run time 10 and nap time 2
philosopher 1 is alive, nap_time = 2
philosopher 2 is alive, nap_time = 2
```

```
philosopher 3 is alive, nap_time = 2
age=6426, philosopher 2 thinking for 756 ms
age=8002, philosopher 1 thinking for 706 ms
age=3840, philosopher 3 thinking for 1934 ms
philosopher 4 is alive, nap_time = 2
philosopher 5 is alive, nap_time = 2
all philosophers started
age=300, philosopher 5 thinking for 809 ms
age=1950, philosopher 4 thinking for 40 ms
age=1990, philosopher 4 hungry
age=2120, philosopher 4 taken forks
age=2120, philosopher 4 eating for 493 ms
age=8711, philosopher 1 hungry
age=7187, philosopher 2 hungry
age=2640, philosopher 4 returned forks
age=8727, philosopher 1 taken forks
age=8727, philosopher 1 eating for 1269 ms
age=2640, philosopher 4 thinking for 1928 ms
age=1120, philosopher 5 hungry
age=5780, philosopher 3 hungry
age=8430, philosopher 2 taken forks
age=2170, philosopher 5 taken forks
age=10043, philosopher 1 returned forks
age=8431, philosopher 2 eating for 1405 ms
age=10051, philosopher 1 thinking for 1275 ms
age=2170, philosopher 5 eating for 1193 ms
age=4580, philosopher 4 hungry
age=3380, philosopher 5 returned forks
age=5080, philosopher 4 taken forks
age=5080, philosopher 4 eating for 176 ms
age=3380, philosopher 5 thinking for 1795 ms
age=11332, philosopher 1 hungry
age=9864, philosopher 2 returned forks
age=7230, philosopher 3 taken forks
age=5290, philosopher 4 returned forks
age=5290, philosopher 4 thinking for 1872 ms
age=9864, philosopher 2 thinking for 1255 ms
age=11469, philosopher 1 taken forks
age=11470, philosopher 1 eating for 754 ms
age=7240, philosopher 3 eating for 1380 ms
age=12256, philosopher 1 returned forks
age=12263, philosopher 1 thinking for 1365 ms
age=11127, philosopher 2 hungry
age=8630, philosopher 3 returned forks
age=11263, philosopher 2 taken forks
age=11263, philosopher 2 eating for 637 ms
age=8630, philosopher 3 thinking for 742 ms
age=5180, philosopher 5 hungry
age=5230, philosopher 5 taken forks
age=5230, philosopher 5 eating for 68 ms
age=5310, philosopher 5 returned forks
age=5310, philosopher 5 thinking for 904 ms
age=7180, philosopher 4 hungry
age=7200, philosopher 4 taken forks
age=7200, philosopher 4 eating for 449 ms
```

```
age=11916, philosopher 2 returned forks
age=9390, philosopher 3 hungry
age=13640, philosopher 1 hungry
age=11917, philosopher 2 thinking for 1900 ms
age=13669, philosopher 1 taken forks
age=13670, philosopher 1 eating for 1466 ms
age=7660, philosopher 4 returned forks
age=9610, philosopher 3 taken forks
age=9610, philosopher 3 eating for 1640 ms
age=7660, philosopher 4 thinking for 1019 ms
age=6230, philosopher 5 hungry
age=8690, philosopher 4 hungry
age=7280, philosopher 5 taken forks
age=15209, philosopher 1 returned forks
age=7290, philosopher 5 eating for 924 ms
age=15231, philosopher 1 thinking for 202 ms
age=13827, philosopher 2 hungry
age=15451, philosopher 1 hungry
age=11260, philosopher 3 returned forks
age=13903, philosopher 2 taken forks
age=13904, philosopher 2 eating for 1128 ms
age=11260, philosopher 3 thinking for 1252 ms
age=9920, philosopher 4 taken forks
age=8230, philosopher 5 returned forks
age=8230, philosopher 5 thinking for 1698 ms
age=9920, philosopher 4 eating for 1158 ms
age=15046, philosopher 2 returned forks
age=16665, philosopher 1 taken forks
age=16671, philosopher 1 eating for 456 ms
age=15047, philosopher 2 thinking for 934 ms
age=12530, philosopher 3 hungry
age=17142, philosopher 1 returned forks
age=17154, philosopher 1 thinking for 863 ms
age=11100, philosopher 4 returned forks
age=13050, philosopher 3 taken forks
age=11110, philosopher 4 thinking for 491 ms
age=13050, philosopher 3 eating for 1054 ms
age=15987, philosopher 2 hungry
age=11610, philosopher 4 hungry
age=9940, philosopher 5 hungry
age=9960, philosopher 5 taken forks
age=9970, philosopher 5 eating for 1160 ms
age=18022, philosopher 1 hungry
must stop now
                                           */
```

Program 7.4: Inter- vs. Intra-Machine Communication Time.

```
resource remote
    import local
    op proc_ping(var a[1:*] : int)
    op send_ping(val a[1:*] : int)
body remote(lcap : cap local; array_size : int)
```

```
   write("remote is alive")
   reply

   proc proc_ping(a)
      fa i := 1 to ub(a) -> a[i]++ af
   end proc_ping

   var a[1:array_size] : int
   do true ->
      receive send_ping(a)
      fa i := 1 to ub(a) -> a[i]++ af
      send lcap.recv_ping(a)
   od
end remote

resource local
   import remote
   op recv_ping(val a[1:*] : int)
body local()
   var num_roundtrips : int := 1000
   var array_size : int := 1000
   var machine_name : string[64] := "king"
   getarg(1, num_roundtrips)
   getarg(2, array_size)
   getarg(3, machine_name)
   if num_roundtrips < 1 ->
      write("num_roundtrips =", num_roundtrips, "is too small."); stop
   fi
   if array_size < 1 ->
      write("array_size =", array_size, "is too small."); stop
   fi
   var machine_cap : cap vm
   machine_cap := create vm() on machine_name
   if machine_cap = null ->
      write("Cannot create vm on", machine_name, "so aborting."); stop
   fi
   write("Virtual machine starting up on machine", machine_name)

   procedure local_ping(ref a[1:*] : int)
      fa i := 1 to ub(a) -> a[i]++ af
   end local_ping

   var rcap : cap remote
   rcap := create remote(myresource(), array_size)
   write("local starting with num_roundtrips=", num_roundtrips,
      "and array_size=", array_size)
   var a[1:array_size] : int := ([array_size] 1)
   var start_time, end_time : int
   write("first a=", a[1], "last a=", a[array_size])

   start_time := age()
   fa i := 1 to num_roundtrips -> rcap.proc_ping(a) af
   end_time := age()
   write("first a=", a[1], "last a=", a[array_size])
   write("average roundtrip time for remote procedure call is",
```

```
            (end_time-start_time)/real(num_roundtrips), "ms")

    start_time := age()
    fa i := 1 to num_roundtrips -> local_ping(a) af
    end_time := age()
    write("first a=", a[1], "last a=", a[array_size])
    write("average roundtrip time for local procedure call is",
        (end_time-start_time)/real(num_roundtrips), "ms")

    start_time := age()
    fa i := 1 to num_roundtrips -> rcap.send_ping(a); receive recv_ping(a) af
    end_time := age()
    write("first a=", a[1], "last a=", a[array_size])
    write("average roundtrip time for send/receive is",
        (end_time-start_time)/real(num_roundtrips), "ms")
    stop
end local

/* .............. Example compile and run(s)

% sr -o ping ping.sr
% ./ping 1000 1 queen
Virtual machine starting up on machine queen
remote is alive
local starting with num_roundtrips= 1000 and array_size= 1
first a= 1 last a= 1
first a= 1001 last a= 1001
average roundtrip time for remote procedure call is 0.119000 ms
first a= 2001 last a= 2001
average roundtrip time for local procedure call is 0.0550000 ms
first a= 3001 last a= 3001
average roundtrip time for send/receive is 0.574000 ms
% ./ping 1000 1000 queen
Virtual machine starting up on machine queen
remote is alive
local starting with num_roundtrips= 1000 and array_size= 1000
first a= 1 last a= 1
first a= 1001 last a= 1001
average roundtrip time for remote procedure call is 4.70300 ms
first a= 2001 last a= 2001
average roundtrip time for local procedure call is 3.40400 ms
first a= 3001 last a= 3001
average roundtrip time for send/receive is 6.20500 ms
% ./ping 1000 10000 queen
Virtual machine starting up on machine queen
remote is alive
local starting with num_roundtrips= 1000 and array_size= 10000
first a= 1 last a= 1
first a= 1001 last a= 1001
average roundtrip time for remote procedure call is 52.8370 ms
first a= 2001 last a= 2001
average roundtrip time for local procedure call is 35.4050 ms
first a= 3001 last a= 3001
average roundtrip time for send/receive is 59.8790 ms
                                          */
```

7.2   Patterns of Communication

The following three programs show different patterns of process communication. Program 7.5 illustrates a way to set up nearest-neighbor communication in an $m \times n$ grid of processes. The program shows that an operation (op) can be declared as a rectangular array:

```
op neighbor[1:m,1:n](item : int)
```

This feature of SR allows one to set up grids or hypercubes of communication channels between processes. Each process in the grid implements one entry in the array **neighbor** of operations with a **receive** and uses it to receive values sent by other processes.

As shown in Section 6.2.3, a **send** to an operation implemented with a **proc** is a form of dynamic process creation. Thus, the **send** to **query** inside the **fa** loop starts up a process for each of the points on the grid. The processes execute in parallel. Each process on the grid generates a random number and sends the number to its north, south, east, and west nearest neighbors (those that exist). Each interior process on the grid then calculates and prints the average of the values it receives from its nearest neighbors.

The processes do not need to share memory since there are no shared variables (the global parameters, m and n, could be broadcast to all processes). This type of communication pattern is compatible with architectures in which the CPUs have local memories and are arranged in a grid with nearest-neighbor hardware communication links and a global broadcast bus.

In the example in Program 7.6, each process in the collection of processes can communicate with all others. After **driver** creates all the **node** processes, **driver** sends to each **node** an array of capabilities to all the **nodes**. Each **node** generates a random number and sends it to all of the other **nodes**, then receives the values generated by all the other **nodes** and computes the average. Program 7.7 does the same thing. This time **driver** sends to each **node** an array of capabilities to the operations implemented in the **nodes** for their communication, rather than an array of capabilities to the **nodes** themselves.

Again, there is no need for the processes to share memory. This communication pattern is suitable for a collection of workstations on a local area network and other distributed memory computing environments that are fully connected.

Program 7.5: Grid Communication Pattern.

```
resource test_query()
    var m : int := 4, n : int := 5; getarg(1, m); getarg(2, n)
    op query(id, jd : int)
    op neighbor[1:m,1:n](item : int)

    write("test_query is alive for", m, "by", n)

    proc query(id, jd) # must be op...proc instead of procedure if sending to it
        var item : int, total : int, average : real
        item := int(random(1,9))
        writes("process query ", id, ",", jd, " generated item ", item, "\n")
        if id < m-1 and jd > 1 and jd < n -> send neighbor[id+1,jd](item) fi
        if id > 2   and jd > 1 and jd < n -> send neighbor[id-1,jd](item) fi
        if jd < n-1 and id > 1 and id < m -> send neighbor[id,jd+1](item) fi
        if jd > 2   and id > 1 and id < m -> send neighbor[id,jd-1](item) fi
```

```
      total := 0
      if id ~= 1 and jd ~= 1 and id ~= m and jd ~= n ->
          fa i:= 1 to 4 -> receive neighbor[id,jd](item)
              total := total + item
          af
          average := total/4.0
          writes("process query ", id, ",", jd, " average is ", average, "\n")
      fi
   end query

   fa i := 1 to m, j := 1 to n -> send query(i, j) af
end test_query

/* .............. Example compile and run(s)

% sr -o grid grid.sr
% ./grid
test_query is alive for 4 by 5
process query 1,1 generated item 4
process query 1,2 generated item 6
process query 1,3 generated item 5
process query 1,4 generated item 4
process query 1,5 generated item 8
process query 2,1 generated item 5
process query 2,2 generated item 3
process query 2,3 generated item 4
process query 2,4 generated item 7
process query 2,5 generated item 7
process query 3,1 generated item 7
process query 3,2 generated item 7
process query 3,3 generated item 7
process query 3,4 generated item 1
process query 3,5 generated item 1
process query 4,1 generated item 2
process query 4,2 generated item 1
process query 4,3 generated item 5
process query 4,4 generated item 7
process query 4,5 generated item 1
process query 2,2 average is 5.50000
process query 2,3 average is 5.50000
process query 2,4 average is 4.00000
process query 3,2 average is 4.50000
process query 3,3 average is 4.25000
process query 3,4 average is 5.50000
                                        */
```

Program 7.6: Totally-Connected Communication Pattern, version 1.

```
resource node
   import driver
   op item_msg(item : int)
   op all_the_caps(node_cap[1:*] : cap node)
body node(id: int; num_nodes : int; driver_cap: cap driver)
```

```
      write("node", id, "is alive"); reply
      var item : int, total : real, average : real
      var node_cap[1:num_nodes] : cap node
      receive all_the_caps(node_cap)
      item := int(random(1,10))
      write("node", id, "generated item", item)
      fa i := 1 to num_nodes st i ~= id -> send node_cap[i].item_msg(item) af
      total := 0
      fa i := 1 to num_nodes-1 -> receive item_msg(item)
         total := total + item
      af
      average := total/(num_nodes-1)
      send driver_cap.avg_msg(id, average)
      write("node", id, "is finished")
   end node

resource driver
   import node
   op avg_msg(id : int; average : real)
body driver()
   write("driver is alive")
   var num_nodes : int := 5; getarg(1, num_nodes)
   var driver_cap : cap driver
   var node_cap[1:num_nodes] : cap node
   var id : int, average : real
   driver_cap := myresource()
   fa i := 1 to num_nodes ->
      node_cap[i] := create node(i, num_nodes, driver_cap)
   af
   fa i := 1 to num_nodes -> send node_cap[i].all_the_caps(node_cap) af
   fa i := 1 to num_nodes -> receive avg_msg(id, average)
      write("node", id, "reporting back average of", average)
   af
   write("driver is finished")
end driver

/* .............. Example compile and run(s)

% sr -o send1 send1.sr
% ./send1
driver is alive
node 1 is alive
node 2 is alive
node 3 is alive
node 4 is alive
node 5 is alive
node 1 generated item 6
node 2 generated item 3
node 3 generated item 4
node 4 generated item 4
node 5 generated item 3
node 5 is finished
node 1 is finished
node 2 is finished
node 3 is finished
```

```
node 4 is finished
node 5 reporting back average of 4.25000
node 1 reporting back average of 3.50000
node 2 reporting back average of 4.25000
node 3 reporting back average of 4.00000
node 4 reporting back average of 4.00000
driver is finished
                                              */
```

Program 7.7: Totally-Connected Communication Pattern, version 2.

```
global Ops
   optype pipe(value : int)
end Ops

resource node
   import Ops, driver
   op item_msg : pipe
   op all_the_caps(pipe_cap[1:*] : cap pipe)
body node(id: int; num_nodes : int; driver_cap: cap driver)
   write("node", id, "is alive"); reply
   var item : int, total : real, average : real
   var pipe_cap[1:num_nodes] : cap pipe
   receive all_the_caps(pipe_cap)
   item := int(random(1,10))
   write("node", id, "generated item", item)
   fa i := 1 to num_nodes st i ~= id -> send pipe_cap[i](item) af
   total := 0
   fa i := 1 to num_nodes-1 -> receive item_msg(item)
      total := total + item
   af
   average := total/(num_nodes-1)
   send driver_cap.avg_msg(id, average)
   write("node", id, "is finished")
end node

resource driver
   import Ops, node
   op avg_msg(id : int; average : real)
body driver()
   write("driver is alive")
   var num_nodes : int := 5; getarg(1, num_nodes)
   var driver_cap : cap driver
   var node_cap[1:num_nodes] : cap node
   var pipe_cap[1:num_nodes] : cap pipe
   var id : int, average : real
   driver_cap := myresource()
   fa i := 1 to num_nodes ->
      node_cap[i] := create node(i, num_nodes, driver_cap)
      pipe_cap[i] := node_cap[i].item_msg
   af
   fa i := 1 to num_nodes -> send node_cap[i].all_the_caps(pipe_cap) af
   fa i := 1 to num_nodes -> receive avg_msg(id, average)
```

```
        write("node", id, "reporting back average of", average)
    af
    write("driver is finished")
end driver

/* .............. Example compile and run(s)

% sr -o send2 send2.sr
% ./send2
driver is alive
node 1 is alive
node 2 is alive
node 3 is alive
node 4 is alive
node 5 is alive
node 1 generated item 6
node 2 generated item 1
node 3 generated item 1
node 4 generated item 6
node 5 generated item 6
node 5 is finished
node 1 is finished
node 2 is finished
node 3 is finished
node 4 is finished
node 5 reporting back average of 3.50000
node 1 reporting back average of 3.50000
node 2 reporting back average of 4.75000
node 3 reporting back average of 4.75000
node 4 reporting back average of 3.50000
driver is finished
                                                                    */
```

7.3   Data Parallelism

If a problem will take a lot of work to solve or if it has a lot of data, and if the work or data
can be split up or subdivided into independent chunks, then a process with its own CPU
can be allocated to each chunk of data or work. These two styles or paradigms of parallel
programming are called *data parallelism* and *master/worker*, respectively. The example SR
programs in this section show some parallel algorithms that split up the data: multiplying
matrices, sorting numbers, and computing a function iteratively over a rectangular domain.
The last example is a parallel algorithm that divides up the work: solving the N queens
problem. Some of the programs require shared memory; others use message passing.

7.3.1   Shared Memory Examples

In matrix multiplication, if there are many CPUs available on a shared-memory machine,
one CPU can be assigned to compute each entry of the product matrix. Programs 7.8 and
7.9 show two ways to do this in SR. The first program starts up as many processes as there
are entries in the product matrix, using a quantifier

```
    (i := 1 to l, j := 1 to n)
```

on the **process multiply** statement. Since we do not want to print the result before it is completely computed, we use a semaphore **done** on which the main program waits. This use of a semaphore is called a *barrier*. The process executing the top-level code cannot continue past the **fa** loop containing P(done) until all of the **multiply** processes have completed. Note that the **multiply** processes are not started up until the **process** statement is reached in the top-level code, at which point the input matrices have been read and initialized. This program needs shared memory to store the matrices so they can be accessed by all the processes. It has coarse-grained concurrency.

Instead of a barrier semaphore to make sure the contents of the product matrix are not printed before the results have been computed, a **final** block can be used. Remove the semaphore **done** from Program 7.8 and change the code that prints the resulting product matrix to

```
    final
        write("The result c is")
        fa i := 1 to l ->
            fa j := 1 to n -> writes(" ", c[i,j]) af
            writes("\n")
        af
    end final
  end matrix_multiply
```

The code in a **final** block in the main resource is not executed until all top-level code in the resource and all processes started with the **process** statement in the resource have finished. As seen in Program 2.16, a **final** block in an instance of a created resource is executed when the resource is destroyed.

We can also change the quantified **process multiply** to an op and **proc multiply(i,j)** pair and use a **send** inside a **fa** loop to start the concurrent processes, as was done in Program 7.5. We would still need either the barrier semaphore or the **final** block technique to delay printing the product matrix until completely computed.

The second version of matrix multiplication, Program 7.9, uses a new language construct. Instead of using an explicit **process** statement, we declare a procedure **multiply** whose arguments are the entry of the product to compute. The SR **co** statement is used to call the procedure concurrently or in parallel for as many times as there are entries in the product matrix. When all concurrent calls are done, the contents of the product matrix can be printed.

The general form of the **co** statement is

   co *statement* // *statement* // ··· **oc**

where each statement is an invocation of an operation, this is, a **send**, a **call**, or an assignment of a function call to a variable. The **co** statement can be quantified in the same way that the **process** statement in Program 7.8 is. In Program 7.9, the quantified **co** does all $l \times n$ calls of **multiply** concurrently. This program requires shared memory and exhibits coarse-grained concurrency.

In Program 7.5, the **fa** loop containing the **send** to **query** can be replaced with the following

```
    co (i := 1 to m, j := 1 to n) call query(i, j)
    oc
```

to achieve the same concurrently executing processes.

The above two matrix multiplication programs start up a fixed number of processes, dependent on the amount of data, for the duration of the computation. Program 7.10

modifies the quicksort algorithm introduced in a sequential SR example, Program 2.14, so that the two recursive calls to procedure qs are done in parallel with a co statement. This is medium-grained concurrency. In this program, the number of processes varies during the computation. The program requires shared memory since the original unsorted array is sorted in place, that is, it is passed by reference (ref).

Many problems in physics can be solved by repeated calculation of the values of some function over a rectangular domain until convergence is achieved. At each successive step, the new value of the function at a point is calculated from the old values of the nearest neighbors of the point. If all the new values are close to the old values, the computation has converged and the algorithm terminates.

This type of algorithm is suitable for the same CPU grid architecture mentioned in connection with Program 7.5. We can assign a process and CPU to each point in the rectangular domain. After each process has used the old values of the function from its nearest neighbors to compute a new value, it has to wait for all the other processes to finish their step before it can do another iteration. One way to implement this synchronization is with a barrier, similar to the one in Program 7.8. Instead of a single semaphore, we use a collection of semaphores and a separate barrier process barrier_coordinator, as shown in Program 7.11. In a lab exercise, you will be asked to discover the race condition that can result if the semaphore barrier_sem_release were a simple semaphore rather than an array.

Since this program uses semaphores, it requires shared memory. In a distributed memory environment, the semaphores could be replaced with a semaphore server process that accepts P and V types of messages from other processes.

Program 7.8: Matrix Multiplication with process.

```
resource matrix_multiply()
    var l, m, n : int
    sem done := 0
    writes("Enter the matrix sizes (l, m, n): "); read(l, m, n)
    var a[1:l,1:m], b[1:m,1:n], c[1:l,1:n] : int
    write("Enter the rows of matrix a one at a time")
    fa i := 1 to l, j := 1 to m -> read(a[i,j]) af
    write("Enter the rows of matrix b one at a time")
    fa i := 1 to m, j := 1 to n -> read(b[i,j]) af

    process multiply(i := 1 to l, j := 1 to n)
        var inner_prod := 0
        fa k := 1 to m ->
            inner_prod := inner_prod + a[i, k]*b[k, j]
        af
        c[i,j] := inner_prod
        V(done)
    end multiply

    fa i := 1 to l, j:= 1 to n -> P(done) af     # wait for 'em
    write("The result c is")
    fa i := 1 to l ->
        fa j := 1 to n -> writes(" ", c[i,j]) af
        writes("\n")
    af
end matrix_multiply
```

```
/* .............. Example compile and run(s)

% sr -o mat1 mat1.sr
% ./mat1
Enter the matrix sizes (l, m, n): 2 3 4
Enter the rows of matrix a one at a time
1 2 3
4 5 6
Enter the rows of matrix b one at a time
7 8 9 10
11 12 13 14
15 16 17 18
The result c is
 74 80 86 92
 173 188 203 218

                                              */
```

Program 7.9: Matrix Multiplication with co.

```
resource matrix_multiply()
    var l, m, n : int
    writes("Enter the matrix sizes (l, m, n): "); read(l, m, n)
    var a[1:l,1:m], b[1:m,1:n], c[1:l,1:n] : int
    write("Enter the rows of matrix a one at a time")
    fa i := 1 to l, j := 1 to m -> read(a[i,j]) af
    write("Enter the rows of matrix b one at a time")
    fa i := 1 to m, j := 1 to n -> read(b[i,j]) af

    procedure multiply(i, j : int)
        var inner_prod := 0
        fa k := 1 to m ->
            inner_prod := inner_prod + a[i,k]*b[k,j]
        af
        c[i,j] := inner_prod
    end multiply

    co (i := 1 to l, j := 1 to n) call multiply(i, j)
    oc

    write("The result c is")
    fa i := 1 to l ->
        fa j := 1 to n -> writes(" ", c[i,j]) af
        writes("\n")
    af
end matrix_multiply

/* .............. Example compile and run(s)

% sr -o mat2 mat2.sr
% ./mat2
Enter the matrix sizes (l, m, n): 4 3 2
Enter the rows of matrix a one at a time
20 19 18
```

```
17 16 15
14 13 12
11 10 9
Enter the rows of matrix b one at a time
8 7
6 5
4 3
The result c is
 346 289
 292 244
 238 199
 184 154
                                                     */
```

Program 7.10: Quicksort with co.

```
resource quicksort()
   procedure print_nums(ref a[1:*] : int; val left, right : int)
      fa i := left to right -> writes(" ", a[i]) af
      writes("\n")
   end print_nums

   var N : int := 10;        getarg(1, N)
   var RANGE : int := 100; getarg(2, RANGE)
   write("sorting", N, "numbers between 1 and", RANGE)
   var nums[1:N] : int

   procedure qs(val left, right : int)
      if right-left <= 0 -> return fi  # allow this for co ... // ... oc below
      var pivot := nums[left]
      var l := left, r := right
      write("qs: sorting", left, "through", right)

      var not_done := true
      do not_done ->
         if nums[l+1] > pivot ->  # needs to be moved to other end of nums
            do (r > l+1) and (nums[r] > pivot) -> r-- od  # find one to swap
            if r > l+1 -> l++; nums[r] :=: nums[l]; not_done := l < r-1
            [] else -> not_done := false  # if can't find one to swap, then
            fi                            # nums now partitioned; we are done
         [] else -> l++; not_done := l < r  # need not be moved to other end
         fi
      od  # when this loop finishes, nums[left] is the pivot,
         # nums[left:l] <= pivot and nums[l+1,right] > pivot
         #
                                    #    [pivot, <= | > ]
                                    #    ^       ^ ^ ^
                                    #    |       | | |
                                    # left       l r right
                                    #    |       | | |
                                    #    v       v v v
      nums[left] :=: nums[l]       #    [<=, pivot | > ]
```

```
        # nums[left,1-1] <= pivot, nums[1] = pivot, and nums[1+1,right] > pivot
        # if right-(1+1) = 0, nums[1+1:right] is singleton so sorted
      co qs(1+1, right)
        # nums[1] = pivot is singleton so sorted
      // qs(left, 1-1)
        # if (1-1)-left = 0, nums[left:1-1] is singleton so sorted
      oc
    end qs

# seed(42.0)   # leave in for reproducible random numbers for debugging
  fa i := 1 to N -> nums[i] := int(random(RANGE)+1) af
  write("original numbers"); print_nums(nums, 1, N)
  qs(1, N)
  write("sorted   numbers"); print_nums(nums, 1, N)
  stop
end quicksort
# See page 90 of the October 1992 issue of UNIX Review (v. 10, no. 10).


/* .............. Example compile and run(s)

% sr -o qsrt qsrt.sr
% ./qsrt
sorting 10 numbers between 1 and 100
original numbers
 83 27 50 76 24 38 63 100 2 38
qs: sorting 1 through 10
qs: sorting 1 through 8
qs: sorting 2 through 8
qs: sorting 4 through 8
qs: sorting 4 through 7
qs: sorting 6 through 7
sorted   numbers
 2 24 27 38 38 50 63 76 83 100
% sr -c qsrt.sr
% srl -L 1 -o qsrt quicksort
% ./qsrt
sorting 10 numbers between 1 and 100
original numbers
 66 27 48 82 13 12 5 91 54 77
qs: sorting 1 through 10
qs: sorting 8 through 10
qs: sorting 1 through 6
qs: sorting 8 through 9
qs: sorting 2 through 6
qs: sorting 5 through 6
qs: sorting 2 through 3
sorted   numbers
 5 12 13 27 48 54 66 77 82 91
                                          */
```

Program 7.11: Iterative Grid Computation Using a Barrier.

```
resource test_query()
    var m : int := 4, n : int := 5, num_iterations : int := 10
    getarg(1, m); getarg(2, n); getarg(3, num_iterations)
    op query(id, jd : int)
    op neighbor[1:m,1:n](value : real)
    sem barrier_sem_arrive := 0, barrier_sem_release[1:m,1:n] := ([m] ([n] 0))

    procedure barrier(i, j : int)
        V(barrier_sem_arrive)
        P(barrier_sem_release[i,j])
    end barrier

    write("test_query is alive for", m, "by", n, "and", num_iterations,
        "iterations")

    proc query(id, jd) # must be op...proc instead of procedure if sending to it
        var value, got, total, average, correction : real
        value := real(int(random(0,10*m*n)))
        writes("process query ", id, ",", jd, " generated value ", value, "\n")
        fa iter := 1 to num_iterations ->
            if id < m-1 and jd > 1 and jd < n -> send neighbor[id+1,jd](value) fi
            if id > 2   and jd > 1 and jd < n -> send neighbor[id-1,jd](value) fi
            if jd < n-1 and id > 1 and id < m -> send neighbor[id,jd+1](value) fi
            if jd > 2   and id > 1 and id < m -> send neighbor[id,jd-1](value) fi
            total := 0
            if id ~= 1 and jd ~= 1 and id ~= m and jd ~= n ->
                fa i:= 1 to 4 -> receive neighbor[id,jd](got)
                    total := total + got
                af
                average := total/4.0; correction := average - value
                value := value + correction
                if iter = 1 or iter = num_iterations ->
                    writes("on iteration ", iter, " process query ", id, ",", jd,
                        " new value is ", value, "\n     (correction was ",
                        correction, ")\n")
                fi
            fi
            barrier(id, jd)
        af
    end query

    fa i := 1 to m, j := 1 to n -> send query(i, j) af

    process barrier_coordinator
        do true ->
            # second semaphore must be an array to avoid a race condition
            fa i := 1 to m, j := 1 to n -> P(barrier_sem_arrive) af
            fa i := 1 to m, j := 1 to n -> V(barrier_sem_release[i,j]) af
        od
    end barrier_coordinator
end test_query
```

```
/* .............. Example compile and run(s)

% sr -o barrier_for_grid barrier_for_grid.sr
% ./barrier_for_grid 4 5 25
test_query is alive for 4 by 5 and 25 iterations
process query 1,1 generated value 83.0000
process query 1,2 generated value 58.0000
process query 1,3 generated value 127.000
process query 1,4 generated value 23.0000
process query 1,5 generated value 104.000
process query 2,1 generated value 192.000
process query 2,2 generated value 20.0000
process query 2,3 generated value 134.000
process query 2,4 generated value 65.0000
process query 2,5 generated value 60.0000
process query 3,1 generated value 101.000
process query 3,2 generated value 137.000
process query 3,3 generated value 118.000
process query 3,4 generated value 59.0000
process query 3,5 generated value 152.000
process query 4,1 generated value 47.0000
process query 4,2 generated value 53.0000
process query 4,3 generated value 80.0000
process query 4,4 generated value 171.000
process query 4,5 generated value 177.000
on iteration 1 process query 2,2 new value is 130.250
      (correction was 110.250)
on iteration 1 process query 2,3 new value is 82.5000
      (correction was -51.5000)
on iteration 1 process query 2,4 new value is 69.0000
      (correction was 4.00000)
on iteration 1 process query 3,2 new value is 73.0000
      (correction was -64.0000)
on iteration 1 process query 3,3 new value is 102.500
      (correction was -15.5000)
on iteration 1 process query 3,4 new value is 126.500
      (correction was 67.5000)
on iteration 25 process query 2,2 new value is 111.400
      (correction was 0.000126025)
on iteration 25 process query 2,3 new value is 104.192
      (correction was -0.000133834)
on iteration 25 process query 2,4 new value is 78.1338
      (correction was 0.000126025)
on iteration 25 process query 3,2 new value is 91.4090
      (correction was -9.46347e-05)
on iteration 25 process query 3,3 new value is 100.236
      (correction was 0.000178227)
on iteration 25 process query 3,4 new value is 125.342
      (correction was -9.46347e-05)
RTS warning: blocked process:
 test_query.barrier_coordinator : file barrier_for_grid.sr, line 47
                                  */
```

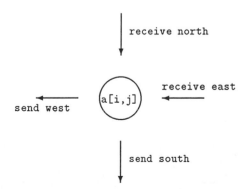

Figure 7.2: One of the Nodes, `multiply(n, i, j, a[i,j])`.

7.3.2   Message Passing Examples

Program 7.12 shows a way, without using a barrier implemented with semaphores in shared memory, to do the iteration synchronization for the processes in Program 7.11. A third dimension is added to the array of operations `neighbor`, one entry for each of the four nearest neighbors. A process that has finished its step will block on its `receive` until its nearest neighbors have finished their steps. The concurrency in both Programs 7.11 and 7.12 is fine-grained because of the extensive communication and synchronization needed during execution.

The final matrix multiplication example, shown in Program 7.13, is based on a *heartbeat* or *systolic* algorithm for multiplying square matrices. See Figures 9.4 and 9.5 of [6] (pages 105-107) for a diagram and pseudo-code of this algorithm. The CPUs, equal in number to the entries in the n-by-n matrices, are arranged in a square array, with only nearest neighbor communication. Therefore, this matrix multiplication algorithm does not need a shared-memory machine to work. To compute $C = A \times B$, each process (CPU) is assigned the entry from matrix A corresponding to its position in the array of CPUs. Zeros are pumped in from the right, and the rows of B are pumped in the top, one per "heartbeat" of the algorithm. The entries of C pop out the left. There are $2n$ heartbeats.

In this program, the processes are arranged in a grid with nearest neighbor communication. The array of operations `sink`, implemented in the main driver resource, is used to absorb the values of B falling off the bottom row of the grid; the array `resu` is used to get the results of the matrix multiplication from the left-most column of the grid. See Figures 7.2 and 7.3. Each `multiply` resource (node) in the grid implements two operations, `north` and `east`, with `receives`. The main driver resource, using the `links` operation of each node, sends to each node the appropriate `north` and `east` capabilities for that node to use for sending to `south` and `west`. Contrast this method of nearest-neighbor communication with the one in Program 7.5, where each process has to "compute" the communication channels of its neighbors using subscripting of the array `neighbor` of operations. This program is an

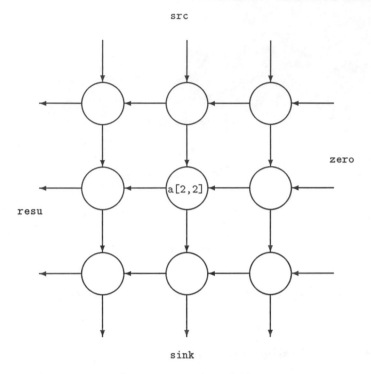

Figure 7.3: A 3-by-3 Grid.

example of fine-grained concurrency.

The last example of this section is a modification of the N queens program presented earlier in Program 2.5. In this version, shown in Program 7.14, the work to be done (counting the ways N queens can be placed on an N-by-N chessboard without attacking each other) is partitioned into chunks. Each chunk consists of counting the ways $N-1$ queens can be placed on an N-by-N chessboard that already has one queen somewhere in the first column. There are N of these chunks of work to be done. The program starts num_processes processes and assigns them chunks of work until all the N chunks are finished. When a process finishes a chunk, it sends its count to the main driver resource and gets another chunk of work to do if there are any chunks left. This is an example of the *master/worker* paradigm of parallel computing. The number of processes is usually less than the number of chunks of work to do, so each worker typically completes several chunks. See Program 7.17 in Section 7.4 for a master/worker shared memory sorting example. Both of these are medium-grained concurrency.

Program 7.12: Iterative Grid Computation Without a Barrier.

```
resource test_query()
    var m : int := 4, n : int := 5, num_iterations : int := 10
    getarg(1, m); getarg(2, n); getarg(3, num_iterations)
    op query(id, jd : int)
    op neighbor[1:m,1:n,1:4](value : real)
```

```
write("test_query is alive for", m, "by", n, "and", num_iterations,
    "iterations")

proc query(id, jd) # must be op...proc instead of procedure if sending to it
    var value, got, total, average, correction : real
    value := real(int(random(0,10*m*n)))
    writes("process query ", id, ",", jd, " generated value ", value, "\n")
    fa iter := 1 to num_iterations ->
        if id < m-1 and jd > 1 and jd < n -> send neighbor[id+1,jd,1](value) fi
        if id > 2   and jd > 1 and jd < n -> send neighbor[id-1,jd,2](value) fi
        if jd < n-1 and id > 1 and id < m -> send neighbor[id,jd+1,3](value) fi
        if jd > 2   and id > 1 and id < m -> send neighbor[id,jd-1,4](value) fi
        total := 0
        if id ~= 1 and jd ~= 1 and id ~= m and jd ~= n ->
            fa i:= 1 to 4 -> receive neighbor[id,jd,i](got)
                total := total + got
            af
            average := total/4.0; correction := average - value
            value := value + correction
            if iter = 1 or iter = num_iterations ->
                writes("on iteration ", iter, " process query ", id, ",", jd,
                    " new value is ", value, "\n      (correction was ",
                    correction, ")\n")
            fi
        fi
        # without third dimension on neighbor op, would need a barrier here
    af
end query

    fa i := 1 to m, j := 1 to n -> send query(i, j) af
end test_query

/* .............. Example compile and run(s)

% sr -o chan4_for_grid chan4_for_grid.sr
% ./chan4_for_grid 4 5 25
test_query is alive for 4 by 5 and 25 iterations
process query 1,1 generated value 120.000
process query 1,2 generated value 67.0000
process query 1,3 generated value 119.000
process query 1,4 generated value 190.000
process query 1,5 generated value 9.00000
process query 2,1 generated value 106.000
process query 2,2 generated value 102.000
process query 2,3 generated value 190.000
process query 2,4 generated value 65.0000
process query 2,5 generated value 59.0000
process query 3,1 generated value 98.0000
process query 3,2 generated value 123.000
process query 3,3 generated value 178.000
process query 3,4 generated value 86.0000
process query 3,5 generated value 155.000
process query 4,1 generated value 95.0000
process query 4,2 generated value 31.0000
process query 4,3 generated value 29.0000
```

```
process query 4,4 generated value 23.0000
process query 4,5 generated value 32.0000
on iteration 1 process query 2,2 new value is 121.500
      (correction was 19.5000)
on iteration 1 process query 2,3 new value is 116.000
      (correction was -74.0000)
on iteration 1 process query 2,4 new value is 131.250
      (correction was 66.2500)
on iteration 1 process query 3,2 new value is 102.250
      (correction was -20.7500)
on iteration 1 process query 3,3 new value is 107.000
      (correction was -71.0000)
on iteration 1 process query 3,4 new value is 105.250
      (correction was 19.2500)
on iteration 25 process query 2,2 new value is 85.1186
      (correction was -2.00090e-05)
on iteration 25 process query 2,3 new value is 96.0685
      (correction was -0.000204908)
on iteration 25 process query 2,4 new value is 108.652
      (correction was -2.00090e-05)
on iteration 25 process query 3,2 new value is 71.4055
      (correction was -0.000144892)
on iteration 25 process query 3,3 new value is 71.5033
      (correction was -2.82970e-05)
on iteration 25 process query 3,4 new value is 89.5388
      (correction was -0.000144892)
                                                   */
```

Program 7.13: Heartbeat or Systolic Matrix Multiplication.

```
global communicate
   optype channel = (x : real)
end communicate

resource multiply
   import communicate
   op north, east : channel
   op links(south, west : cap channel)
body multiply(n, id, jd : int; a : real)
   write("multiply", id, jd, "is alive with n =", n, "and a =", a)
   reply
   var south, west : cap channel
   receive links(south, west)
   var sum, x : real
   fa i := 1 to n ->
      receive north(x)
      send south(x)
      receive east(sum)
      sum +:= a*x
      send west(sum)
   af
end multiply
```

```
resource matrix_multiply()
   import communicate, multiply
   var n : int
   var toss : real
   writes("Enter the matrix size (n): "); read(n)
   var a[1:n,1:n], b[1:n,1:n], c[1:n,1:n] : real
   var mcap[1:n,1:n] : cap multiply
   op resu[1:n], sink[1:n] : channel
   var south, west : cap channel
   write("Enter the rows of matrix a one at a time")
   fa i := 1 to n, j := 1 to n -> read(a[i,j]) af
   write("Enter the rows of matrix b one at a time")
   fa i := 1 to n, j := 1 to n -> read(b[i,j]) af
   fa i := 1 to n, j := 1 to n ->
      mcap[i,j] := create multiply(n, i, j, a[i,j])
   af
   fa i := 1 to n, j := 1 to n ->
      if i < n -> south := mcap[i+1,j].north
      [] else -> south := sink[j]
      fi
      if j > 1 -> west :=   mcap[i,j-1].east
      [] else -> west := resu[i]
      fi
      send mcap[i,j].links(south, west)
   af
   fa i := 1 to n, j := 1 to n -> send mcap[1,j].north(b[j,i]) af  # src
   fa i := 1 to n, j := 1 to n -> send mcap[i,n].east(0.0) af      # zero
   fa i := 1 to n, j := 1 to n -> receive sink[j](toss) af
   fa j := 1 to n, i := 1 to n -> receive resu[i](c[i,j]) af
   write("The result c is")
   fa i := 1 to n ->
      fa j := 1 to n -> writes(" ", c[i,j]) af
      writes("\n")
   af
end matrix_multiply

/* .............. Example compile and run(s)

% sr -o mat3 mat3.sr
% ./mat3
Enter the matrix size (n): 3
Enter the rows of matrix a one at a time
1 2 3
4 5 6
7 8 9
Enter the rows of matrix b one at a time
10 11 12
13 14 15
16 17 18
multiply 1 1 is alive with n = 3 and a = 1.00000
multiply 1 2 is alive with n = 3 and a = 2.00000
multiply 1 3 is alive with n = 3 and a = 3.00000
multiply 2 1 is alive with n = 3 and a = 4.00000
multiply 2 2 is alive with n = 3 and a = 5.00000
multiply 2 3 is alive with n = 3 and a = 6.00000
```

```
multiply 3 1 is alive with n = 3 and a = 7.00000
multiply 3 2 is alive with n = 3 and a = 8.00000
multiply 3 3 is alive with n = 3 and a = 9.00000
The result c is
 84.0000 90.0000 96.0000
 201.000 216.000 231.000
 318.000 342.000 366.000

                                      */
```

Program 7.14: N Queens Problem Revisited.

```
resource helper
   import EightQueens
   op my_assignment(r: int) {send}
body helper(id : int; n : int; qcap : cap EightQueens)
   write("Helper", id, "starting up with board size", n)
   reply
   var solutions : int
   var board[1:n]: int := ([n] 0)

   procedure safe(row, column: int; board[1:*]: int) returns answer: bool
   # Check whether it is safe to place a queen at row, column;
   #    i.e., is board[column]=row a safe configuration?
      fa j := 1 to column-1 ->
         if board[column-j] = row
               or board[column-j] = row-j
               or board[column-j] = row+j ->
            answer := false
            return
         fi
      af
      answer := true
   end safe

   procedure place(column: int; board[1:*]: int)
   # Place a queen in all safe positions of column c,
   # then try placing a queen in the next column.
   # If a position in column n is safe, print the board.
      fa row := 1 to n ->
         board[column] := row   # try placing a queen in (row,column)
         if safe(row, column, board) ->
            if column = n -> solutions++   # have a solution
            [] column<n -> place(column+1, board)   # try next column
            fi
         fi
         board[column] := 0   # unrecord that a queen was placed
      af
   end place

   var r : int
   solutions := 0
   do true ->
      send qcap.give_assignment(id, solutions)
```

```
         receive my_assignment(r)
         solutions := 0
         board[1] := r
         write("Helper", id, "to handle queen in column 1, row", r)
         place(2, board)
         write("Helper", id, "that handled queen in column 1, row", r,
            "finished at", age(), "ms")
      od
end helper

resource EightQueens
   import helper
   op give_assignment(id : int; solutions : int) {send}
body EightQueens()
   const N := 8
   var board_size : int := N
   var num_processes : int := N
   var id : int
   # First argument on command line is board size.
   getarg(1, board_size)
   if board_size <= 1 ->
      write("board_size =", board_size, "is too small"); stop
   fi
   getarg(2, num_processes)
   if num_processes <= 0 ->
      write("num_processes =", num_processes, "is too small"); stop
   fi
   var helper_cap[1:num_processes] : cap helper
   var my_cap : cap EightQueens
   var total_solutions : int
   var solutions : int
   my_cap := myresource()
   fa i := 1 to num_processes ->
      helper_cap[i] := create helper(i, board_size, my_cap)
   af
   write("Solutions to the", board_size,
      "queens problem will be farmed out to", num_processes,
      "processes")
   total_solutions := 0

# Send all the different initial board positions (queen in some row of column
# one) to any process waiting for an assignment. The parameter solutions in
# give_assignment will be zero the first time it is received from a process.
   fa r := 1 to board_size ->
      receive give_assignment(id, solutions)
      if solutions > 0 ->
         total_solutions := total_solutions + solutions
         write("Helper", id, "found", solutions, "solutions")
      fi
      send helper_cap[id].my_assignment(r)
   af
# All initial positions have been passed out.  Wait for processes to finish.
   fa i := 1 to num_processes ->
      receive give_assignment(id, solutions)
      total_solutions := total_solutions + solutions
```

```
        write("Helper", id, "found", solutions, "solutions and is done")
    af
    write("Total number of solutions found was", total_solutions)
    stop
end EightQueens


/* .............. Example compile and run(s)


% sr -o Nqueens Nqueens.sr
% ./Nqueens
Helper 1 starting up with board size 8
Helper 2 starting up with board size 8
Helper 3 starting up with board size 8
Helper 4 starting up with board size 8
Helper 5 starting up with board size 8
Helper 6 starting up with board size 8
Helper 7 starting up with board size 8
Helper 8 starting up with board size 8
Solutions to the 8 queens problem will be farmed out to 8 processes
Helper 1 to handle queen in column 1, row 1
Helper 1 that handled queen in column 1, row 1 finished at 367 ms
Helper 2 to handle queen in column 1, row 2
Helper 3 to handle queen in column 1, row 3
Helper 3 that handled queen in column 1, row 3 finished at 888 ms
Helper 4 to handle queen in column 1, row 4
Helper 5 to handle queen in column 1, row 5
Helper 5 that handled queen in column 1, row 5 finished at 1347 ms
Helper 6 to handle queen in column 1, row 6
Helper 7 to handle queen in column 1, row 7
Helper 7 that handled queen in column 1, row 7 finished at 1845 ms
Helper 8 to handle queen in column 1, row 8
Helper 1 found 4 solutions and is done
Helper 3 found 16 solutions and is done
Helper 5 found 18 solutions and is done
Helper 7 found 8 solutions and is done
Helper 2 that handled queen in column 1, row 2 finished at 2149 ms
Helper 4 that handled queen in column 1, row 4 finished at 2345 ms
Helper 8 that handled queen in column 1, row 8 finished at 2591 ms
Helper 2 found 8 solutions and is done
Helper 4 found 18 solutions and is done
Helper 8 found 4 solutions and is done
Helper 6 that handled queen in column 1, row 6 finished at 2717 ms
Helper 6 found 16 solutions and is done
Total number of solutions found was 92
% sr -c Nqueens.sr
% srl -L 1 -o Nqueens helper EightQueens
% ./Nqueens
Helper 1 starting up with board size 8
Helper 2 starting up with board size 8
Helper 3 starting up with board size 8
Helper 4 starting up with board size 8
Helper 5 starting up with board size 8
Helper 6 starting up with board size 8
Helper 7 starting up with board size 8
Helper 8 starting up with board size 8
```

```
Solutions to the 8 queens problem will be farmed out to 8 processes
Helper 1 to handle queen in column 1, row 1
Helper 2 to handle queen in column 1, row 2
Helper 3 to handle queen in column 1, row 3
Helper 4 to handle queen in column 1, row 4
Helper 5 to handle queen in column 1, row 5
Helper 6 to handle queen in column 1, row 6
Helper 7 to handle queen in column 1, row 7
Helper 8 to handle queen in column 1, row 8
Helper 1 that handled queen in column 1, row 1 finished at 13497 ms
Helper 1 found 4 solutions and is done
Helper 8 that handled queen in column 1, row 8 finished at 13520 ms
Helper 8 found 4 solutions and is done
Helper 3 that handled queen in column 1, row 3 finished at 14473 ms
Helper 3 found 16 solutions and is done
Helper 6 that handled queen in column 1, row 6 finished at 14484 ms
Helper 6 found 16 solutions and is done
Helper 4 that handled queen in column 1, row 4 finished at 14511 ms
Helper 5 that handled queen in column 1, row 5 finished at 14517 ms
Helper 4 found 18 solutions and is done
Helper 5 found 18 solutions and is done
Helper 2 that handled queen in column 1, row 2 finished at 14581 ms
Helper 2 found 8 solutions and is done
Helper 7 that handled queen in column 1, row 7 finished at 14589 ms
Helper 7 found 8 solutions and is done
Total number of solutions found was 92
                                   */
```

7.4   Integrating Animator into SR

It is possible to write an SR resource that serves as an interface to the XTANGO animation interpreter so that its drawing and moving procedures can be called directly from an SR program.

The original XTANGO animator interpreter program, `animator.c`, is a C program that parses lines of input containing commands and their arguments. Once a command is parsed, a procedure of the name of the command is called to interface with the XTANGO system.

To integrate the animator interpreter into SR, the input line parsing code of `animator.c` was taken out. An SR global resource, Program 7.15, was written that consists of an **in** statement (rendezvous) inside a "do forever" loop. The **in** statement accepts calls to the interface routines, exported by the global, which have the same names as the animator commands, preceded by '`A_`.' The body of each branch of the **in** statement calls the corresponding command procedure in `animator.c`.

Program 7.16 is a simple example using the `SRanimator` interface. Another example is parallel quicksort, Program 7.17. This is another example of the master/worker paradigm, introduced in Section 7.3. As the numbers are partitioned and assigned to a worker process, each partition set is enclosed in a box and the circles representing the numbers to be sorted in that partition set are all colored the color of the worker process sorting the partition set. Figure 7.4 contains a snapshot of an animation of 100 random numbers between 1 and 10000 being sorted using six processes. By watching several of these animations, the effect of a poor pivot value and why there is limited speedup can be seen.

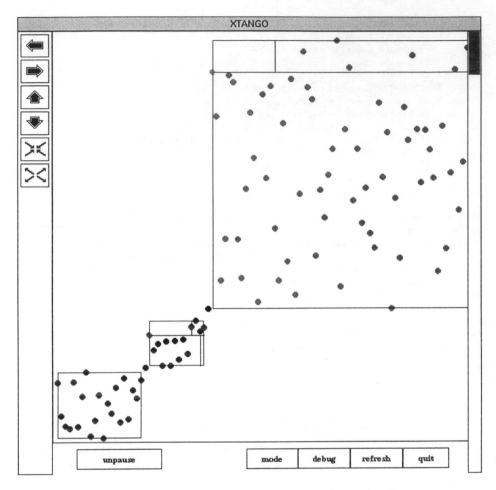

Figure 7.4: Animation Snapshot of Quicksort using SRanimator.

The SR language environment contains an interface to the X-windows graphics system, called SRWin. It is possible to animate SR programs without using XTANGO. Since it is a lower level interface to the X-windows libraries, the SRWin package may be more difficult to use than the XTANGO animation interpreter program. For example, compare the two "Hello, world!" programs, 7.16 and 7.18. SRWin does have the advantage, though, of being able to accept input in the animation window. Program 7.19 contains the source code for a quicksort program using the SRWin X-windows interface. This program appears in [26]. An animation snapshot is shown in Figure 7.5.

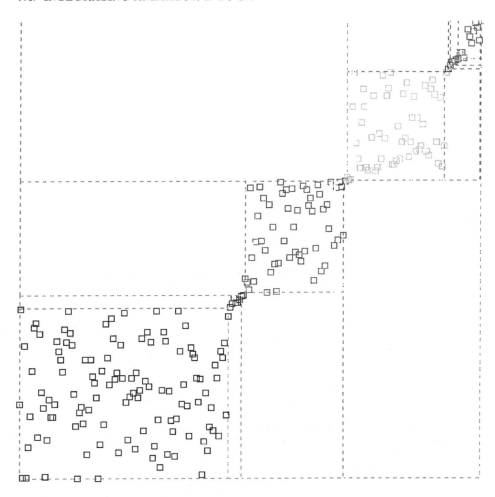

Running: '+'/'-' to adjust speed

Figure 7.5: Animation Snapshot of Quicksort using SRWin.

Program 7.15: SRanimator Interface to XTANGO.

```
global SRanimator
    op A_bg(colorr : string[*])
    op A_coords(lx, byy, rx, ty : real)
    op A_delay(frames : int)
    op A_line (id : int; lx, ly, sx, sy : real; colorr, width : string[*])
    op A_rectangle(id : int; lx, ly, sx, sy : real; colorr, filll : string[*])
    op A_circle(id : int; lx, ly, rad : real; colorr, filll : string[*])
    op A_triangle(id : int; lx, ly, vx0, vy0, vx1, vy1 : real;
       colorr, filll : string[*])
```

```
    op A_text(id : int; lx, ly : real; cen : int; colorr, str : string[*])
    op A_bigtext(id : int; lx, ly : real; cen : int; colorr, str : string[*])
    op A_delete(id : int)
    op A_move(id : int; tx, ty : real)
    op A_moverelative(id : int; tx, ty : real)
    op A_moveto(id1, id2 : int)
    op A_jump(id : int; tx, ty : real)
    op A_jumprelative(id : int; tx, ty : real)
    op A_jumpto(id1, id2 : int)
    op A_color(id : int; colname : string[*])
    op A_fill(id : int; filll : string[*])
    op A_vis(id : int)
    op A_raise(id : int)
    op A_lower(id : int)
    op A_exchangepos(id1, id2 : int)
    op A_switchpos(id1, id2 : int)
    op A_swapid(id1, id2 : int)
    op A_end()
body SRanimator
    external BEGIN_TANGOalgoOp(), IDS_ASSOCmake(), END_TANGOalgoOp()
    external bg(colorr : string[*])
    external coords(lx, byy, rx, ty : real)
    external delay(frames : int)
    external line (id : int; lx, ly, sx, sy : real; colorr, width : string[*])
    external rectangle(id : int; lx, ly, sx, sy : real; colorr, filll : string[*])
    external circle(id : int; lx, ly, rad : real; colorr, filll : string[*])
    external triangle(id : int; lx, ly, vx0, vy0, vx1, vy1 : real;
        colorr, filll : string[*])
    external text(id : int; lx, ly : real; cen : int; colorr, str : string[*])
    external bigtext(id : int; lx, ly : real; cen : int; colorr, str : string[*])
    external delete(id : int)
    external move(id : int; tx, ty : real)
    external moverelative(id : int; tx, ty : real)
    external moveto(id1, id2 : int)
    external jump(id : int; tx, ty : real)
    external jumprelative(id : int; tx, ty : real)
    external jumpto(id1, id2 : int)
    external color(id : int; colname : string[*])
    external fill(id : int; filll : string[*])
    external vis(id : int)
    external raise(id : int)
    external lower(id : int)
    external exchangepos(id1, id2 : int)
    external switchpos(id1, id2 : int)
    external swapid(id1, id2 : int)

    BEGIN_TANGOalgoOp()
    IDS_ASSOCmake()
    reply

    do true ->
        in A_bg(colorr) ->
            bg(colorr)
        [] A_coords(lx, byy, rx, ty) ->
            coords(lx, byy, rx, ty)
```

```
        [] A_delay(frames) ->
            delay(frames)
        [] A_line (id, lx, ly, sx, sy, colorr, width) ->
            line (id, lx, ly, sx, sy, colorr, width)
        [] A_rectangle(id, lx, ly, sx, sy, colorr, filll) ->
            rectangle(id, lx, ly, sx, sy, colorr, filll)
        [] A_circle(id, lx, ly, rad, colorr, filll) ->
            circle(id, lx, ly, rad, colorr, filll)
        [] A_triangle(id, lx, ly, vx0, vy0, vx1, vy1, colorr, filll) ->
            triangle(id, lx, ly, vx0, vy0, vx1, vy1, colorr, filll)
        [] A_text(id, lx, ly, cen, colorr, str) ->
            text(id, lx, ly, cen, colorr, str)
        [] A_bigtext(id, lx, ly, cen, colorr, str) ->
            bigtext(id, lx, ly, cen, colorr, str)
        [] A_delete(id) ->
            delete(id)
        [] A_move(id, tx, ty) ->
            move(id, tx, ty)
        [] A_moverelative(id, tx, ty) ->
            moverelative(id, tx, ty)
        [] A_moveto(id1, id2) ->
            moveto(id1, id2)
        [] A_jump(id, tx, ty) ->
            jump(id, tx, ty)
        [] A_jumprelative(id, tx, ty) ->
            jumprelative(id, tx, ty)
        [] A_jumpto(id1, id2) ->
            jumpto(id1, id2)
        [] A_color(id, colname) ->
            color(id, colname)
        [] A_fill(id, filll) ->
            fill(id, filll)
        [] A_vis(id) ->
            vis(id)
        [] A_raise(id) ->
            raise(id)
        [] A_lower(id) ->
            lower(id)
        [] A_exchangepos(id1, id2) ->
            exchangepos(id1, id2)
        [] A_switchpos(id1, id2) ->
            switchpos(id1, id2)
        [] A_swapid(id1, id2) ->
            swapid(id1, id2)
        [] A_end() ->
            END_TANGOalgoOp()
        ni
    od

    final
        # should check queue on in statement above and service first
        END_TANGOalgoOp()
    end final
end SRanimator
```

Program 7.16: "Hello, world!" using **SRanimator** Interface.

```
resource hello_world()
   import SRanimator
   call A_coords(1.0, 1.0, 3.0, 3.0)
   call A_bg("azure")
   call A_text(777, 2.0, 2.0, 1, "red", "Hello, world!")
   call A_delay(10000)
   call A_delete(777)
   call A_end()
end hello_world

/* .............. Example compile and run(s)

% cc -g -c -I. animator.c
% sr -c SRanimator.sr
% sr -c hello_world.sr
% srl -o hello_world SRanimator hello_world animator.o xtango.o \
-lXaw -lXmu -lXext -lXt -lX11 -lm
% ./hello_world
Press RUN ANIMATION button to begin

XTANGO Version 1.52

Press QUIT button to end
                                                  */
```

Program 7.17: Animation of Quicksort using **SRanimator** Interface.

```
resource quicksort()
   import SRanimator

   procedure print_nums(ref a[1:*] : int; left, right : int)
      const MAX_PER_LINE : int := 15
      var count : int := 0
      fa i := left to right -> writes(" ", a[i]); count++
         if count mod MAX_PER_LINE = 0 -> writes("\n") fi
      af
      if count mod MAX_PER_LINE != 0 -> writes("\n") fi
   end print_nums

   var N : int := 10;        getarg(1, N)
   var RANGE : int := 100; getarg(2, RANGE)
   var NCPU : int := 4;      getarg(3, NCPU)
   if NCPU > 6 -> write(stderr, "too many CPUs, must be <= 6"); stop(1) fi
   write("sorting", N, "numbers between 1 and", RANGE, "using", NCPU, "CPUs")
   var nums[1:N] : int

##### animator #####v
   procedure scale_x(x : int) returns x_scaled : real
      x_scaled := real(x)/(N+1)
```

```
    end scale_x

    procedure scale_y(y : int) returns y_scaled : real
        y_scaled := real(y)/(RANGE+1)
    end scale_y

    procedure maxx(ref number[1:*] : int; left, right : int) returns mx : int
        mx := number[left]
        fa i := left+1 to right -> if number[i] > mx -> mx := number[i] fi af
    end maxx

    procedure minn(ref number[1:*] : int; left, right : int) returns mn : int
        mn := number[left]
        fa i := left+1 to right -> if number[i] < mn -> mn := number[i] fi af
    end minn

    # set up colors
    var colors[1:6] : string[16]   # := ("red    ", "green ", "blue   ", "orange",
                                   #      "maroon", "yellow")
                                   # trailing blanks confuse SRanimator
    colors[1] := "red"
    colors[2] := "green"
    colors[3] := "blue"
    colors[4] := "orange"
    colors[5] := "maroon"
    colors[6] := "yellow"
    var worker_object : int := 100000    # race condition possible!
##### animator #####^

    op task(left, right : int)
    op done_count()

    procedure qs(worker_id, left, right : int)
        if right-left <= 0 -> write(stderr, "right-left<=0, error!"); return fi
        var pivot := nums[left]
        var l := left, r := right

##### animator #####v
        # enclose what this worker is working on in a black outline rectangle
        var rectangle_id : int := worker_object++
        var ymin := minn(nums, left, right)
        var ymax := maxx(nums, left, right)
        var xpos, ypos, xsize, ysize : real
        xpos := scale_x(left); ypos := scale_y(ymin)
        xsize := scale_x(right-left); ysize := scale_y(ymax-ymin)
        # enclose what this worker is working on in a black outline rectangle
        send A_rectangle(rectangle_id, xpos, ypos, xsize, ysize, "black",
            "outline")
        # change items sorted to this worker's color
        fa i := left to right ->
            send A_color(i, colors[worker_id])
            send A_fill(i, "solid")
        af
        # make pivot half color
        send A_fill(left, "half")
```

```
        # draw a black horizontal line from the pivot across the rectangle
        var line_id_h : int := worker_object++
        xpos := scale_x(left); ypos := scale_y(pivot)
        xsize := scale_x(right-left); ysize := 0.0
        send A_line(line_id_h, xpos, ypos, xsize, ysize, "black", "thin")
        # draw two verticle lines at left+1 and right
        var line_id_v_l : int := worker_object++
        var line_id_v_r : int := worker_object++
        xpos := scale_x(l+1); ypos := scale_y(pivot)
        xsize := 0.0; ysize := scale_y(ymax-pivot)
        send A_line(line_id_v_l, xpos, ypos, xsize, ysize, "black", "thin")
        xpos := scale_x(r); ypos := scale_y(ymin)
        xsize := 0.0; ysize := scale_y(pivot-ymin)
        send A_line(line_id_v_r, xpos, ypos, xsize, ysize, "black", "thin")
##### animator #####^

        var not_done := true
        do not_done ->
            if nums[l+1] > pivot ->  # needs to be moved to other end of nums
                do (r > l+1) and (nums[r] > pivot) -> r--  # find one to swap

##### animator #####v
                    # move the right verticle line one to the left
                    if not_done ->
                        send A_moverelative(line_id_v_r, scale_x(-1), 0.0)
                    fi
##### animator #####^

                od
                if r > l+1 -> l++; nums[r] :=: nums[l]; not_done := l < r-1

##### animator #####v
                    # swap locations and ids of the objects
                    send A_move(r, scale_x(l), scale_y(nums[l]))
                    send A_move(l, scale_x(r), scale_y(nums[r]))
                    send A_swapid(r, l)
##### animator #####^

##### animator #####v
                    # move the left verticle line one to the right
                    if not_done ->
                        send A_moverelative(line_id_v_l, scale_x(1), 0.0)
                    fi
##### animator #####^

                [] else -> not_done := false  # if can't find one to swap, then
                fi                             # nums now partitioned; we are done
            [] else -> l++; not_done := l < r  # need not be moved to other end

##### animator #####v
            # move the left verticle line one to the right
            if not_done ->
                send A_moverelative(line_id_v_l, scale_x(1), 0.0)
            fi
##### animator #####^
```

```
            fi
        od # when this loop finishes, nums[left] is the pivot,
           # nums[left:1] <= pivot and nums[1+1,right] > pivot
           #
                              #    [pivot, <= | > ]
                              #    ^         ^ ^ ^
                              #    |         | | |
                              # left         l r right
                              #    |         | | |
                              #    v         v v v
        nums[left] :=: nums[l]  #    [<=, pivot | > ]
                  # nums[left,1-1] <= pivot, nums[l] = pivot, and nums[1+1,right] > pivot

##### animator #####v
        # swap locations and ids of the objects
        send A_move(left, scale_x(l), scale_y(nums[l]))
        send A_move(l, scale_x(left), scale_y(nums[left]))
        send A_swapid(left, l)
##### animator #####^

        if right-(1+1) > 0 -> send task(1+1, right)
        [] right-(1+1) = 0 -> send done_count() # nums[1+1:right] singleton sorted

##### animator #####v
            # color the object solid black to indicate it is in final position
            send A_color(right, "black")
            send A_fill(right, "solid")
##### animator #####^

        fi

##### animator #####v
        # delete the line and rectangle objects
        send A_delete(rectangle_id)
        send A_delete(line_id_h)
        send A_delete(line_id_v_l)
        send A_delete(line_id_v_r)
##### animator #####^

        send done_count() # nums[l] = pivot is singleton so sorted

##### animator #####v
        # color the object solid black to indicate it is in final position
        send A_color(l, "black")
        send A_fill(l, "solid")
##### animator #####^

        if (l-1)-left > 0 -> qs(worker_id, left, l-1)
        [] (l-1)-left = 0 -> send done_count() # nums[left:l-1] singleton sorted

##### animator #####v
            # color the object solid black to indicate it is in final position
            send A_color(left, "black")
            send A_fill(left, "solid")
```

```
##### animator #####^

      fi
   end qs

   sem worker_alive := 0

   process worker(id := 1 to NCPU)
      var left, right : int
      writes("*DEBUG* worker: id=", id, " is alive", "\n")
      V(worker_alive)
      do true ->
         receive task(left, right)
         writes("*DEBUG* worker: id=", id, " received task, left=", left,
            " right=", right, "\n")
         qs(id, left, right)
      od
   end worker

   fa id := 1 to NCPU -> P(worker_alive) af

#  seed(42.0)   # leave in for reproducible random numbers for debugging
   fa i := 1 to N -> nums[i] := int(random(RANGE)+1) af
   write("original numbers"); print_nums(nums, 1, N)

##### animator #####v
   # display original numbers
   fa i := 1 to N ->
      A_circle(i, scale_x(i), scale_y(nums[i]), 0.75*scale_x(1), "black",
         "outline")
   af
##### animator #####^

   send task(1, N)
   var count : int, total : int := 0
   do total < N ->
      receive done_count()
      total++
   od
   write("sorted   numbers"); print_nums(nums, 1, N)
   call A_end()
   stop
end quicksort

/* .............. Example compile and run(s)

% cc -g -c -I. animator.c
% sr -c SRanimator.sr
% sr -c quicksort.sr
% srl -L 1 -S 50000 -o quicksort SRanimator quicksort animator.o xtango.o \
-lXaw -lXmu -lXext -lXt -lX11 -lm
% ./quicksort 100 10000 6
Press RUN ANIMATION button to begin

XTANGO Version 1.52
```

```
sorting 100 numbers between 1 and 10000 using 6 CPUs
*DEBUG* worker: id=1 is alive
*DEBUG* worker: id=2 is alive
*DEBUG* worker: id=3 is alive
*DEBUG* worker: id=4 is alive
*DEBUG* worker: id=5 is alive
*DEBUG* worker: id=6 is alive
original numbers
 3249 5645 6547 4704 7599 6327 7347 2467 3259 6446 1133 88 4721 5319 3783
 7127 6510 552 1256 2605 5459 6130 1051 2236 8636 1849 9515 521 8830 4395
 7759 2145 3936 2963 8666 6913 3936 9007 7928 1816 4947 9585 9606 4938 3996
 6171 8019 635 3419 8467 6425 390 5197 2804 375 1104 1709 3585 6039 686
 2392 8341 4539 1444 1499 1549 483 9783 1324 7613 9109 5875 7133 2789 6180
 5070 934 8248 1862 7533 140 5931 4482 8144 2003 9419 7607 2493 1464 7118
 6430 4153 7684 316 2707 9072 2453 6817 8759 8926
*DEBUG* worker: id=1 received task, left=1 right=100
*DEBUG* worker: id=2 received task, left=38 right=100
*DEBUG* worker: id=3 received task, left=23 right=36
*DEBUG* worker: id=4 received task, left=33 right=36
*DEBUG* worker: id=5 received task, left=18 right=21
*DEBUG* worker: id=6 received task, left=27 right=31
*DEBUG* worker: id=4 received task, left=24 right=25
*DEBUG* worker: id=3 received task, left=94 right=100
*DEBUG* worker: id=5 received task, left=30 right=31
*DEBUG* worker: id=4 received task, left=97 right=100
*DEBUG* worker: id=6 received task, left=9 right=16
*DEBUG* worker: id=5 received task, left=3 right=7
*DEBUG* worker: id=3 received task, left=6 right=7
*DEBUG* worker: id=4 received task, left=10 right=14
*DEBUG* worker: id=1 received task, left=81 right=92
*DEBUG* worker: id=5 received task, left=86 right=92
*DEBUG* worker: id=6 received task, left=82 right=84
*DEBUG* worker: id=3 received task, left=83 right=84
*DEBUG* worker: id=4 received task, left=87 right=90
*DEBUG* worker: id=1 received task, left=77 right=79
*DEBUG* worker: id=6 received task, left=54 right=75
*DEBUG* worker: id=3 received task, left=44 right=52
*DEBUG* worker: id=5 received task, left=55 right=75
*DEBUG* worker: id=4 received task, left=46 right=48
*DEBUG* worker: id=1 received task, left=66 right=75
*DEBUG* worker: id=6 received task, left=57 right=64
*DEBUG* worker: id=2 received task, left=69 right=75
*DEBUG* worker: id=3 received task, left=73 right=75
*DEBUG* worker: id=4 received task, left=60 right=61
sorted    numbers
 88 140 316 375 390 483 521 552 635 686 934 1051 1104 1133 1256
 1324 1444 1464 1499 1549 1709 1816 1849 1862 2003 2145 2236 2392 2453 2467
 2493 2605 2707 2789 2804 2963 3249 3259 3419 3585 3783 3936 3936 3996 4153
 4395 4482 4539 4704 4721 4938 4947 5070 5197 5319 5459 5645 5875 5931 6039
 6130 6171 6180 6327 6425 6430 6446 6510 6547 6817 6913 7118 7127 7133 7347
 7533 7599 7607 7613 7684 7759 7928 8019 8144 8248 8341 8467 8636 8666 8759
 8830 8926 9007 9072 9109 9419 9515 9585 9606 9783
Press QUIT button to end
                                    */
```

Program 7.18: "Hello, world!" using SRWin.

```
resource hello_world()
   import SRWin
   var mywin : winWindow := WinOpen("", "Hello", null, UseDefault, 100, 30)
   if mywin = null -> write("Cannot open a window."); stop(1) fi
   WinSetForeground(mywin, "red")      # color for text
   WinSetBackground(mywin, "azure")    # color of background
#     I was trying to change the background of A. Zhao's qsort.sr program
#    (in the examples/srwin directory of the SR distribution) from black to
#    white.  I couldn't figure out how to do it, so I started playing with
#    the "Hello, world!" program on page 1 of his SRWin technical report
#    (TR-93-14).  I discovered that just setting the background from the
#    default black to white with WinSetBackground(mywin, "white") wouldn't
#     work.  Putting a WinClearArea(...) after it didn't help either.  Finally
#    I discovered WinEraseArea(...) did the trick.  The manual page for srwin
#    is not very clear about the difference between WinClearArea(...) and
#    WinEraseArea(...).
   WinEraseArea(mywin, winRectangle(0, 0, 100, 30))
   WinDrawString(mywin, winPoint(10, 20), "Hello, world!")
   WinFlush(mywin)                     # flush pending output
   nap(3000)
   WinClose(mywin)                     # destroy window
end hello_world

/* .............. Example compile and run(s)

% sr -o hello_world srwin.o hello_world.sr -lX11
hello_world.sr:
hello_world.sr:
linking:
% ./hello_world
                                        */
```

Program 7.19: Animation of Quicksort using SRWin.

```
# Quick Sort
#
# Qiang A. Zhao, October 92
#
# Usage: qsort WindowSize Points DotSize

resource qsort()

   const  JS := 4                            # number of job servers
   import SRWin

   op banner(win: winWindow; str: string[*])
   op regenerate()
   op drawDot(win: winWindow; idx, value, slp: int)
   op part(id, left, right: int; var x, y, w, h: int) returns mid:int
```

```
op job(left, right: int)
op done(int)

var SIZE := 500;        getarg(1, SIZE)
var NP := SIZE/2;       getarg(2, NP)
var DOT := 6;           getarg(3, DOT)

if (SIZE < 100) or (NP < 10) ->
  write("Invalid Value, sorry...")
  stop(1)
fi

const  OFF := 40
const  DOT2 : int := DOT/2
const  SCALE : real := real(SIZE-DOT)/real(NP-1)

const  MSG_READY := "Press 'g' to go"
const  MSG_RUNNING := "Running: '+'/'-' to adjust speed"
const  MSG_DONE := "Done, 'r' to regenerate numbers"

var numbers[NP] : int
var mainwin, ww, boxw, textw: winWindow
var cwins[1:JS] :winWindow
var colors[1:JS] : string[6]
        colors[1] := "red"
        colors[2] := "yellow"
        colors[3] := "green"
        colors[4] := "cyan"
op  ec : winEventChannel
var ev: winEvent
var slp: int := 0
var started := false

## Draw a string at the bottom
proc banner(win, str)
  # WinClearArea turned window black eventhough background set to white
  WinEraseArea(mainwin, winRectangle(0, SIZE+DOT, SIZE, OFF-DOT))
  WinDrawString(win, winPoint(OFF, SIZE+30), str)
end

## Generate random numbers
proc regenerate()
  WinEraseArea(mainwin, winRectangle(0, 0, SIZE, SIZE+DOT))
  fa i:= 1 to NP ->
    numbers[i] := int(random(SIZE)+1)
    drawDot(ww, i, numbers[i], 0)
  af
end

## Draw a box stands for a point being sorted
proc drawDot(win, idx, value, slp)
  if slp > 0 -> nap(slp) fi
  WinDrawRectangle(win,
    winRectangle(int(SCALE*(idx-1)), SIZE-value-DOT2, DOT, DOT))
end
```

```
###
# Partition
proc part(id, left, right, x, y, w, h) returns mid
  var minv := SIZE+1, maxv := -1
  var i : int
  fa i := left to right ->
    minv := min(minv, numbers[i])
    maxv := max(maxv, numbers[i])
  af
  x := int((left-1) * SCALE + DOT2)
  h := maxv - minv + 1
  y := SIZE - minv - h
  w := int((right-left) * SCALE)
  #
  WinDrawRectangle(boxw, winRectangle(x, y, w, h))
  # recolor to my color
  fa i:= left to right ->
    drawDot(cwins[id], i, numbers[i], 0)
  af
  WinSync(mainwin, false)                    # intended to slow things down
  #
  var  pivot := numbers[left]
  var  lx := left+1, rx := right
  do lx <= rx ->
    if numbers[lx] <= pivot -> lx++
    [] numbers[lx] > pivot ->
       drawDot(mainwin, lx, numbers[lx], 0)
       drawDot(mainwin, rx, numbers[rx], 0)
       numbers[lx] :=: numbers[rx]
       drawDot(cwins[id], lx, numbers[lx], slp)
       drawDot(cwins[id], rx, numbers[rx], slp)
      WinSync(mainwin, false)                # intended to slow things down
       rx--
    fi
  od
  if rx > left ->
    drawDot(mainwin, left, numbers[left], 0)
    drawDot(mainwin, rx, numbers[rx], 0)
    numbers[rx] :=: numbers[left]
    drawDot(cwins[id], left, numbers[left], slp)
    drawDot(cwins[id], rx, numbers[rx], slp)
  fi
  #
  mid := rx
  return
end

####################################################################
# open main window
mainwin := WinOpen("", "Quick Sort", ec, UseDefault, SIZE, SIZE+OFF)
if mainwin = null ->
  write("Ouch, can't open window")
  stop(1)
fi
```

```
WinSetBackground(mainwin, "white")
WinSetEventMask(mainwin, Ev_KeyUp)
ww := WinNewContext(mainwin)
boxw := WinNewContext(mainwin)
textw := WinNewContext(mainwin)
fa i:= 1 to JS ->
  cwins[i] := WinNewContext(mainwin)
  WinSetForeground(cwins[i], colors[i])
  WinEraseArea(cwins[i], winRectangle(0, 0, SIZE, SIZE+OFF))
af
WinSetForeground(mainwin, "white")
WinSetForeground(boxw, "orange")
WinSetForeground(textw, "black")
WinSetLineAttr(boxw, 0, LineDoubleDash, CapButt, JoinMiter)

## a taste of flavor
seed(0)

## sorting control
regenerate()
banner(textw, MSG_READY)
slp := 40

## workers, get job from bag...
process worker(id := 1 to JS)
  var lo, mid, hi: int
  var x, y, w, h: int
  var mywork: int := 0

  receive job(lo, hi)
  do true ->
    mid := part(id, lo, hi, x, y, w, h)
    WinDrawRectangle(boxw, winRectangle(x, y, w, h))
    if lo < mid - 1 ->
      if mid + 1 < hi ->
        send job(mid+1, hi)
      [] else ->
        mywork +:= hi - mid + 1
      fi
      hi := mid -1
    [] else ->
      mywork +:= mid - lo + 1
      if mid + 1 < hi ->
        lo := mid + 1
      [] else ->
        mywork +:= hi - mid + 1
        if lo = hi -> mywork -= 1        # one work counted twice
        send done(mywork)
        mywork := 0
        receive job(lo, hi)
      fi
    fi
  od
end
```

```
    ##########
    var got, tmp : int
    do true ->
      in ec(ev) ->
        if (ev.event_type = Ev_KeyUp) ->

            var ch := char(ev.data)
            if ch = 'q' | ch = 'Q' | ch = '\177' | ch = '\003' ->
              stop
            [] ch = 'g' ->
              if not started ->
                started := true
                WinEraseArea(mainwin, winRectangle(0, 0, SIZE, SIZE+DOT))
                banner(textw, MSG_RUNNING)
                got := 0
                send job(1, NP)
              [] else ->
                WinBell(mainwin, 0);
              fi
            [] ch = '-' ->
              slp +:= 5
            [] ch = '+' ->
              slp := max(slp - 5, 0)
            [] ch = 'r' ->
              if not started ->
                regenerate()
                banner(textw, MSG_READY)
              [] else ->
                WinBell(mainwin, 0)
              fi
            fi

        [] ev.event_type = Ev_DeleteWindow ->
          stop
        fi

      [] done(tmp) ->                    # in
        got +:= tmp
        if got >= NP ->
          banner(textw, MSG_DONE)
          started := false
        fi
      ni
    od

    ### Final
    final
      WinClose(mainwin)
    end

end qsort

/* .............. Example compile and run(s)

% sr -o quicksort srwin.o quicksort.sr -lX11
```

```
quicksort.sr:
quicksort.sr:
linking:
% ./quicksort
```
                                                           */

7.5   Lab: Parallel Computing

Objectives

To observe how the number of CPUs available to an SR program affects its execution time.

Preparation Before Lab

Read Section 7.1 on concurrency. Program 7.1 is a version of the N queens program in which a **helper** resource counts the number of solutions with a queen already placed somewhere in the first column.

7.5.1   Assignment: Speedup

Compile Program 7.1 on a multiple CPU machine with at least 8 CPUs, such as a Sequent Symmetry or a Silicon Graphics Iris, and run four times as follows:

```
sr -o queens queens.sr
setenv SR_PARALLEL 1
time queens
setenv SR_PARALLEL 2
time queens
setenv SR_PARALLEL 4
time queens
setenv SR_PARALLEL 8
time queens
```

Observe the output, particularly the times reported by the **age** function and the **time** built-in of **csh**. Explain what you see.

7.5.2   Assignment: Race Condition

Explain exactly why Program 7.11 is incorrect if there is no call to **barrier** at the end of **query**. Discover the race condition that can result if the semaphore **barrier_sem_release** is a simple semaphore rather than an array.

7.5.3   Assignment: No Race Condition

Explain exactly why Program 7.12 has the correct per iteration synchronization.

List of Example Programs

References

[1] Gregory R. Andrews, Ronald A. Olsson, Michael Coffin, Irving Elshoff, Kevin Nilsen, Titus Purdin, and Gregg Townsend, "An Overview of the SR Language and Implementation," *ACM Trans. Prog. Lang. and Sys.*, Vol. 10, No. 1, Jan. 1988.

[2] Gregory R. Andrews and Ronald A. Olsson, "Report on the SR Language Version 1.1," TR 89-6, Dept. of Computer Science, The University of Arizona, May 1989.

[3] Gregory R. Andrews, *Concurrent Programming: Principles and Practice*, Benjamin/Cummings Publishing, 1991.

[4] Gregory R. Andrews and Ronald A. Olsson, *The SR Programming Language: Concurrency in Practice*, Benjamin/Cummings Publishing, 1993 (the SR language is available by anonymous `ftp` from machine `cs.arizona.edu` in file `/sr/sr.tar.Z`).

[5] Henri E. Bal, "A Comparative Study of Five Parallel Programming Languages," EurOpen Spring 1991 Conference on Open Distributed Systems, Tromso, May 20-24, 1991.

[6] M. Ben-Ari, *Principles of Concurrent and Distributed Programming*, Prentice-Hall, 1990.

[7] Thomas Bräunl, *Parallel Programming: An Introduction*, Prentice-Hall, 1993.

[8] Harvey M. Deitel, *An Introduction to Operating Systems*, second edition, Addison-Wesley, 1990.

[9] Stephen J. Hartley, "Experience with the Language SR in an Undergraduate Operating Systems Course," *ACM SIGCSE Bulletin*, Vol. 24, No. 1, March 1992.

[10] Stephen J. Hartley, "An Operating Systems Laboratory Based on the SR (Synchronizing Resources) Programming Language," *Computer Science Education*, Vol. 3, No. 3, 1992.

[11] Stephen J. Hartley, "Animating Operating Systems Algorithms with XTANGO," *ACM SIGCSE Bulletin*, Vol. 26, No. 1, March 1994.

[12] Maurice P. Herlihy and Jeannette M. Wing, "Linearizability: A Correctness Condition for Concurrent Objects," *ACM Transactions on Programming Languages and Systems*, Vol. 12, No. 3, 1990.

[13] David Hemmendinger, "A Correct Implementation of General Semaphores," *ACM Operating Systems Review*, Vol. 22, No. 3, 1988.

[14] Phil Kearns, "A Correct and Unrestrictive Implementation of General Semaphores," *ACM Operating Systems Review*, Vol. 22, No. 4, 1988.

[15] Brian W. Kernighan and Dennis M. Ritchie, *The C Programming Language*, Prentice-Hall, 1978.

[16] Ted G. Lewis and Hesham El-Rewini, *Introduction to Parallel Computing*, Prentice-Hall, 1992.

[17] David Mosberger, *Memory Consistency Models*, Department of Computer Science Technical Report 93-11, University of Arizona, May 1993 (available by anonymous **ftp** from machine **cs.arizona.edu** in file **/reports/1993/TR93-11.ps**).

[18] Ronald A. Olsson, "Experience Using the C Preprocessor to Implement CCR, Monitor, and CSP Preprocessors for SR," submitted July 1994 for publication to *Software-Practice and Experience*.

[19] Michael J. Quinn, *Parallel Computing: Theory and Practice*, second edition McGraw-Hill, 1994.

[20] Abraham Silberschatz and Peter B. Gavin, *Operating System Concepts*, fourth edition, Addison-Wesley, 1994.

[21] William Stallings, *Operating Systems*, Macmillan, 1992.

[22] John T. Stasko and Doug Hayes, "XTANGO Algorithm Animation Designer's Package," available by anonymous **ftp** from machine **par.cc.gatech.edu** (from directory **pub**, retrieve file **xtango.tar.Z**, then uncompress and extract file **xtangodoc.ps** from directory **./xtango/doc** in the archive file **xtango.tar**).

[23] Andrew S. Tanenbaum, *Operating Systems: Design and Implementation*, Prentice-Hall, 1987.

[24] Andrew S. Tanenbaum, *Modern Operating Systems*, Prentice-Hall, 1992.

[25] Kathleen Jensen and Niklaus Wirth, *PASCAL User Manual and Report*, second edition, Lecture Notes in Computer Science, Vol. 18, Springer-Verlag, 1976.

[26] Qiang A. Zhao, *SRWin, a Graphics Library for SR*, Department of Computer Science Technical Report 93-14, University of Arizona, May 1993 (available by anonymous **ftp** from machine **cs.arizona.edu** in file **/reports/1993/TR93-14.ps**).